Will This Be China's Century?

Will This Be
China's Century?

A Skeptic's View

Mel Gurtov

LYNNE
RIENNER
PUBLISHERS

BOULDER
LONDON

Published in the United States of America in 2013 by
Lynne Rienner Publishers, Inc.
1800 30th Street, Boulder, Colorado 80301
www.rienner.com

and in the United Kingdom by
Lynne Rienner Publishers, Inc.
3 Henrietta Street, Covent Garden, London WC2E 8LU

Library of Congress Cataloging-in-Publication Data
Gurtov, Melvin.
Will this be China's century?: a skeptic's view / Mel Gurtov.
Includes bibliographical references and index.
ISBN 978-1-58826-898-3 (hc: alk. paper)
ISBN 978-1-58826-874-7 (pbk.: alk. paper)
   1. China—Politics and government—2002– 2. China—Relations—United States.
3. United States—Relations—China. I. Title.
DS779.4.G87 2013
327.51—dc23   2012041549

British Cataloguing in Publication Data
A Cataloguing in Publication record for this book
is available from the British Library.

Printed and bound in the United States of America

The paper used in this publication meets the requirements
of the American National Standard for Permanence of
Paper for Printed Library Materials Z39.48-1992.

5   4   3   2   1

To my precious grandchildren,
Brynn Appel and Gavin Joseph

Contents

Preface

This book is my seventieth birthday present to myself. Beyond being a research project, the book is an appeal for common sense about China and US-China relations. I have devoted a good part of my life to studying both Chinese and US foreign policy. Following the lead of some of my early mentors, I have tried to find ways to promote a clearer understanding of China and a path to partnership with the United States in international affairs. Politically, this is (once again) not a popular time for such ideas. But I don't think we have much choice: either we will find common ground with China or we will eventually find ourselves in a new Cold War with that large country. And let's be clear: a rising, self-confident China is a far tougher, more demanding adversary than it ever was under Chairman Mao.

I wish to thank Larry Kirsch and Neal Hirschfeld for their helpful comments on the manuscript, and two anonymous reviewers for providing detailed critiques. I'm also grateful to Sam Kim, Mark Selden, Peter Van Ness, and Dali Yang for their comments and thoughtfulness, and to Milton Leitenberg for his usual diligence in sending me helpful research materials. Thanks also to David Plott at *Global Asia* for permission to reproduce an article by Wang Jisi in the appendix of this book. As always, Lynne Rienner was a valued guide to improving the presentation. All authors should have such a wonderful publisher.

And thank you, Jodi, for always being there for me.

—*Mel Gurtov*

1

Exploring the "Century" Issue

In an attention-grabbing speech delivered before overseas Chinese in Mexico, China's new leader, Xi Jinping, said in 2009: "There are some foreigners who have eaten their fill and have nothing better to do than criticize [*zhi shou hua jiao*: point their fingers at] our affairs. First, China does not export revolution; second, it does not export poverty and hunger; third, it does not cause unnecessary trouble. What else is there to say?"[1] China's nationalistic press was quick to support these lines, saying it was time to stand up to "foreigners" (i.e., Westerners) and stop being so defensive about China. In fact, although Xi's comment reflects a bold self-confidence in China, it doesn't end the story. There is a lot more to say about what China "exports," and even more to say about what is actually going on in fast-rising China.

The chief purpose of this book is to challenge the notion that the new century belongs to China in the same way that the preceding century was claimed to belong to the United States. This is no small issue. The notion of an "American century," as explained in Chapter 2, has been used by political leaders and foreign-policy pundits right up to the present to explain and justify a unique role for the United States as world leader. This exceptionalism embodies both the realities of global military and economic power and a nationalistic conviction with regard to the universal relevance of US values and ideals. China's leaders do not claim a "Chinese century"; nor do they claim a Chinese exceptionalism. Yet the extraordinary pace of China's economic development has led to numerous predictions that just such evidences of global leadership are forthcoming or have already taken hold. The question mark in the book's title is there to propose that, whether in domestic or international terms, a Chinese century is far into the future, if it will happen at all.

The United States occupies a good portion of this book. In part that is because Sino-US relations have become the most important bilateral

1

relationship in world affairs, as leaders of both countries assert. Another reason is that while comparisons of China and the United States are often inappropriate, there are points of similarity worth noting, such as increasing income inequality, weak positions on global warming, and a sometimes dangerous nationalism. Moreover, leaders in both countries eye one another with a mixture of awe and wariness; they find each other's political institutions unpalatable and their militaries potentially threatening. Yet, especially in China's case, many decisions are framed with the United States in mind.

Lastly, I do not want to leave the impression that the improbability of a Chinese century means that US citizens can rest secure in the belief the new century will still belong to the United States. As in my other writings, I take a human-interest approach to international affairs, which puts the global community's security and well-being—specifically, the impoverished and repressed peoples of the world—ahead of any one country's priorities. From that perspective, as stated in my concluding chapter, this century should not belong to any great power. The United States, like China, has a multitude of pressing domestic concerns that demand attention—*and*, in some cases, also demand renewed efforts to engage with one another for their own sake as well as for the sake of the planet. In our time, leaders and publics of both countries should recognize, to invest in global security is to invest in national security.

Analyzing China's strengths and weaknesses, then, here involves both traditional and nontraditional approaches. On the traditional side, I explore the usual indicators of national power, hard and soft; China's relations with various countries, regions, and international organizations; and issues of internal governance, such as leadership, social controls, the behavior of institutions such as the military and the Chinese Communist Party (CCP), and political legitimacy. But I also examine how China measures up, primarily at home but also abroad, when it comes to human development and human security. In that category are income distribution, respect for human rights, protection of the environment, and social welfare. In the end, my desire is to produce a brief but fair assessment of how far China has come, and how far it still has to go, to be a global leader.

Note

1. Speech of February 11, 2009; at http://chinadigitaltimes.net/2009/02/xi-jinping-%E4%B9%A0%E8%BF%91%E5%B9%B3-on-foreigners-pointing-fingers-at -china-with-video/.

2

Interpreting China's Rise

A television ad that appeared in the fall of 2010, sponsored by a conservative US group opposed to government waste, showed a Chinese "professor" lecturing on the decline of empires such as the United States. The ad depicted a snide, self-assured lecturer suggesting that the US government was spending the country into oblivion with its huge health-care and job-stimulation costs. China will be eating America's lunch, the "professor" predicted: "*xianzai tamen dou dei gei women ganhuo*" (now they have to work for us). The students laughed approvingly.[1] The message was that government intervention accounted for the failed US economy, a poorly informed point to make considering China's success with a managed economy and its own high health-care costs. But of course the real intent of the group's message was to convey fear and loathing of China.

How times have changed! In 1941, Henry Luce, magnate of the Time-Life magazine empire, argued in a widely discussed editorial that the United States had the means and the moral obligation to make the post–World War II years the "American century." Well before the war ended, strategic planners inside and outside the US government created a global financial and commercial network—institutions later collectively labeled the Washington Consensus—that would make Luce's dream come true.[2] Until the Vietnam War, the preeminent US role in world affairs was questioned only in the world dominated by the Soviet Union. But the "Vietnam syndrome" that supposedly eliminated interventions abroad proved to be temporary; the combination of Ronald Reagan's revivalism and the first Iraq war led to assertions from conservatives that the United States' "unipolar moment" had arrived. When, in the view of neoconservatives, the Bill Clinton administration failed to seize that moment, their Project for the New American Century sought to restore Luce's (and Reagan's) dream, this time more around US military

3

than around economic power. But that effort, which gained new vitality after the 9/11 terrorist attacks, was brought down by a "war on terror" that lacked credibility, entailed huge political as well as financial costs, and helped promote economic and social decline at home.

Now, as the "antiwaste" ad shows, some people in the United States worry that China, the very country in which Luce grew up, is waiting in the wings to become the new global powerhouse. Didn't paramount leader Deng Xiaoping once advise, "*tao guang yang hui,*" which is often translated as "bide time and keep a low profile"? This phrase, though spoken sometime after the Tiananmen disaster, when China was on the defensive, is often cited as a reason to distrust China. But the phrase is open to interpretation. A more literal translation is "hide brightness, nourish obscurity," which seems to be a better reflection of Deng's actual thinking: avoid confrontations, take advantage of opportunities, focus on rapid economic development. The notion that Chinese triumphalism has replaced US triumphalism is being pushed mainly *outside* China. *Inside* China one finds great national pride and suspicions about the US response to China's rise. But few Chinese are hailing the dawn of a China-centered century.

That China's rise should arouse pride of achievement is hardly surprising given the economic austerity and mass campaigns of the Maoist past. Its status as the world's second-largest economy, its currency reserves of more than $3 trillion, its impressive poverty reduction, its leadership in solar-energy panels and wind-power generation, and its glitzy hosting of the 2008 Olympic Games all testify to how far and how fast China has transformed. Add to these advances China's remarkable achievements in science and technology, such as its rapid advance to the front ranks of supercomputing and, in June 2012, the launch of a spacecraft with three astronauts aboard that linked up with an orbiting docking station, the first step toward establishing a permanent space station.

While the United States bends under the weight of huge public debt, two overseas wars, high unemployment, and doubts abroad and at home about its ability to lead, China seems to have infinite financial resources and a competitive spirit that make it look like a challenger for top dog. Once simply the world's largest developing country, China has become the fastest-growing economy since 1979. Its leaders clearly believe China has earned the right to raise questions about the lead country, including about its creditworthiness. That happened in 2010 when Premier Wen Jiabao very publicly worried over whether or not the United States could "guarantee" that it was able to preserve the value of

China's US Treasury bill holdings, which by then had surpassed $1 trillion. He got reassurances, but he made his point. With the Barack Obama administration forced to give economic recovery priority over anything else, with US resources spread thin by wars in Iraq and Afghanistan, and with the economies of key US allies in Europe and Asia in turmoil, was China staking out a claim to leadership? *Can* China lead? And what does international leadership mean today?

The View from China

Chinese leaders insist that China "will never seek hegemony" *(yongyuan bucheng ba)*. Their view, at least as it is presented to Western audiences, is that seeking hegemony would require confronting the United States. China not only lacks the capacity to do so, such as having comparable military forces and reliable allies; more crucially, China would have to divert vast resources away from its economic development program in order to challenge the United States.[3] But in this new era of foreign-policy debate in China, other voices contest the acceptance of US predominance. Some Chinese foreign-policy professionals, along with younger nationalistic intellectuals and probably some senior military officers, believe China should be more assertive when dealing with the United States. This group tends to see the United States as a threat to China's rise both from without—seeking to contain China militarily and weaken it economically—and from within, by pressing China on currency revaluation, human-rights abuses, and business practices.[4] For now, however, the dominant view in China's leadership seems in accord with US leaders' view that common interests should be stressed, requiring cooperation along with inevitable competition and occasional friction.

This is also the prevailing view of China's foreign-policy specialists, as Roger Irvine's thorough review of the journals in which they write brings out. Though their university institutes and think tanks are government-controlled, the new era in China has allowed for diversity of opinion and a flow of information and ideas between them and senior officials.[5] These analysts say that the United States will remain the sole superpower for some time. China's domestic weaknesses require that economic development, not international affairs, receive highest priority. Consequently, we are urged to take seriously the official emphasis in the People's Republic of China (PRC) on "peaceful development" and a low profile; these will remain key elements of China's policy well into the future. Only a direct threat to China's "core interests"—border security, sovereignty (reunification with Taiwan in particular), maintenance of the party-state system, and international acceptance as a great power—would alter those directions.

The minority view among these analysts sees a progressive weakening of US primacy and criticizes the Chinese leadership for being too submissive to the United States. The global financial crisis of 2008 was the pivotal event for these writers, coming as it did on the heels of US involvement in two Middle East wars. As an example, Gao Zugui, director of world politics at the China Institutes of Contemporary International Relations, argued in 2010 that China's international status had risen as a consequence of a narrowing gap in comprehensive power between it and the United States. Not only had the United States lost its "monopoly of the right to discourse on world issues" as a result, but the West as a whole was losing its grip in the balance of power between developed countries and emerging economies.[6]

Despite these criticisms, very few Chinese analysts have argued for a confrontational foreign policy or for a Chinese effort to create an alternative international order. Thus, the real difference between these schools of thought has to do with assessments of the *relative decline* of the United States and not with questioning either the unique power position of the United States or China's capacity to challenge it. As Irvine puts it, China's specialists do not

> endorse the views of . . . outside observers that China is destined to become the dominant global power; the majority are cautious regarding suggestions of abandoning the old order or overturning it with undue haste. They are wary of China being charmed into taking on a too ambitious or burdensome role. Priority is still given to keeping a relatively low profile internationally and to ensuring that the current favorable environment for economic development is not wasted.

The View from the West

In the West, the world of China-watchers, too, is divided, with opinion ranging from disregard for what Chinese officials and experts say to acceptance of their word as being confirmed by China's actual behavior.

We start with the China Critics, of whom there are several types. Some are not simply opposed to specific PRC policies—critics may be found in all the schools—but are viscerally predisposed to seeing China in the worst possible light. The Critics are convinced that China is a looming military threat to the United States; that its reforms should not take attention away from the political reality that China is a Communist dictatorship; and that engaging China is fruitless. A strong US military to contain the "China challenge" is the remedy.[7] If this sounds familiar to students of the Cold War, it should: for the China Critics, China has replaced the former Soviet Union as an implacable enemy that needs to be contained or at least constrained. "Partnership" with China is a bad idea.[8]

China Critics may also be found on the left, where Beijing comes under constant assault for its repression of human rights—religious rights, labor rights, media rights, and ethnic-minority rights. These liberal Critics typically belong to nongovernmental organizations (NGOs) that lobby in Washington, DC, often with great effectiveness. A third group of Critics is present among international relations theorists of the realist persuasion. They contend that China, either because it is a rising but dissatisfied power or simply because it is becoming a great power, will sooner or later act to alter the balance of power in its favor. Power-transition theorists perceive the China danger in terms of the structural imbalance between a rapidly rising China and a United States that will seek to maintain its number-one status. Offensive realists predict that a newly empowered China will behave like great powers of the past and seek hegemony to ensure its security.[9]

The China Engagers, on the opposite end from the Critics, have held sway in the US government ever since Richard Nixon's ground-breaking trip to Beijing in 1972. They also are the dominant voice in the European Union (EU). Though engagement has always meant different things to different government leaders, business leaders, and academic specialists, it rests on the search for common ground with China as a matter of national self-interest. Engagers have diverse answers to the question, What makes it necessary and desirable to engage China? So-called liberal Engagers rest their case on globalization, arguing that the more China's rise rests on deep economic interdependence and acceptance of the rules of the multilateral trade and financial institutions, the more likely it is that China will become a democratic and peace-seeking country. For all their differences, George W. Bush and Bill Clinton agreed on that much about China. Realist Engagers, on the other hand, see China as fast becoming a rule maker and status-quo power like the United States even though China is not democratizing. For realists, China acknowledges the realities of the current international system, understands the limits of China's power to change it, and has learned lessons from the former Soviet Union and the United States about the dangers of imperial over-stretch.[10]

Engagers also differ among themselves about when, how, and what to engage China about.[11] Moreover, Engagers find no contradiction in occasionally advocating confronting China even while insisting that engagement is their policy preference—a circumstance that occurred during the Clinton and Obama presidencies. But in seeking ways to work with China, the distinguishing characteristic of the Engagers may be that they regard diplomacy as the preferable tool of foreign policy and are optimistic about the prospects for engagement itself. Though some Engagers may believe in the virtues of US primacy in international affairs, all prefer to treat China as a great power in a world where shared power is becoming very important.

China Critics and China Engagers have been around for some time. Two new schools have emerged more recently as China's rise has become *the* topic in international circles. The China Duopolists believe in taking engagement to the next level: a US-China duopoly. This "G-2" or, in the historian Niall Ferguson's phrasing, "Chimerica," is based on the assumption that these are the two most important countries in world affairs, that they can and must cooperate in the common cause of international peace and stability, and that their economic interdependence has already created a single fused economy.[12] The China Leads school argues that China is on the verge of replacing the United States as the most important power.[13] Like the "declinists" of two decades ago, who predicted the demise of US global leadership—a prediction that is being made again[14]—this school's adherents believe that a "Beijing Consensus" (BC, discussed below) has already supplanted the US-led Washington Consensus as the source of new rules to govern the international economy. They may also uphold the notion that the Chinese are pushing a China Model (CM) in developing countries as a counterpoint to Western development models.

Among the indicators the China Leads school points to as evidence of China's top rank is its share of world gross domestic product (GDP). Table 2.1 shows GDP for China, the United States, and Africa. In percentage terms, China has gone from 4.6 percent of world GDP in 1977, the last year before the economic reforms officially began, to 17.4 percent in 2008. By contrast, the United States has gone from about 21.3 percent of world GDP in 2003 to 18.6 percent in 2008. The rapidity of China's rise is reflected not only in how quickly it is catching up to the United States in GDP but also in the contrast between China and all of Africa: China's GDP rose roughly tenfold between 1977 and 2008, whereas Africa's rose not quite threefold. Such evidence, however, is easily disputed. Among the categories of economic growth neglected by

Table 2.1 China, Africa, United States, and World GDP ($ millions)

	1977	1987	1997	2003	2008
China	843,097	1,883,027	3,706,647	6,187,983	8,908,894
Africa	645,985	829,468	1,057,077	1,320,915	1,734,918
US	3,868,829	5,290,129	7,109,775	8,431,121	9,485,136
World	18,157,093	24,693,769	33,241,788	40,809,563	50,973,935

Source: From the work of Prof. Angus Maddison at www.ggdc.net/maddison/Maddison .htm (Statistics on World Population, GDP, and Per Capita GDP, 1–2008 AD, horizontal file 02-2010).

the GDP figures—and the China Leads school—is GDP *per person*, in which case we find that US income levels are roughly ten times China's today.

There is a fifth school, America Firsters—analysts and politicians who believe the days of the United States are far from numbered. This school finds little reason to presume that China will replace the United States as global leader even if it tries. Representative of this school is Vice President Joseph R. Biden. After visiting China and spending considerable time with his counterpart, Xi Jinping, the heir-apparent to Hu Jintao, Biden wrote that the United States has nothing to fear from China since it is far ahead of China in size of the economy, per capita income, scientific innovation, and educational excellence, among other indicators.[15] Many prominent US political scientists agree, even while pointing to serious shortcomings in US society and politics.[16] Sometimes analysts who belong to this school have an unblinking optimism about the US-China relationship, failing to see that while a cooperative relationship is essential, it contains as many elements of difference as of commonality.[17] A more sophisticated version accepts the widespread view of a United States in decline, but argues that the United States has put in place a set of international institutions and rules, and has so many powerful economic and political partners, that China would do well to stay within the Western-dominated system.[18]

Coming to Grips with China's Future

Each of these Western schools makes presumptions about China's motives and objectives in world affairs. Some lay claim to world leadership for China even though China's leaders—unlike some intellectuals—do not. By contrast, US leaders have claimed leadership at least over the past one hundred years, and especially since the end of World War II. US intentions to preserve the top position are clear enough; China's must be inferred, or presumed. Nonetheless, each school proposes an agenda for US policy toward China based on what it perceives to be China's real intentions. My analysis is no different, though hopefully it is informed by a lifetime of study of China as well as of US foreign policy.

I take the part of the Engagers and make the following argument: those who proclaim that China's rise might displace the United States greatly overstate China's strength, ambitions, and most of all its capacity to lead. Understandably, the rapidity of China's rise raises concerns about the direction that country's international relations and security policies will take. Chinese power, especially economic power, introduces a new factor in world politics. But analysts who dwell on this change focus far too much on the "China challenge" and far too little on the challenges *to* China. They also exaggerate the extent of US decline in leadership capacity and international capabilities. Still, the United States also is seriously limited in its claim to leadership of the new century. It, too, has domestic problems that run wide and deep. None of them can be remedied by adding to its military edge or by continuing to resort to interventions abroad. The policy conclusion from this analysis is that engaging China at every opportunity, and treating China as a respected partner, remain the best option for the United States as well as for Japan and the European Union—not just because China's support is vital to dealing effectively with problems of global scope but also because helping China confront its own social and environmental problems is in every country's interest.

By demonstrating the benefits of a collaborative approach to China, we may hope to contribute to its emerging civil society and reinforce the views of key figures in and around the Chinese state who believe cooperation with the United States is the wisest course. Democratizing China is not, however, the principal rationale for engaging it; that is the task of the Chinese themselves. But creating a mutually nonthreatening and beneficial relationship is an appropriate, and achievable, goal for the United States. Acting on the presumption of an existing or probable China threat, on the other hand, exaggerates China's intentions and capabilities and opens the door to a new Cold War.

Leadership

Analyzing the notion of China's century can be done on two levels. One involves aspirations and intentions: Do Chinese leaders believe their country should, and can, supplant the United States as global leader? The second level concerns capabilities: Does China possess the soft and hard power to take charge in world affairs and command a large following? We might remind ourselves of the unique qualities that accounted for US hegemony at the end of World War II: the dominant country with respect to trade, finance (the dollar backed by gold), and technology; the one major economy that emerged from the war not only physically intact but with unique attributes, such as nearly full employment and a military-industrial-scientific complex; military superiority, symbolized by the atomic bomb; and a global vision that embraced the spread of both US values and economic and political influence.

To displace or compete with the United States for global leadership, China would need to have assets *comparable* to those of the United States since World War II. "Comparable," for the obvious reason that in this post–Cold War, post-9/11 world, the indicators of leadership are not all the same as those that defined US hegemony at the end of World War II and afterward. Today's indicators might include:

- Generosity: sharing wealth, technical, human, and other resources with the rest of the world while also providing "public goods"— benefits to all comers
- Commanding loyalty: the ability to bring together allies and other supporters around specific policies
- Policy initiator and innovator: being first to articulate and implement foreign policies, programs, and activities, including dispensing rewards and punishments
- Model: having the values, culture, language, laws, and social and political practices that others seek to emulate
- Risk-taker: a willingness to act alone when believed necessary and regardless of others' (including allies') opinions

On this basis, China's capacity to lead might be judged by its ability to adapt to globalization, the strength of its ideas for dealing with climate change and other challenges to the global commons, its record of meeting its obligations under the United Nations Charter, the global influence of its culture and values, the attractiveness and strength of its domestic institutions, its success at responding to the demands of disadvantaged and alienated people, its ability to gain allies for its political causes, and of course its military capabilities.

As I see it, therefore, world leadership has both material and non-material elements—both soft power, such as ideas and vision, and hard power, such as money and weapons. In the next chapter, I assess ideas about the meaning of China's rise for developing countries, for China's place in the world, and for its military power. Here we will see the contrast between the perceptions of many Western analysts, especially those belonging to the China Leads school, and the words and actions of Chinese leaders. In Chapters 4 and 5, I look at the policy side of China's international relations, in three dimensions: relations with different world regions; with international institutions and multilateral organizations; and with two of its key Asian neighbors, South Korea and India. I conclude from that examination that China's capacity to exert influence is lower, and its self-proclaimed role as a "responsible great power" *(fuziren de daguo)* is less credible, than is often presumed.

We must therefore look *inside* China to answer questions about China's capacity to lead. Chapter 6 assesses how well China's leadership is handling large-scope problems common to many countries, such as poverty, social inequities, and environmental degradation. I also evaluate China's political leadership and soft-power resources, such as the educational and public health systems. In Chapters 7 and 8, I turn the skeptical focus from China to the United States, questioning the capacity and desirability for either country to dominate in the new century. Deeper US-China cooperation is a more appropriate policy direction than US efforts to remain the sole superpower, I conclude, and in Chapter 9 I explore ways to strengthen US engagement with China even while acknowledging the many issues that divide the two countries. The book closes with some specific suggestions for reducing the US-China gap in understanding and policy.

Notes

1. The one-minute ad appeared at www.theatlantic.com/politics/archive/2010/10/the-phenomenal-chinese-professor-ad/64982/.

2. These were the World Bank (formally, the International Bank for Reconstruction and Development), the International Monetary Fund, and the General Agreement on Tariffs and Trade (GATT, forerunner of the World Trade Organization).

3. Wang Jisi, "China's Search for a Grand Strategy: A Rising Great Power Finds Its Way," *Foreign Affairs* 90, no. 2 (2011): 68–79; Zheng Bijian, "China's 'Peaceful Rise' to Great-Power Status," *Foreign Affairs* 84, no. 5 (2005): 18–24.

4. Wang Jisi, China's leading authority on the United States, has characterized the view of China's leaders this way: "The United States will attempt to constrain and even block China's rise": Wang Jisi and Kenneth Lieberthal, "Addressing U.S.-China Strategic Distrust," Beijing University International Strategy Research Institute, March 2012, p. 10. This publication is the Chinese version of the Brookings Institution report cited in Chapter 9, n. 15.

5. Roger Irvine, "Primacy and Responsibility: China's Perception of Its International Future," *China Security*, no. 18 (2010); at www.chinasecurity.us. On the influence of these policy intellectuals, see also Rex Li, *A Rising China and Security in East Asia: Identity Construction and Security Discourse* (London: Routledge, 2009), pp. 225–226.

6. Gao Zugui, "The International Strategic Situation and Its Prospects in a Post-crisis Era," *Peace and Development Studies* (Beijing), February 2010, p. 70, cited in Irvine, "Primacy and Responsibility."

7. See, for example, Robert D. Kaplan, "The Geography of Chinese Power," *Foreign Affairs* 89, no. 3 (2010): 22–41, and Aaron L. Friedberg, *A Contest for Supremacy: China, America, and the Struggle for Mastery in Asia* (New York: W. W. Norton, 2011).

8. Condoleezza Rice was among those who banished the word when she became national security special assistant under George W. Bush. Rice wrote that China should be regarded as a "strategic competitor" because its goal was "to alter Asia's balance of power in its own favor." See her "Promoting the National Interest," *Foreign Affairs* 79, no. 1 (2000): 56.

9. For example, John Mearsheimer, who states in the introduction to *The Tragedy of Great Power Politics* (New York: W. W. Norton, 2001) that "a policy of engagement [with China] is doomed to fail. If China becomes an economic power-house it will almost certainly translate its economic might into military might and make a run at dominating Northeast Asia."

10. See, for example, the essays by Alastair Iain Johnston, Thomas G. Moore, and Samuel S. Kim in Kim, ed., *The International Relations of Northeast Asia* (Lanham, MD: Rowman & Littlefield, 2004), and David Shambaugh, *Beautiful Imperialist: China Perceives America, 1972–1990* (Princeton, NJ: Princeton University Press, 1991).

11. Contrast, for example, David M. Lampton, *Power Constrained: Sources of Mutual Strategic Suspicion in U.S.-China Relations* (Seattle, WA: National Bureau of Asian Research, 2010); Elizabeth C. Economy and Adam Segal, "The G-2 Mirage: Why the United States and China Are Not Ready to Upgrade Ties," *Foreign Affairs* 88, no. 3 (2009): 14–23; and Thomas J. Christensen, "The Advantages of an Assertive China: Responding to Beijing's Abrasive Diplomacy," *Foreign Affairs* 90, no. 2 (2011): 54–67.

12. Zbigniew Brzezinski has been particularly vocal about the possibilities for US-China ("G-2") cooperation in dealing with global problems. See, for example, his "The Group of Two That Could Change the World," *Financial Times*, January 13, 2009. On the notion of a China-US fusion, see Zachary Karabell, *Superfusion: How China and America Became One Economy and Why the World's Prosperity Depends on It* (New York: Simon & Schuster, 2009).

13. For example, Martin Jacques, *When China Rules the World: The End of the Western World and the Birth of a New Global Order* (New York: Penguin, 2009).

14. For example, by Alfred McCoy, "The Decline and Fall of the American Empire"; TomDispatch.com, December 5, 2010.

15. Biden, "China's Rise Isn't Our Demise," *New York Times*, September 7, 2011, online ed.

16. For example, Joseph S. Nye, Jr., "The Future of American Power," *Foreign Affairs* 89, no. 6 (2010): 2–12.

17. For example, Henry Kissinger, *On China* (New York: Penguin, 2011).

18. G. John Ikenberry, "The Rise of China and the Future of the West," *Foreign Affairs* 87, no. 1 (2008): 23–37.

3

Evaluating China's Place in the World

An old debate is currently resurfacing in China: "What about the West is worth adopting or adapting? Modern arms? Popular education? Marxism?" Or, in larger terms, "Does Westernization mean sacrificing our essential Chineseness?" The debate has its origins in China's difficult effort to come to grips with Westernization in the final decades of the Qing dynasty (1644–1911), in the ensuing Republican era (1912–1949), and then in Mao's China.[1] "We should not eat Western food in one gulp," Mao decided. Yet as an avid student of Marxism, a Western import, Mao could hardly say the Chinese shouldn't "eat Western food" at all. And when Deng Xiaoping came to supreme power and authorized the economic reforms in 1977–1978, he had no problem with Western food—so long as China controlled the menu.

So the debate goes on, but with a new twist today. China's new generation of leaders has literally imported a great deal from the West, including important elements of market capitalism. But it has put a wall up against liberal political models. Thus we have, in essence, a Chinese model that, some writers claim, is being systematically *exported* to developing countries. Below I examine that claim.

Beijing Consensus or Business as Usual?

Beijing Consensus is a term coined in 2004 by Joshua Cooper Ramo, a British economist and onetime Goldman Sachs managing partner. He treated China's developing-country (or Third World) policies as a major departure from the so-called Washington Consensus (WC), the group of policy preferences—such as privatization of state assets, deregulation, and liberalization of private investment terms—often pressed on developing countries by the International Monetary Fund (IMF), the World

15

Bank, and the US Treasury Department in return for loans and grants. The BC and its successor, the China Model, defy easy definition since Chinese officials do not refer to these terms in public and seem to discourage their use, probably out of fear that they will be taken as fixed formulas and become a target of criticism, just as has happened with the WC. But both the BC and the CM have been the subject of numerous articles by Chinese intellectuals since Deng's inauguration of the "opening up" policy.

In more recent years, Joseph Fewsmith tells us, this debate has pitted China's "new left," a loosely knit group of young nationalists that believes in a distinctive China model and rejects neoliberal reforms as well as Western-style democracy, and more cosmopolitan writers who support China's opening as essential to progressing economically and politically. Among the latter group are those who dismiss the notion that there *is* a China model, since China's development is still a work in progress, still searching for answers to numerous social ills and the capacity to innovate. But one thing these economic reformers accept is the reality of globalization and the determination to use it to China's advantage. Post-Mao leaders have done precisely that.

Outside China, however, the BC is a reality to analysts such as Ramo—a template for Chinese policies that emphasize a non-Western economic-development program, supposedly modeled on China's own experience, and an absolutist approach to state sovereignty. In Ramo's words, the BC both prefigures a "new development approach . . . driven by a desire to have equitable, peaceful high-quality growth" and applies "the increasingly thoughtful accumulation of tools of asymmetric power projection."[2] Critics argue that "Ramo's Beijing Consensus is a misguided and inaccurate summary of China's actual reform experience. It not only gets the empirical facts wrong about China, it also disregards the similarities and differences China's experience shares with other countries, and it distorts China's place in international politics."[3] Some detractors offer a harsher judgment: the Beijing Consensus is a subterfuge, meant to justify China's aid and investments to governments with blood on their hands.

Whether we agree or not that the Beijing Consensus or China Model is a conscious element of China's foreign policy may be beside the point. The essential matter is that China's rise brings a newly successful and powerful state to a world order in which the United States for too long has called the shots. Without directly challenging the United States, China offers another way of doing business—and with a degree of self-confidence and credibility that was often absent in Mao's era of "making revolution." That alternative, however it might be labeled, reflects the latest stage of the historical debate over Westernization referred to above—a debate now that concerns not just how much China's development should require accommodating the West, but also how China's policies toward developing countries should be distinguished from Western models if they are to serve Chinese interests.

With that understanding, we may say that China's alternative for developing economies seems to boil down to state capitalism imposed on weak societies. The state guides the economy, relying heavily on key enterprises and banks it privileges, adroit use of market mechanisms, and capital from long-term foreign investment rather than from short-term flows (in part to avoid excessive foreign indebtedness).[4] Central direction of the economy protects against excessive foreign entry while strengthening the roles of political leaders and government bureaucrats. Externally, this approach emphasizes state sovereignty, national interests, and noninterference by one state in another's affairs—all part of what the Chinese call their "new security concept," but which also amounts to favoring state power over civil society. Chinese commentaries stress the opportunity that the investments and aid they offer presents to developing countries to avoid the hazards of reliance on Western-dominated financial institutions: austerity programs that call for severe cuts in state-subsidized social welfare, deregulation of state-owned facilities, trade liberalization, and an open door for multinational corporation investment. To these so-called conditionalities that are the hallmarks of the Washington Consensus are other threats to state sovereignty: sanctions for nonperformance, such as withdrawal or stoppage of assistance; and at the outside, economic strangulation to induce a change of policy or even of regime.

Does this alternative Chinese approach to economic development—economically state-centered, politically illiberal—amount to an exportable model? While China's aid and investment pattern certainly emphasizes national development and a central role for government in steering the economy, critics of the BC are correct to say that this is not a model that conforms to China's actual economic practices at home. That could hardly be otherwise: the assets China brings to its economic reforms—an entrepreneurial spirit that survived the Mao era, the experiences of export-led economies nearby, the lure of the vast China market for overseas Chinese and other sources of capital and technology, and in recent times huge financial reserves for the state to disburse—are not found or easily duplicated elsewhere. Moreover, *de*centralization of economic decisionmaking has become a hallmark of China's reforms, though at the cost of putting regulatory authority in the hands of local politicians who often are also businessmen.

Perhaps most importantly, China's path to success, dubbed "socialism with Chinese characteristics"—the Chinese don't like the term *state capitalism*—incorporates Beijing's reliance on the "Washington" model of liberal internationalism. More than one-half of China's exports, for instance, are actually the exports of multinational corporations. China's principal trade and investment partners are the other major capitalist trading countries, just as is true of the United States, Japan, and the European Union. (The US and European markets account for about 37 percent of China's total exports.) China is a force in the World Trade Organization (WTO), which it joined in 2001 after a long battle against US objections. Now China is also a key player in the IMF and the World Bank, in which it is seeking greater voting power. And China is very active in concluding free-trade agreements with its East Asia neighbors. In a word, China has fully embraced globalization, capitalist style.

Relevant as well are the specific cases of China's approach to global warming and energy, two issues on which it has been a key player. China is now the world's largest carbon emitter by volume, while the United States leads on a per-person basis. Together, these two countries account for around 40 percent of total carbon emissions. In the quest for a new international treaty to replace the 1997 Kyoto Protocol, which the United States did not sign but China did, Beijing has been as unyielding as Washington when it comes to making climate policy conform to the global interest. Both countries reject specific targets for reduction of carbon dioxide. Beijing, moreover, insists that developing countries must be given special consideration if they are going to reduce carbon emissions. (China's method for calculating carbon dioxide emissions, which India and other countries have adopted—on the basis of carbon intensity in relation to output—is another obstacle to a binding treaty.) Likewise on energy issues, China's enormous demand drives the many oil and gas agreements it has concluded with producer countries. In 2010, China, which became a net oil importer in 1993, was the world's largest energy consumer, fourth-largest oil producer, and second-largest oil importer. It is already dependent on external sources for 54 percent of its oil, and many experts predict it will be the world's largest importer of oil by 2025. (For comparison, the United States ranked third as an oil producer, producing more than twice as much as China, and first among oil importers in 2010.)[5]

What these two cases show is not merely China's importance in the global environment and energy pictures, but also its fundamentally self-interested policies—just as we would expect of a great power that practices what passes for realism. China is no more likely to sacrifice its economic priorities for the sake of the global community than is the

United States or any other country. In a pattern set long ago by the most developed countries and their global corporations, China is busily extracting resources to promote its own growth. Its increasing dependence on external sources of energy has led it to befriend any number of authoritarian regimes, from Saudi Arabia, Iran, and Angola (China's top energy suppliers) to Sudan, Venezuela, and Kazakhstan. China is thus following a path similar to that set by the United States after World War II, when it gave unstinting support to undemocratic governments in the Middle East on the promise of long-term access to low-priced oil—though without the huge arms transfers that accompanied, and remain a key component of, US political support.

Abroad as at home, growth can carry a high price tag, as we shall see: official corruption and cronyism, widening income and opportunity gaps, and the need to enforce "stability" through increased repression. The notion of some writers that people's well-being is at the center of a Chinese model is a considerable exaggeration. China's "respect for sovereignty" has often been used to justify ignoring the human rights of people abroad when those rights conflict with state power, as we shall see in later chapters. China's foreign aid—which, in the Chinese definition, consists mainly of government-supported investment and low- to no-interest loans[6]—has certainly benefited people in many instances, as noted in the Africa and Latin America cases below. But aid always first serves the donor's own economic and political interests. China is no exception.

Thus, even as Beijing preaches statist economics and remains in important respects a developing country, it is also a key member of the global club of the rich. And as China gets richer and its status as a great economic power solidifies, we may predict—and I say this with emphasis: *its relevance to developing countries as a development model will decline.* China may continue seeking changes in the global financial and commercial order dominated by the West; but as Samuel Kim concluded some time ago, when one examines China's behavior in international organizations such as the UN, and its adherence to multilateral treaties, one finds a general conformity with existing rules and practices rather than a pattern of obstructionism. To be sure, there are important exceptions that are indicated later. But for the most part China is a system maintainer, not a system reformer or system transformer.[7]

Still, China's distinctive policies in developing countries have great appeal, particularly to those governments that, often for sound historical reasons, reject Western intrusions and aid with few results. Here is where China's "model" is most poignant, for Beijing is now better able than ever before to resist those external pressures it finds unacceptable, such as on currency reform, carbon emissions, and human rights.[8] Other developing countries may not find Chinese policies on these issues or their own development path relevant to their situations, but they surely admire China's ability to "say no." The problem that arises is whether or not these same governments will one day be able to say no to China, whose loans and businesses make it an imposing *foreign* presence. Even though Chinese aid, unlike the WC's, does not have "structural adjustment" rules that must be adopted by recipients, they often do forfeit some of their economic sovereignty. China's "noninterference" doctrine does not preclude its asserting—or at least being perceived as using—the power that comes from being the dominant investor.

China's Defensiveness

China's approach to the developing world has less to do with staking out a claim to leadership than with its effort to construct an international *identity* as a great power.[9] That effort, so different from the Mao era, includes not only its wide-ranging aid and investment but also membership in regional economic and political groups, a worldwide diplomacy, and active involvement in international organizations, particularly those in which Western countries are *not* members. Nevertheless, as Chinese foreign-policy intellectuals freely acknowledge,[10] these activities clearly do not amount to a grand strategy that seeks to redefine the international order and proclaim China's leading role in it. Hu Jintao's repeated references to building a "harmonious world" cannot be considered a serious plan. Unlike the United States, China does not have an outsized ideology that claims an exceptional history, global mission, and universal values; nor does it equate "national defense" with *inter*national security. Indeed, as one Chinese scholar lamented, China needs to find an alternative to the US notion of "interests above all else" and "human rights above state sovereignty" if it is going to be an influential player in global affairs.[11]

The role of nationalism is also fundamentally different for the two countries. US nationalism, which mixes a high degree of national pride with a belief in the superiority of US values and institutions,[12] has profoundly shaped a foreign policy of offensive realism—an expansive approach to national security. Yet US nationalism is also insular: It results in a consistent failure to comprehend and accept the legitimacy of others' nationalism. By contrast, Chinese nationalism is defensive and instrumental: it reflects China's modern history of vulnerability to external threats (including border insecurity) and the leadership's fear of internal political chaos, both of which are used by the Communist Party to mobilize the public during troubled times. As one China-watcher has put it, these features make Chinese nationalism "pragmatic" rather than ideological.[13]

Illustrative of that evaluation and the Chinese leadership's use and fear of popular nationalism is China's response to the rupture with Japan in 2012 over Tokyo's purchase of the Senkaku Islands (called Diaoyudao or Diaoyutai in China), the disputed island group in the East China Sea. As in past years of demonstrations against Japan, the leadership was caught between approving people's patriotism and keeping it from causing an irreparable rift with Japan, a country with which China has trade approaching $350 billion a year (China's second-largest trade partner after the United States) and which is the number-one foreign investor in China. A signed editorial in *Renmin ribao* (People's Daily), the official newspaper, referred more than once to "irrational conduct," and pointed out that wild anti-Japanese actions would be no more logical than Japan's actions. (Subsequently, a Chinese mob in Xian attacked a Japanese-made car and nearly killed the Chinese driver.) China would act in accordance with international norms, the editorial said. Yet it took issue with Deng's guideline on keeping a low profile. "A bloodied people is destined to be bullied, and a country that always maintains a low profile will inevitably be defeated."[14]

Yet one searches in vain for a Chinese counterpart to Henry Luce's vision or to any history of belief in a global Chinese mission. The Chinese do not believe, as many in the United States do, that what is good for their country is good for the world. Nor is there evidence that China today seeks to restore the ancient Sinocentric order and thus reverse the "century of humiliation" that began in the early 1800s. The notion of China as the Middle Kingdom—the center of the civilized world—was built on a glorious isolationism and ethnic superiority, precisely the opposite of Luce's idealism. Like many earlier and later US political leaders, Luce was inspired by the belief that its values should be proclaimed abroad. But he was also convinced that the strength of the postwar US economic system made it the obvious center of a restored global economy. And there was more: Luce spoke of "America as the Good Samaritan, really believing again that it is more blessed to give than to receive, and America as the powerhouse of the ideals of Freedom and Justice." Here was the traditional missionary impulse in US foreign policy—bestowing the "blessings of liberty" on one and all, whether invited or not—that is missing from the Chinese lexicon.

If anything, China's worldview, even in the heady days under Chairman Mao when revolution was declared "the main trend in the world today," has always been defensively motivated and riveted on domestic achievement. The models of correct international relationships—the five principles of peaceful coexistence—and independent economic development, whether Mao's self-reliance or Deng's market socialism, have been presented as virtuous alternatives to interventionist Western models built on capitalist individualism. China's singular purpose has been to deflect Western power and thus contribute to the security needed for China to carry out socialist development while maintaining political order—that is, unchallenged Communist Party rule. As China's "opening to the outside world" that began under Deng Xiaoping makes clear, this is not a rejectionist program: large-scale economic engagement with the West is perfectly acceptable so long as China maintains freedom of action in domestic and foreign policy and avoids war with the major powers. But it is not the stuff of hegemonic dreams.[15]

We can understand what China has been up to over the last thirty years from this inside-out perspective. Under Deng, the appeal to "keep a low profile, never take the lead" was based on the conviction, which still holds, that China's first priority is rapid development of the economy. "Economic construction," he said, "is at the core of [foreign policy] tasks; it is the basis for the solution of our external and internal problems."[16] What he meant—and what Mao meant, using similar language, and what today's leaders also mean—is that attaining development goals is the essential precondition for strengthening China's external security and maintaining social order. As Deng frequently said, China can only achieve its goals if it has social stability and the elimination of poverty.[17] (See Appendix, document 1 for a contemporary Chinese view of the primacy of domestic issues.)

Consider former premier Wen Jiabao's remarks in an interview:

China is not a superpower. Although China has a population of 1.3 billion and although in recent years China has registered fairly fast economic and social development since reform and opening up, China still has this problem of unbalanced development between different regions and between China's urban and rural areas. China remains a developing country. We still have 800 million farmers in rural areas, and we still have dozens of millions of people living in poverty. As a matter of fact, over 60 million people in rural and urban areas in China still live on allowances for basic living costs in my country. And each year, we need to take care of about 23 million unemployed in urban areas and about 200 million farmers come and go to cities to find jobs in China. We need to make committed and very earnest efforts to address all these problems. To address our own problems, we need to do a great deal. China is not a superpower. That's why we need to focus on our own development and on our efforts to improve people's lives.[18]

The only point missing from Wen's presentation is that the Chinese party-state, in order to preserve its right to rule and its development path, will continue to vigorously *enforce* public order against all manner of opposition, whether from the left or right—again, just as Deng Xiaoping did.[19] When the social fabric seemed about to tear apart in the winter of 1986/87 and then most dramatically in June 1989, Deng had no compunctions about cracking down, not just on demonstrating students and workers but also on some of the top leaders who disagreed with his get-tough strategy. The same mindset prevailed under the so-called fourth generation of PRC leaders, led by Hu Jintao. Beginning in 2004, Hu called for creating a "harmonious society" in a "harmonious world," concepts that embraced and expanded Deng's mission: not only to make the country strong enough to resist foreign pressure, regardless of the issue, but also to insist on recognition as a "responsible great power" whose views must count on all important international issues. But, as an authoritative editorial in the official *People's Daily* stated in 2005, "Protecting stability comes before all else. Any behavior that wrecks stability and challenges the law will directly damage the people's fundamental interests."

These ominous words came amid widening income inequality and growing popular anger at illegal land seizures, issues we will return to later.[20] The warning also applied to high-ranking colleagues, as Wen Jiabao made clear when, toward the end of his tenure in 2012, he indirectly criticized a fellow Politburo member and party secretary of Chongqing, Bo Xilai, saying that another Cultural Revolution might occur if wrongheaded (read "leftist" or "Mao-era") policies were followed.[21] Bo's evident ambition to join the Politburo's standing committee, the apex of party power, and his ruthless pursuit of personal enemies as well as criminals in Chongqing probably raised questions about his acceptance of rule by consensus. Tales of corruption involving Bo's and his wife's families soon emerged—blatant use of their powerful patron's *guanxi* with businesses and foundations, the sort that always arouses public anger. Adding to the drama, Bo was found to have wiretapped the telephones of top officials.[22] Once again the official press called for the support of party leaders, linked Bo's dismissal to China's future stable development, and censored blogs that commented on the case.[23] Ahead of the eighteenth party congress in November, Bo was expelled from the CCP and ordered to face charges that include bribery and abuse of power.

It is no exaggeration to say that Chinese leaders are obsessed with maintaining social order and fearful of anyone who might pose a challenge to their authority. Instability is the obverse of "harmonious society" and, by extension, a "harmonious world." Chinese leaders reason that without extensive social controls, economic growth will be at the mercy of popular forces—labor, farmers, ethnic minorities, migrant workers, and ordinary citizens angry at the privileged lives of the high and mighty—that seek to improve their lot by challenging the existing power structure. For if instability reigned in China, the country's rising role in world affairs would again be severely curtailed both by the need to devote even more resources to dealing with it and by the blow to China's reputation.[24] Bo Xilai's apparent abuse of power was not only a potential source of popular unrest; it also cast an unfavorable light on all members of the political elite.

"Harmonious World"

The term *harmonious world* encompasses a new Chinese assertiveness when dealing with core interests such as retaking Taiwan and protecting China's sovereignty.[25] It also embraces high-minded principles such as equity and consultation among states, common prosperity, and the peaceful resolution of disputes, ideas that if implemented would strengthen China's role in world politics at the expense of the United States and the West.[26] How these elements mesh is a matter of ongoing debate in Beijing, particularly concerning how to respond to the United States, a country China both needs and resents, and how to be a "good citizen" on regional and global issues. Here, official PRC policy is informed, and constrained, by factors that were not present in Mao's time: epistemic communities of experts who are attentive to the views of specialists outside China; the importance of collegiality and consensus in decisionmaking; the influence of netizens, bloggers, and other sources of critical opinion; the bureaucratization of foreign policy, due largely to the emergence of influential think tanks and research institutes; and the views of local power holders such as province leaders and businesspeople.[27] Even China's military, the People's Liberation Army (PLA), usually regarded as the most nationalistic institution, is thought by some observers to be embracing a more nation-centered rather than simply party-centered perspective.[28]

While none of these factors detracts from the absolute authority of China's top leaders, least of all on critical national-security problems, they indicate how policymaking today has become increasingly "normal" or pluralized, that is, subject to an array of domestic political, social, and economic forces in much the same way as happens in other major countries. The paramount leader cannot simply order that China "seek hegemony" even if he wanted to. But by the same token, neither can he afford to ignore his people's nationalist sensitivities that may stem from perceived slights or historical memory. Chinese thinking has its share of rationalizations that justify all manner of behavior, but using power politics to promote globalist ideals is not one of them.

The Chinese are proud of their long cultural traditions, but they are careful to avoid arguing on behalf of a Chinese cultural sphere that would rationalize subordinating neighboring countries. National pride looks forward to China's modernization, symbolized by Shanghai's skyscrapers, and not backward to dynastic rule symbolized by the dragon. Nor do the Chinese make grand pronouncements on specific international issues such as international law, global warming, and governance in particular countries. While US leaders will not hesitate to use domestic and international forums to expound on major international issues, including political developments in other countries, Chinese leaders are normally reticent.

Contrasting ideas of leadership flow from these differences. Modern US leaders have never doubted that the United States is born to lead, or that being number one is virtually a God-given right. Strangely, although China is sometimes criticized for being unable to get past its historical grievances, it is the United States that consistently sees itself as a country destined by history to lead the world to freedom and democracy. The idea is part and parcel of the US foreign-policy ideology.[29] "We are the indispensable nation," Secretary of State Madeleine Albright intoned during the Clinton administration. President Obama expressed the same thought in his 2012 State of the Union address. "We must lead the world," he said in Chicago in April 2007.[30] Benevolence and selflessness, US leaders insist, guide foreign policy. Accepting the Nobel Peace Prize in 2009, Obama sounded very much like John F. Kennedy when he said:

> Whatever mistakes we have made, the plain fact is this: The United States of America has helped underwrite global security for more than six decades with the blood of our citizens and the strength of our arms. The service and sacrifice of our men and women in uniform has promoted peace and prosperity from Germany to Korea, and enabled democracy to take hold in places like the Balkans. We have borne this burden not because we seek to impose our will. We have done so out of enlightened self-interest—because we seek a better future for our children and grandchildren, and we believe that their lives will be better if others' children and grandchildren can live in freedom and prosperity.[31]

Political party does not matter when world leadership is the issue. Mitt Romney, campaigning for the presidency in 2011, said: "In an American Century, America has the strongest economy and the strongest military in the world. In an American Century, America leads the free world and the free world leads the entire world."[32] Thus do Henry Luce's ideas remain alive nearly seventy years later.

US leaders representing both major parties—not just presidents and their chief advisers, but also most members of Congress—have invariably insisted that they are guided by traditional Western values: democracy, individual freedom, human rights, the rule of law, free markets. The uniquely US claim is that "American values are universal," as former national-security special assistant Condoleezza Rice wrote.[33] US leaders believe they are duty-bound to extend US values abroad. Hence, the frequent comments on other countries' political processes, the direct interventions abroad in the name of democracy and freedom, and the numerous US attempts at nation building, from Cuba to Afghanistan, in the conviction that the US experiment with democracy can and should be transposed to other societies, *in their own best interests.* Yet at the same time, US officials have asserted that "pragmatism" and "enlightened self-interest" are also guiding tenets of foreign policy. How then explain the fact that the United States has often backed tyrants with generous amounts of money and arms (from Chiang Kai-shek in pre-1949 China to Muammar Qaddafi in Libya), trained their secret police (in many Latin American countries, for example), flouted international law (for example, the Convention Against Torture) or refused to sign or ratify it (as with the Convention on the Law of the Sea and the Comprehensive Test Ban Treaty), and erected trade barriers to protect its industries (such as cotton, steel, and tobacco)? The answer lies in the US understanding of national interest, which embraces an expansive interpretation of both realism *and* idealism—hence a foreign policy that practices engagement *and* the use of force, working through coalitions *and* taking unilateral action, promoting democracy everywhere *and* supporting dictators.

For some countries, balancing these seemingly contradictory forces may seem impossible, but not for the United States. As President Obama said, "we must try as best we can to balance isolation and engagement, pressure and incentives, so that human rights and dignity are advanced over time." The practical significance of this conception of national interest was demonstrated by Bush in Iraq and Obama in Libya; namely, that interests and values may compel intervention even if US security is not directly threatened. "Great powers don't just mind their own business," as Condoleezza Rice went on to assert—a recipe for endless interventions abroad and a justification of interference in the internal affairs of other countries. When, for example, Secretary of State Clinton commented critically on Russia's parliamentary elections at the end of

2011, she said: "The United States and many others around the world have a strong commitment to democracy and human rights. It's part of who we are. It's our values."[34] Clinton purported to speak for the Russian people's quest for democracy, which naturally drew an angry response from Prime Minister Vladimir Putin. Similarly, at the height of the crisis with Libya in 2011, Secretary Clinton said during a tour of Africa that too many rulers were determined to hold on to power and needed to be more accountable, otherwise "it is time for them to go." Despotic rulers who resisted democratic reforms, she warned, put them "on the wrong side of history."[35]

This is precisely the kind of dialogue that US and Chinese officials frequently engage in, though it is a dialogue of the deaf. The United States pressures China to liberalize its politics and the Chinese are piqued at what they see as an assault on their sovereignty and national pride. US officials urge Chinese leaders to be on the right side of history; the Chinese resent being lectured to about their place in history. Washington expresses concern about human rights abuses in China and urges China to release or grant a fair hearing to dissidents; Chinese authorities deny the abuses but on occasion will release a prisoner just to quiet US protests. In all such cases, the Chinese are on the defensive: they have yet to turn the tables on US leaders and lecture *them* on history and human rights.

The Practice of Leadership

Equally important as talking like a leader is acting like one—taking the initiative, pointing the direction for others, developing coalitions, and building trust. Even if Chinese leaders were to make a determined effort to displace the United States, there are plenty of reasons to think this would prove immensely difficult. In Asia, suspicions of China rank second only to suspicions of Japan. Aside from Japan, publics in India, Indonesia, and Vietnam are among those where China's rise is not popular even though much admired. The reasons are clear enough: memories of Maoist support of insurgencies against several governments during the Cold War; uncertainty about the scope of China's ambitions, especially given its unresolved territorial and national integration issues; fear of China's economic power, including its trade competition and the purposes of its foreign aid and investments; China's export of environmental problems such as deforestation and desertification; and, where large overseas Chinese communities exist, questions about their loyalties and envy of their commercial prominence. In fact, China's own missteps in

Asia in recent years have helped the US image: Beijing's refusal to criticize, much less pressure, North Korea over its nuclear-weapons program, its provocative behavior toward South Korea, and its run-ins with Japan and some of the Southeast Asian countries over ownership of disputed islands in the South and East China Seas.

Whereas the United States has assumed highly visible roles in international affairs even in the midst of an economic crisis, China has not. In the international economy, for instance, the dollar remains almighty. Some PRC officials have stated that the yuan (or renminbi) will be fully convertible in another decade, meaning that international businesses can trade, raise money, and settle bills in yuan. But while the yuan is increasingly circulating outside China, including in its foreign trade, and despite Chinese expressions of concern about the dollar's soundness, Beijing does not seem anxious to challenge the dollar's supremacy.[36] To the contrary, and as another example of the extent of China-US economic interdependence, the Chinese continue to invest in US bonds—roughly $1.5 trillion at last count—because, when all is said and done, the US Treasury is still the safest place in the world for their money.

One might well say that the 2011 debt crisis in Washington severely tested that conclusion. The outcome, which included Standard & Poor's downgrading of the US credit rating, reinforced a view—strongly pushed by some Chinese editorial writers[37]—that the United States, having long been engaged in reckless spending, might not be able to remain the country of choice for the world's money. But so far it is, for China as for everyone else. And when the Greek debt crisis threatened to engulf Europe later in 2011, China hesitated to cut a deal it could easily have afforded—loaning several billion dollars in exchange for political concessions, such as recognition as a market economy—that would have dramatically increased its global stature. Even though the European Union is China's largest export market, Hu Jintao stood in the background at G-20 meetings in Paris while Barack Obama took center stage, urging the Europeans to solve their own problems.

Similarly on the global stage, the foreign-policy and international security capabilities of the United States are without peer. It often acts as a peace broker in major international conflicts, whether external (such as Israel-Palestine) or internal (such as Iraq after US withdrawal). US military officers train the militaries of numerous countries abroad and at home; "advise and assist" missions are in place from Uganda to the Philippines; and defense department personnel are constant visitors to partner countries. The United States leads the way in imposing sanctions on defiant regimes (North Korea, Iran, Libya, and Syria, for example), ignores the United Nations when US interests are judged to require unilateral intervention (such as in Iraq and Kosovo), and is the player whose support is most sought when it comes to making breakthroughs on certain global issues (such as global warming and trade). No other country provides as many "public goods" as does the United States, such as acting as the global market of choice and accepting large annual trade deficits in order to ensure fluidity in the global economy. China, by contrast, protects its domestic market from international competition in many sectors. It is not a dependable market of last resort for its Asian neighbors. They rely on China to import their products, such as machinery, for use in Chinese exports; but when PRC exports fall, so do its imports from around Asia.

Myanmar (Burma) offers a good illustration of the differences between US and PRC diplomacy. Until late in 2011, the United States had treated Myanmar's military leadership as a pariah, imposing sanctions and keeping official relations to a minimum. China, meanwhile, had developed a close political and economic relationship with Myanmar, becoming its leading investor and trade partner, but in the process occupying a perhaps too preponderant position there. When a new Myanmar leadership unexpectedly began dismantling some of the more onerous restrictions on human and political rights, the US State Department commented favorably and dispatched Secretary of State Clinton to Yangon (Rangoon). Unlike Chinese diplomats, who never commented publicly on the Myanmar government's political or economic situation, Clinton complimented the new Myanmar leaders, held two meetings with the longtime prodemocracy opposition leader Aung San Suu Kyi, and urged the government to take further steps, such as the release of all political prisoners and an end to the oppression of ethnic minority groups. (When an activist monk who had been released was subsequently detained, Washington demanded an explanation.) Clinton also promised to provide a modest aid package and left open the possibility of removing the sanctions if Myanmar extended the reforms. The Chinese were left to ponder whether the US move was part of an effort to contain their ambitions in South Asia or a response to Myanmar's effort to introduce greater balance in its international relations.[38]

China's voting pattern in the UN Security Council reflects China's multiple, and often contradictory, roles as a great power, a socialist country, and a Third World leader. When it comes to conflicts in Africa, the Middle East, and other regions, Beijing's voice is rarely heard or sought. When its diplomats address ongoing conflicts, they urge only that the contending sides talk—good advice, but also safely distant. China votes for some UN Security Council–sanctioned humanitarian interventions, such as in East Timor (1999) and Côte d'Ivoire (Ivory Coast, 2011), but rejects them when (as in Syria in 2012) they believe a humanitarian intervention might (as in Libya) involve the use of force to bring to power a regime that will support Western interests. PRC policy on international interventions in the Third World may sometimes be influenced in part by whether or not a regional consensus has formed on them. When it voted along with all the other members of the Security Council in favor of a French and UN attack to remove Laurent Gbagbo from office in Côte d'Ivoire, African opinion was decisively against his coup. On the other hand, Beijing went against the strong consensus on Syria within the Arab League, which demanded in 2012 that President Bashar al-Assad step down and end his brutal crackdown on dissidents.[39]

Washington, on the other hand, is far more likely than Beijing to support interventions in the Third World, whether they have Security Council support or not and regardless of any humanitarian motivation. The United States dispenses opinions and advice not only on conflicts everywhere, but on many countries' internal political practices as well—their elections (including China's and Taiwan's), the fairness of their laws, the probity of their officials, and the viability of their institutions. Congressionally funded organizations—the International Republican Institute and the National Democratic Institute—are among the US groups that carry out training in democracy and other political activities in those countries, moreover, and the US government often contributes money and advice to foreign political parties it favors. Such activities would never be tolerated if carried out by foreigners within the United States.

China's economic prowess is widely respected and even held in awe around Asia, as various Pew Research Center polls show.[40] But where, China's friends may have asked, is Beijing's authority when regime change hangs in the balance? The fact that China would not exercise a veto in the Security Council to prevent a NATO attack on Qaddafi's forces is a potent reminder of which countries usually call the shots on questions of war and peace. Beijing evidently found that it could not oppose a UN action that was favored by the African Union and was consistent with the 2005 "responsibility to protect" resolution passed in the General Assembly.

Unlike the United States, China *has no one to lead*. As one prominent Chinese analyst has written, China needs to find "high-quality friends"—military and political allies on a par with US partners around the world.[41] Until it can achieve what the analyst called moral stature, China's foremost task, mainly in Asia, is to lower fears of it so that it can improve its economic and military position. This is defensive realism: competing with the United States, trying to weaken its paramount position, but not attempting to displace it.

When President Hu Jintao visited Washington in late 2010, and then–Vice President Xi Jinping in early 2012, their consistent message was that China seeks "mutual respect and mutual benefit." The contrast with the message of US leaders was striking: President Obama and other senior officials reiterated the theme, first promoted in 2005 under President George W. Bush, that China should be a "responsible stakeholder" and "play by the rules." They meant that China should align with certain US policy preferences—on North Korea, trade, and currency valuation, for example. Hu and Xi stressed cooperation, too, but as an equal player and not a follower or junior partner—a "win-win" (*huli gongying*) approach, in Xi's words. Xi's view of responsibility was that the United States should respect China's "core interests" in Taiwan and Tibet as well as allow for more technology sales to China. The decisive difference lies in the two countries' different roles in the international system—one a rising power, the other already risen and determined to remain in charge.[42]

China Threat?
The Contentious Debate over China's Military

China has a long way to go to become a great military power, much less challenge US preeminence. Only the United States has been willing and able to fight two wars simultaneously. Only the United States maintains a global network of bases and military access points, and from these places it conducts overflights, training exercises, and prepositioning of war matériel. Its military spending exceeds that of all other countries combined. Carrying out regime change by military and nonmilitary means, undertaking covert military actions around the world, and acting both multilaterally and unilaterally have long been staples of US foreign policy. China's military profile is more akin to that of a second-tier power. Its actual military spending is a mystery since from year to year some categories of spending are left off the books, for example a portion of weapons research and development, subsidies for certain military industries, and acquisitions of weapons from other countries. While China has significantly increased military spending every year since the late 1980s—officially, it was 601 billion yuan (about $91.5 billion) in 2011, and 670 billion yuan (about $111 billion) was announced for 2012—even the addition of another $25 billion to cover extrabudgetary spending would still leave China's spending about six times lower than the US military officially spends (and the Pentagon's budget, too, does not include some items, such as spending on nuclear weapons, interest on deficit spending for past wars, veterans' benefits, and supplementary funds voted for undeclared wars, such as in Iraq and Afghanistan).

China has no prospect of catching up to the United States militarily without a major long-term reordering of budget priorities. In fact, Chinese military spending is not out of line with that of some neighbors, such as India and Taiwan, or that of the United States and its NATO partners when calculated on a per capita basis, as a percentage of the central government budget (about 6 percent), or as a percentage of GDP (around 2 percent). China's top military officer was right to ask aloud, during a visit to the United States in 2011, why questions were being raised about his country's military capabilities and intentions when the United States was so far ahead of China in both weapons and military doctrine.[43] Indeed, in the Chinese view one major factor that worries their leaders about US intentions is precisely their awareness of China's relative military inferiority.[44]

Furthermore, despite ongoing weapons modernization, China's military reach and capabilities remain limited (see Table 3.1). Its approximately $5.3 billion in arms exports (delivered), for instance, ranked sixth in the world for 2006–2011, far below US exports of about $46.5 billion and Russia's $35.6 billion for those years. Pakistan, a US ally, has been China's biggest customer, while the United States has focused on arming a host of Persian Gulf allies. In terms of arms sales, the gap between the United States and China—and the rest of the world—grew even larger in 2011, when US sales accounted for an astounding 79 percent of global arms sales, compared with China's of about 3 percent.[45] Among arms importers from 2006 to 2011, China ranked second in the world to India ($9.2 billion compared with $13.9 billion) and just ahead of two US allies: South Korea and Pakistan.

Then there is the oft-discussed matter of China building an aircraft carrier. Beijing announced in 2011 that it will start building two; one is expected to be in service by the end of 2012, but it is a refurbished Soviet-era carrier and is intended mainly for training purposes. The United States, on the other hand, has ten aircraft carriers (plus one under construction) attached to the Fifth, Sixth, and Seventh Fleets. Nor does China's arsenal of nuclear weapons compare with the enormous capabilities of the US force: more than eight thousand US operational and inactive warheads, as against China's 240, many of which apparently are not deployed; nearly two thousand US nuclear weapons with strategic (intercontinental) range, compared with China's twenty; sixteen US bal-

Table 3.1 US-China Military Comparisons

	United States	China
Spending 2010 2000–2010	$685.1 billion[a] $5.85 trillion[b]	$114 billion $758 billion
Arms exports, 2006–2011	$46.5 billion	$5.3 billion
Arms imports, 2006–2011	$5 billion	$9.3 billion
Foreign aid	$244 bil. (total, 2000–2008), of which $65.9 bil. was military. (In 2008, military aid was about 31% of total aid.)	$74 bil. (2002–2007), of which $174 million was military aid[c]
Bases abroad[d]	823 in 39 countries	None
Nuclear Weapons	About 8,500 (including more than 1,900 strategic and operational)	240 (possibly 20 strategic in stockpile)
Active personnel	1.38 million	2.25 million

*Sources:*http://en.wikipedia.org/wiki/Military_budget_of_the_United_States#Budget_for_2 010; Stockholm International Peace Research Institute (SIPRI) at http://armstrade.sipri.org /armstrade/html/export_toplist.php and http://milexdata.sipri.org/result.php4; www.census.gov /compendia/statab/2011/tables/11s1297.pdf; Lum et al., "Chinese Foreign Aid Activities," pp. 2–5; US Department of Defense, *Base Structure Report: Fiscal Year 2007 Baseline*, p. 6, at www.defense.gov/pubs/BSR_2007_Baseline.pdf; Federation of American Scientists, "Status of World Nuclear Forces 2011," www.fas.org/programs/ssp/nukes/nuclearweapons /nukestatus.html.
Notes: a. Includes the wars in Iraq and Afghanistan, but does not include other military-related costs such as interest on the debt, medical care for wounded soldiers, and veterans' future benefits. b. In constant dollars. c. China clearly does not want to publicize its military aid, hence the tiny sum it has reported, which omits weapons transfers among other items. See Lum et al., "Chinese Foreign Aid Activities," table 5, p. 8. d. The base figure does not include bases in seven US territories. Bases in Germany, Japan, and South Korea account for 523 of the 823 total.

listic missile submarines, compared with one for China; and more than one thousand US nuclear cruise missiles, compared with none for China.[46]

While Taiwan remains China's, and the PLA's, major security concern, the People's Liberation Army is venturing farther from China than ever before. Its military-to-military contacts continue to increase. It is devoting considerable attention to so-called nontraditional threats, including terrorism but also counterpiracy operations in the Gulf of Aden, disaster relief in Haiti, and noncombat evacuation operations in Kyrgyzstan—actually, the kinds of activities that *support* US and international efforts. China has invested substantially to carry out these operations, such as in large amphibious ships, long-range transport aircraft, at-sea replenishment vessels, and hospital ships.[47] Just over two thousand Chinese soldiers have also taken part in twelve UN peacekeeping operations, though these have not been combat troops.[48] (See Appendix, document 2, for the official PRC report on national defense.)

Rather than interpret Chinese military developments as signs of aggressive intent or power projection, a more reasonable assessment should take into account China's greater wealth and prestige compared with the Mao era, the leadership's concern about *internal* security problems ("a critical task," the national defense report says), and the military's normal quest to modernize. The PLA's involvement in international missions is a way to demonstrate China's claim to being a "responsible great power." At the same time, more and more national-security resources are being devoted to dealing with domestic disorder, "keep[ing] insolvent defense factories afloat, or simply ensur[ing] the military's loyalty."[49] The size and capability of China's military forces, the PLA navy in particular, are bound to increase. So, as a consequence, is China's search for points of military access in East and South Asia. But aggressive intent is another matter entirely, and a strong argument can be made that what the Chinese are really about is protecting their security interests from legal or political assault. The PRC is increasingly assertive about its national interests, yet remains essentially reactive when it comes to protecting them.[50]

Some US military planners and their academic supporters present China as building toward a naval challenge to the United States that includes preventing or neutralizing US access to the Taiwan Strait, using international law to limit US military access to China's EEZ (exclusive economic zone), laying claim to large swaths of the East Asian seas, and seeking bases in Myanmar and elsewhere.[51] The evidence for these objectives is sparse and unconvincing. In fact, US Navy officials find that while the Chinese are indeed upgrading their naval capabilities, they seem mainly intended for "antiaccess" missions, primary among them being to deny or delay a US response should another crisis emerge over Taiwan. Moreover, these officials see no sign that the Chinese navy has achieved "operational proficiency" with the other services or has sufficient combat experience.[52]

One may make the argument that, nevertheless, the trend line of China's military capabilities is upward and therefore it is only a matter of time before the PRC becomes a military rival of the United States in the Asia-Pacific and eventually a global military power. But as Chinese military capabilities increase and improve, so do those of the United States—and that is precisely what is happening now with US air and naval power in the Asia-Pacific region.[53] Furthermore, such worst-case hypothesizing presumes several dramatic reversals, not only in PRC military thinking but also, and especially, in China-US relations. As I argue later, both countries have every opportunity to forestall arms racing and confrontations that would lead to the worst case. Trends occur for a reason; there is nothing inevitable about them.

Notes

1. Joseph Fewsmith, "Debating 'the China Model,'" *China Leadership Monitor*, no. 35 (2011); at http://media.hoover.org/sites/default/files/documents/CLM35JF.pdf.

2. Joshua Cooper Ramo, *The Beijing Consensus* (London: Foreign Policy Centre, 2004), pp. 3-4; online at http://fpc.org.uk/fsblob/244.pdf.

3. Scott Kennedy, "The Myth of the Beijing Consensus," *Journal of Contemporary China* 19, no. 65 (2010): 461–477.

4. Here, China's economic model is part of a global trend, at least among emerging market countries: see Ian Bremmer, "State Capitalism Comes of Age: The End of the Free Market?" *Foreign Affairs* 88, no. 3 (2009): 40–55.

5. Statistics from the US Energy Information Agency, May 2011; at www.eia.gov/countries/cab.cfm?fips=CH. For background on China see Denise Eby Konan and Jian Zhang, "China's Quest for Energy Resources on Global Markets," *Pacific Focus* 23, no. 3 (2008): 382–399.

6. Thomas Lum, Hannah Fischer, Julissa Gomez-Granger, and Anne Leland, "China's Foreign Aid Activities in Africa, Latin America, and Southeast Asia," CRS Report R-40361, February 25, 2009. The CRS study is based on one by the New York University Wagner School, "Understanding Chinese Foreign Aid: A Look at China's Development Assistance to Africa, Southeast Asia, and Latin America," April 25, 2008.

7. Samuel S. Kim, "China in World Politics," in Barry Buzan and Rosemary Foot, eds., *Does China Matter? A Reassessment* (London: Routledge, 2004), pp. 37–53.

8. "We will not yield to any pressure of any form forcing us to appreciate" the yuan, said Premier Wen Jiabao at the end of 2009. He reportedly described such pressure as an effort to contain China's development: Reuters, "China to Stay the Course on Currency, Wen Says," *New York Times*, December 28, 2009, online ed.

9. Lee, *A Rising China*. Lee's book, however, focuses on China's relations with the major powers in East Asia and not with the Third World.

10. For example, Wang Jisi, "China's Search for a Grand Strategy."

11. Liu Kang, "'Interest Above All' Cannot Become the Foundation of China's Foreign Policy," *Renmin wang*, February 16, 2012; at http://world.people.com.cn/GB/17126233.html.

12. Minxin Pei, "The Paradoxes of American Nationalism," *Foreign Policy* (May–June 2003): 31–37; at www.foreignpolicy.com/articles/2003/05/01/the_paradoxes_of_american_nationalism.

13. See Suisheng Zhao, "China's Pragmatic Nationalism: Is It Manageable?" *Washington Quarterly* 29, no. 1 (2005–2006): 131–144.

14. "How Should We Protect Diaoyudao?" *Renmin ribao*, September 15, 2012; at http://opinion.people.com.cn/n/2012/0915/c1003-19018681.html.

15. For an extended discussion of these points in relation to China's Third World policies, see my "Changing Perspectives and Policies" in Lowell Dittmer and George T. Yu, eds., *China, the Developing World, and the New Global Dynamic* (Boulder, CO: Lynne Rienner Publishers, 2010), pp. 13–35.

16. Speech of September 1, 1982, in Deng Xiaoping, *Fundamental Issues in Present-Day China* (Beijing: Foreign Languages Press, 1987), p. 4.

17. "To achieve genuine political independence a country must first lift itself out of poverty," Deng said. That required removing barriers to world trade and other essential contacts with the rest of the world; otherwise, "if our country were plunged into disorder and our nation reduced to a heap of loose sand, how could we ever prosper? The reason the imperialists were able to bully us in the past was precisely that we were a heap of loose sand": Deng, *Fundamental Issues*, pp. 173 and 165, respectively.

18. Interview with Fareed Zakaria of CNN in 2008; at http://articles.cnn.com /2008-09-29/world/chinese.premier.transcript_1_financial-crisis-interview-vice -premier/4?_s=PM:WORLD.

19. See Willy Lam, "Hu Jintao's Great Leap Backward," *Far Eastern Economic Review* (January–February 2009): 19–22.

20. See Jim Yardley, "China Warns Citizens It Won't Tolerate Threats to Stability," *New York Times*, August 1, 2005, p. A5.

21. "Talking About a Cultural Revolution," *Financial Times*, March 14, 2012. Bo Xilai mixed policies popular with the poor with harsh crackdowns on criminals and corrupt officials that often violated the rule of law.

22. Jonathan Ansfield and Ian Johnson, "Ousted Chinese Leader Is Said to Have Spied on Other Top Officials," *New York Times*, April 25, 2012, online ed.

23. See, for example, the *Renmin ribao* editorials: Commentator, "Consciously Abide by Party Discipline and the Law" and "Using Practical Actions to Protect the Excellent Situation in the Stability of Reform and Development," April 13, 2012.

24. For a similar view, see Susan L. Shirk, *China: Fragile Superpower* (New York: Oxford University Press, 2007).

25. Wang Yizhou, "China's Path: Growing and Learning," *Global Asia* 5, no. 1 (2010): 12–16.

26. Hongying Wang and James N. Rosenau, "China and Global Governance," *Asian Perspective* 33, no. 3 (2009): 5–39.

27. David M. Lampton, ed., *The Making of China's Foreign and Security Policy in the Era of Reform, 1978–2000* (Stanford, CA: Stanford University Press, 2001); Linda Jakobson and Dean Knox, "New Foreign Policy Actors in China," SIPRI (Stockholm International Peace Research Institute) Policy Paper no. 26, September 2010.

28. Jakobson and Knox, "New Foreign Policy Actors," p. 15.

29. For relevant quotations from various US foreign-policy leaders, see my *United States Against the Third World: Anti-nationalism and Intervention* (New York: Praeger, 1971).

30. "I dismiss the cynics who say that this new century cannot be another [in which] we lead the world in battling immediate evils and promoting the ultimate good," Obama also said in that speech. Quoted in Richard Dreyfuss, "Obama's Evolving Foreign Policy," *Nation*, July 21–28, 2008, p. 22.

31. Text in *New York Times*, December 10, 2009, online ed.

32. Ashley Parker, "In Foreign Policy Speech, Romney Calls for an 'American Century,'" *New York Times* blog; at http://thecaucus.blogs.nytimes.com /2011/10/07/in-foreign-policy-speech-romney-calls-for-an-american-century/?hp.

33. Rice, "Promoting the National Interest."

34. David M. Herszenhorn and Steven Lee Myers, "Putin Says Clinton Incited Protests over Russian Vote," *New York Times*, December 8, 2011, online ed.

35. Steven Lee Myers, "Clinton Presses Africans to Abandon Authoritarian Rulers, Singling Out Qaddafi," *New York Times*, June 14, 2011, p. A9.

36. From time to time, Chinese officials have floated the idea of creating a new international currency. In 2009, for instance, following on Wen Jiabao's criticisms of US financial policy and concern in China about the declining value of its holdings in the United States, the head of China's central bank proposed that at some point the international community should consider creating a new international currency reserve that includes other currencies besides the dollar: see David Barboza, "China Urges New Reserve to Replace the Dollar," *New York Times*, March 24, 2009, p. 5. China-Japan trade transactions now use renminbi.

37. One editorial said: "The U.S. government has to come to terms with the painful fact that the good old days when it could just borrow its way out of messes of its own making are finally gone. It should also stop its old practice of letting its domestic electoral politics take the global economy hostage and rely on the deep pockets of major surplus countries to make up for its perennial deficits. A little self-discipline would not be too uncomfortable for the United States, the world's largest economy and issuer of international reserve currency, to bear." The writer went on to suggest the need for a new "global reserve currency": Wang Yamei, "After Historic Downgrade, U.S. Must Address Its Chronic Debt Problems," *Xinhuanet*, August 6, 2011 at http://news.xinhuanet.com/english2010/indepth/2011-08/06/c _131032986_2.htm.

38. Jason Burke and Tania Branigan, "India and China Move to Protect Burmese Interests from US Influence," *Guardian*, December 1, 2011; online at www.guardian.co.uk/world/2011/dec/01/india-china-move-to-protect-burmese -interests.

39. China was pushed into a spoiler's role in the evolving Syrian civil war in 2012. Following Russia's lead, the Chinese took no part in international discussions with the Syrian opposition, with Turkey and the Arab states, or with human-rights groups about how best to pressure Assad and end the killing. All Beijing could do was sit on its veto power in the Security Council to ensure that a Libya-style military intervention in Syria would not be approved.

40. These are polls regularly conducted under the Pew Global Attitudes Project. See www.pewglobal.org.

41. Yan Xuetong, "How China Can Defeat America," *New York Times*, November 20, 2011, online ed.

42. The Chinese have been saying this for some time. See the comment report-ed by David M. Lampton: "China is most concerned with its own internal develop-ment and the United States is most concerned with trying to maintain international order. Therefore, our agendas are different": Lampton, "A Growing China in a Shrinking World: Beijing and the Global Order," in Ezra F. Vogel, ed., *Living with China: U.S./China Relations in the Twenty-first Century* (New York: W. W. Norton, 1997), p. 121.

43. The officer was General Chen Bingde, chief of the PLA general staff. See Elisabeth Bumiller, "Chinese General Says China Won't Challenge U.S. Military," *New York Times*, May 19, 2011, p. A3.

44. Wang and Lieberthal, "Addressing U.S.-China Strategic Distrust."

45. Based on an annual Congressional Research Service report. Chinese arms sales have been flat at around 3 percent a year for the past several years. See Thom

Shanker, "U.S. Arms Sales Make Up Most of Global Market," *New York Times*, August 27, 2012, p. A6. Total US arms sales in 2011 were reported as over $66 billion, compared with about $21 billion in 2010. The United States sells nearly half of all arms sold to developing countries. Russia occupies second place in all categories of arms sales. See also Thom Shanker, "Global Arms Sales Dropped Sharply in 2010, Congressional Study Finds," *New York Times*, September 24, 2011, p. A10.

46. Arms Control Association, "Nuclear Weapons: Who Has What at a Glance"; at www.armscontrol.org/factsheets/Nuclearweaponswhohaswhat#1 (November 2011); Hans M. Kristensen and Robert S. Norris, "Chinese Nuclear Forces, 2011," *Bulletin of the Atomic Scientists* 67, no. 6 (2011): 81–87; Stockholm International Peace Research Institute, "World Nuclear Forces, January 2011"; at www.sipri.org/research/armaments/nbc/nuclear; Donald G. Gross, "Transforming the U.S. Relationship with China," *Global Asia* 2, no. 1 (2007), fig. 2, p. 85.

47. Jeffrey Engstrom, "PLA's Growing Force Projection Capabilities," *China Brief* 10, no. 25 (2010); at www.jamestown.org/programs/chinabrief/single/?tx_ttnews[tt_news]=37295&tx_ttnews[backPid]=25&cHash=23a98efe4e.

48. For background, see International Crisis Group, *China's Growing Role in UN Peacekeeping*, Report no. 166, April 17, 2009.

49. Murray Scot Tanner, "China Rethinks Unrest," *Washington Quarterly* 27, no. 3 (2004): 154.

50. The strongest such argument has been made by Michael D. Swaine and M. Taylor Fravel, "China's Assertive Behavior, Part Two: The Maritime Periphery," *China Leadership Monitor*, no. 35 (2011): 1–32.

51. For examples, see Ronald O'Rourke, "U.S. Navy Capabilities—Background for Congress," Congressional Research Service Report no. RL33153, July 22, 2011; and Aaron L. Friedberg, "China's Challenge at Sea," *New York Times*, September 4, 2011, online ed.

52. Ronald O'Rourke, "China's Naval Modernization: Implications for U.S. Navy Capabilities—Background and Issues for Congress," CRS Report no. RL33153, July 22, 2011, esp. pp. 3–4.

53. See remarks by Deputy Secretary of Defense Ashton Carter, October 3, 2012, in O'Rourke, *China Naval Modernization,* p. 49.

4

China's Reach

A Chinese deputy foreign minister had the following to say about doing business with Sudan's government, whose army was committing genocide in Sudan's Darfur region: "Business is business. We try to separate politics from business."[1] That is partly true: while actively cultivating trade and investment ties with African and other governments, China has refrained from commenting on certain of their internal problems—their abuses of labor and political rights, for example, and their use of force against their own people or other countries. We don't find China criticizing such excesses, much less endorsing or carrying out meaningful sanctions endorsed by the UN against repressive regimes. Far from it: in Sudan's case, the Chinese initially supplied weapons to the government, as indicated below, and when Sudan split in two, courted both governments for their oil. Such is the full meaning of "business," for if nothing else the Chinese are political realists; they well understand that diplomacy should promote China's political as well as economic interests. We therefore find that, as in the past, China wants the developing world's support for its international policies and expects silence on China's own internal problems in return for China's silence on theirs.

The Third World's Importance for China

The developing countries have always been a high priority in Chinese diplomacy. The reasons for their importance are totally different from those in the past, however. In Mao's time, the Third World was considered the central factor in a revolutionary united front against Western imperialism and, later, "Soviet revisionism." Under Deng, relations among the developing countries (called "South-South" relations) were regarded as significant for China in its battle with "hegemonism," particularly on economic issues. Now that China's own economic and security interests are so closely tied to global developments, its Third World diplomacy has become more active than ever. Africa, discussed below, has been the object of an intense high-level wooing by senior Chinese officials since the early 1990s. Beijing has become Africa's largest trade partner and a major loan giver.[2] In East Asia, Beijing is deeply involved, politically as well as economically, such as in the multilateral ASEAN (Association of Southeast Asian Nations) process, notably ASEAN+3 (China–Japan–South Korea); in the creation of a number of free-trade agreements;[3] and on the Korean peninsula, where China has become South Korea's number-one trade partner while simultaneously keeping North Korea afloat through food and energy assistance. And in the Middle East and Latin America, Chinese resource investments and trade ties have mushroomed in recent years.

These few facts are enough to convey that China now has a global diplomacy. But do they reflect a quest for a leadership position, such as an effort to edge out rivals, rewrite the rules of international commerce, or bring a global interest such as energy conservation in line with China's national interest? Or do they simply reflect China's singular determination to become a large, influential, economically strong country? To address these questions, we turn now to evaluating China's policies as practiced in the developing countries.

China in Africa

Africa has always received considerable attention from the PRC, going back to the early 1960s when the breakup of colonial rule led to the formation of numerous new nations. Appeals to anticolonialism and antiimperialism were at the heart of China's attempt to forge a global united front with independent Africa. In a sense, China's Africa policy today is a reprise of the 1960s, when it made a few strategic aid commitments to projects—the most notable being construction of the Tan-Zam (Tanzania-Zambia) Railway—that the West had turned its back on. Today, China can still be found engaging in economic development projects that Western governments, multinational companies, and the IMF hesitate to support. But we are not talking about just a few projects now, for Beijing has an ambitious agenda backed by substantial financial and corporate resources. Oil has become the centerpiece of China's trade with Africa. Angola, Sudan, and other African countries together supply somewhat more than one-quarter of China's oil imports, and oil constitutes roughly two-thirds of Africa's exports to China.

China's road to becoming the most important outside actor in Africa may be explained by four factors.[4] First is an emphasis on a history of Sino-African solidarity marked by common experiences: antiimperialism and civil war, exploitation by the West, and attempts by outsiders to marginalize Africa as they had China. Second is a professed commitment to the principle of noninterference. Third is stress on mutual gain: trade, aid, and investments that, Chinese sources maintain, benefit Africa no less than they do China. Last is active PRC diplomacy: a fairly constant parade of high-level Chinese visitors to Africa, regular visits to China by African dignitaries, and large-scale meetings under the China-Africa Forum. One payoff is that China has won the contest with Taiwan for diplomatic recognition, since now only four of Africa's fifty-four countries recognize Taiwan. In the end, though, China's Africa policy is informed by its own recent development experiences—combining foreign assistance with local resources while minimizing the role of powerful outside institutions.

Specialists on the subject differ on how to interpret China's economic activities in Africa: Are they purely self-interested? Or do they actually benefit African recipients—and which ones? Is China behaving in ways different from the West with respect to trade, aid, and investment in Africa? Does China have political as well as economic motives? As the best studies of China in Africa show, it is not easy to generalize about China's motives or the consequences of its activities there.[5]

Something of a Chinese exodus to Africa has occurred—not just investors, engineers, and laborers but also individuals seeking their fortune in small businesses such as restaurants and pharmacies. Altogether they may number as many as three-quarters of a million—not all permanently settled—and they reflect the enormous leap in China's economic engagement with the continent.[6] Sino-African trade went from around $10 billion in the 1990s to $55 billion by 2006.[7] In 2008, China's "Year of Africa," trade ballooned to around $100 billion, and by 2011 exceeded $161 billion.[8] Official PRC development assistance and loans rise every year—from an estimated $303 million in 2001 to $625 million in 2006 and $1.3 billion in 2009. Chinese investments have likewise leaped ahead—into major construction projects, such as roads, dams, and railroads, as well as into mining and oil production. By 2010, about two thousand PRC companies had invested a total of about $10 billion during the decade.[9] As with trade, foreign direct investment (FDI) is concentrated in a few countries, mainly those with oil and minerals, such as South Africa and Nigeria.[10] To a far greater degree than is true of Western investment in Africa, China's investments are promoted by corporations that receive substantial government support, such as export credits, loan guarantees, and information.[11] Its revisiting of the Tan-Zam Railway project in the 1990s, assisting the private sector to correct management and labor problems, is an example.[12]

Many Africans express gratitude to the Chinese for bringing in consumer goods, factories, and technology that were previously absent and for establishing schools and clinics.[13] Many express admiration for the way China has overcome a history of oppression and humiliation at the hands of foreign powers and has dramatically reduced poverty. They appreciate the fact that China's foreign-aid program has long favored Africa over other developing-country regions and that China has tried to offset Africa's trade deficit with it through debt forgiveness and the reduction or elimination of tariffs.[14] Indeed, at the China-Africa Forum in 2012, Hu Jintao committed to a new credit line of $20 billion over three years, mainly to support business development, training programs, and scholarships, and China announced a further lowering of tariffs on imports from Africa.

But to critics, African and otherwise, the price of China's increasing footprint is high: taking away the best jobs, sending money home rather than investing it locally, flooding markets with goods at prices that local businesses cannot match (such as Chinese textile exports), sticking to their own, acting as arrogant and sometimes violent overseers, relying on low health and safety standards for workers, tying aid to the purchase of Chinese goods, building stadiums and office complexes for elites, and exporting raw materials to China for value-added processing.[15] This last factor, some African politicians say, replicates the colonial pattern of extracting resources and selling the Africans manufactured goods.[16] In such cases, China's supposedly alternative development model is sometimes no more relevant than the West's when it comes to meeting the needs of ordinary people, offering fair trade terms, and respecting local cultures.

Charges of exploitation are sometimes justified, sometimes not, just as in the case of Western governments and private investors in developing countries. Chinese media, which devote considerable space to the country's role in African development, explicitly dismiss charges of neocolonialism. Occasionally a Chinese writer will acknowledge that China, while "not a colonialist, is . . . a successful capitalist in Africa," a status that may backfire if China's presence becomes so dominating that it will look like a colonizer by creating dependent economies.[17] Whether that possibility is already a reality may depend on how one understands "China." The behavior of Chinese state-owned companies, for example, may or may not reflect PRC government preferences, just as is true of Western multinational corporations in relation to their home governments. Two specialists have predicted that as time goes on, the "contradictions" between the Chinese government's interests in Africa and those of its corporations will multiply, mainly because the government's aid bureaucracy has become very large at the same time that the number of Chinese agents requiring oversight—company heads, workers, shopkeepers—has greatly increased.[18]

Plenty of negative experiences involving China in Africa have been reported. In South Africa, for example, cheap Chinese imports, by undercutting local suppliers, add to already massive unemployment. Environmentally destructive practices by Chinese firms have generated a local backlash in some countries. Instances of bribery, underpricing, and other corrupt practices designed to get a foot in the door (as in Sudan and Ethiopia) may reflect China's (or its corporations') determination to get access regardless of cost or corporate decisions to maximize profits. Lack of transparency in Chinese aid programs also invites criticism. In Namibia, a visit by Hu Jintao in 2007 was followed by a Chinese low-interest loan that was to be used in part to purchase anti-smuggling devices. But then, according to a *New York Times* report: "Namibia charged that the state-controlled company selected by China to provide the scanners—a company until recently run by President Hu's son—had facilitated the deal with millions of dollars in illegal kickbacks. And [then] China threw up barriers when Namibian investigators asked for help looking into the matter."[19] The reason for the barriers seems to have been that China did not want to reveal the terms of the loan and repayment, the fact that the loans were tied to purchases of Chinese goods, and that no opportunity was allowed for competitive bidding among Chinese suppliers.

When China's economic presence creates a large footprint, it involves China in a country's politics. In Zambia, for instance, China's exploitive coal-mining practices have led to protests and violence. The Chinese presence became a major issue in presidential elections in September 2011, and the ruling party lost power after twenty years.[20] A strike for a new minimum wage at a Chinese mine in August 2012 led to the death of a Chinese supervisor. Investments can be risky: Early in 2012, about seventy Chinese as well as Sudanese road workers in an oil-rich area of Sudan were kidnapped by a rebel group, showing the danger of exporting so many workers without protection. In South Africa, where China has become the leading trade partner, the political price became apparent on two occasions, both of which involved the Dalai Lama. In response to Chinese pressure, South Africa barred the Dalai Lama from attending a peace conference in March 2009 to promote the 2010 World Cup.[21] Then, in 2011, China evidently again twisted arms to get South Africa to deny a visa to the Dalai Lama on the occasion of the eightieth birthday celebration for the Reverend Desmond Tutu.

Political interference may also arise out of arms trading. Even though Chinese arms aid to Africa is very small on a volume basis, it can play an important role in internal conflicts—precisely what China is supposedly committed to avoid. In each case Chinese arms have abetted repression. China has supplied arms, ammunition, and intelligence equipment to Robert Mugabe's forces in Zimbabwe as well as to groups of human-rights violators in the Democratic Republic of Congo (DRC). The shipments went through, and directly to, the DRC in violation of a UN embargo. One such shipment was attempted in 2008, when Mugabe's election was widely disputed and his opposition was under assault. The arms were reportedly valued at about $1.2 million. Several African governments refused to unload the shipment at their docks, and various African nongovernmental groups joined in criticizing China's action. Beijing supposedly ordered the ship to return home, but whether or not it did so before delivering the goods remains uncertain.[22]

Waltzing with dictators like Mugabe may show respect for sovereignty, but it puts Beijing on the side of repression. Sudan, mentioned at the start of this chapter, is another case in point: Throughout much of the genocidal war in the Darfur region, China resisted an international response of any kind. Then it sent about three hundred engineering troops there in 2007 in support of a UN and African Union peacekeeping force, but China also sold arms to the Sudanese government, justifying it as "small-scale."[23] Sudan's leader, Omar al-Bashir, survived the international criticism, the sanctions, the International Criminal Court's warrants for his arrest on genocide charges, and even the secession of South Sudan in 2011. China welcomed him on a state visit in June 2011, arguing (predictably) that it was more productive to work directly with him than censure him. But the actual reason probably was simply to protect the China National Petroleum Company's stake in al-Bashir's country.[24] A year later, China was reportedly seeking a similar stake in South Sudan's oil sector despite an ongoing civil war and unresolved differences between north and south over oil revenue.[25]

Similarly in Guinea, where the military junta's use of force against protesters in 2009 drew international condemnation, a private Chinese company reportedly signed a huge agreement to invest in that country's electricity and aviation industries in return for rights to mine bauxite and iron ore. The deal was something of a coup for the Guinean government in trying to create a pretense of stability and legitimacy.[26] It also represented an about-face for China, whose ambassador to Guinea had said the country was not politically stable enough, and the market for minerals was not strong enough, to warrant a major investment stake.[27] These are the kinds of deals that undermine the argument of those who contend that under the Beijing Consensus, people's welfare is taken seriously. They are purely business transactions on a state-to-state basis and are no more focused on human development than are, say, the overseas investments of many Western and Japanese multinational corporations.

In the end, perhaps the fairest summation of China in Africa is that it is neither a unique nor a one-dimensional story. China's economic projects have sometimes performed better and sometimes worse than Western projects. Sometimes China takes the heat for wrongdoing that mainly is the responsibility of African authorities. Where China's practices have been criticized, they have sometimes reportedly been corrected—such as its labor abuses in Mozambique, which seem to be turning around with the hiring of more local workers and promises of greater investment and better terms of trade.[28] The Western media's focus on China's oil imports from Africa, labor problems, profit taking, and association with oppressive regimes is accurate and important, but it tends to neglect the total picture of infrastructure investments. The problems that arise in China's aid and investment projects are publicized, while the success stories, and African appreciation of them, are overlooked. Meantime, the West's own aid failures usually go unmentioned, and the "myth"—as it has been characterized in many sources—that China is competing with the United States in Africa is accepted as fact.[29]

It must also be kept in mind that, taken together, Western countries still dominate Africa's trade and investment picture, whereas Chinese aid has stepped in at a time when US aid to Africa has been negligible or when investing has been judged too risky. Even then, China's total aid to Africa—counting official assistance, concessional loans, and private sources—while substantial, is a good deal less than US, French, and German aid.[30] Finally, the cultural dimension should not be overlooked. The Western colonial era has left a deep imprint in terms of language, education, religion, and other cultural preferences. Money talks; but ordinary people in Africa, even if they have heard about a Chinese aid program and China's economic renaissance, may be only dimly aware of China itself, and may harbor unflattering stereotypes of Chinese as being unapproachable and potentially threatening to young people's job prospects.[31]

Southeast and South Asia

After decades of hostility during the Cold War, beginning in the early 1990s China came to embrace the "ASEAN way." It joined the ASEAN prime ministerial dialogue group and the ASEAN Regional Forum (ARF), a political and security dialogue group. China then vigorously pursued creation of the China-ASEAN Free Trade Agreement (CAFTA). Now the ten-nation ASEAN and China are each other's fourth-largest trade partner. In 2002, moreover, China agreed with ASEAN on a code of conduct for the settlement of disputes and freedom of navigation,[32] and the following year signed ASEAN's Treaty of Amity and Cooperation (TAC). These undertakings, which the United States for some time ignored,[33] accepted ASEAN's norms of noninterference and nonuse of force. The chief impediment to making those norms a reality has been the competing claims (involving China and five other countries) to the Spratly Islands (Nansha, in Chinese) and the Paracel Islands (Xisha) in the South China Sea.

China's initial turnaround on relations with ASEAN reflected not just economic incentives but a fundamental rethinking about how to win friends and build networks. The "new security concept" that Beijing unveiled in the late 1990s was essentially an updating of the "five principles of peaceful coexistence," the calling card of Chinese diplomacy since the 1950s. The PRC's stress on noninterference, consultation, and peaceful dispute resolution in its public diplomacy meshed with ASEAN's central principles. The new security concept, Hu Jintao said, provided a certain amount of reassurance at a time when the United States was preoccupied elsewhere.[34]

Verbal promises are cheap, however, and while they have been accompanied by concrete actions, in more recent years tension over the South China Sea claims has increased. Chinese policy has toughened, though exactly why is unclear: it might have occurred for mainly domestic reasons, perhaps related to leadership cohesion and consensus, or for strategic reasons, such as the opportunity created by US absorption with conflicts in the Middle East. As one scholar has remarked, the main elements of this assertiveness can be found not only in the way China has brusquely advanced its territorial claims in the South China Sea but also in its uncooperative stance on North Korea, its strong reaction to US arms sales to Taiwan, and its questioning of US financial stability at about the same time.[35]

None of the contending parties is innocent, however; all appear to be driven in some part by nationalistic politics and resource needs. In 2011, China and Vietnam exchanged threats, as did China and the Philippines in April 2012 when Chinese fishing boats were boarded in contested waters that the Philippines had invited foreign oil and gas companies to explore. Chinese patrol boats interfered with the vessels of other claimants. Vietnam threw oil on the fire by claiming sovereignty over the Paracels and the Spratlys in June 2012, and the Philippine government, with new security assurances from the United States in hand, vowed not to cave in to Chinese territorial demands. Five of the disputing countries have established outposts of one sort or another in the Spratlys.

The United States has gotten directly into the act, with Secretary of State Hillary Clinton asserting a US "national interest" in the South China Sea dispute based on "freedom of navigation." The Chinese resent this intrusion into an area of "core interest," particularly when Washington, in support of the Philippines, carried out joint military exercises following the April 2012 skirmish and reaffirmed the US commitment to the Philippines' defense. When Clinton visited China in September 2012, she was greeted with thinly disguised warnings to stay out of territorial disputes.[36]

These tensions have raised concerns in Southeast Asia about the veracity of PRC professions of peaceful intentions and opposition to big-power politics. The patrol boat incidents may have embarrassed Chinese military and party leaders.[37] As one well-informed analyst has put it, China is "looking for influence rather than spoiling for a fight."[38] To demonstrate their commitment to good neighborliness, Chinese diplomats in July 2011 signed "guidelines" for implementing the 2002 declaration. But these are sketchy and nonbinding. Moreover, specialists on the South China Sea controversy in some of China's leading think tanks are virtually unanimous in support of PRC policy and blame the United States for enabling the Philippines and Vietnam to be assertive about their claims. Quite a few of these specialists, as well as some Chinese military leaders, want to see a much tougher Chinese stance, and in mid-2012 they got their wish: China deployed troops and inaugurated a legislative body with administrative powers over the South China Sea islands' inhabitants and the surrounding waters.[39] As one Chinese scholar who has studied these experts' views concludes, "Beijing cannot afford to be seen as losing territory to foreign powers."[40]

None of the contending parties to the South China Sea dispute has rock-solid historical arguments to support its territorial claims. In such a situation, adherence to the principle of peaceful resolution of disputes and a willingness to strictly abide by the 1982 Convention on the Law of the Sea—which the United States has not ratified—are essential for all the interested parties: China, ASEAN, and the United States.[41] In a nutshell, though the parties *could* try to forge an agreement to share the South China Sea's resources, the continuing failure to conclude a binding code of conduct remains the overriding obstacle. At the same time, the dispute does not appear to mark a shift in China to confrontation of rivals, small or large; more likely, China's approach displays its increased power and self-confidence. Few observers expect a firefight to break out, but the ratcheting up of tensions certainly bodes poorly for China's much publicized good-neighbor policy.[42]

There is yet another side to the territorial question: China's concerns about aggressive US intelligence probing in adjacent waters, close to its new submarine base on Hainan Island. These missions have already led to confrontations at sea between PRC and US vessels, most notably over the surveillance activities of the USS *Impeccable* in March 2009.[43] On a wider scale, Obama's announcement in November 2011 that the United States would be building a military presence in western Australia, in which twenty-five hundred troops would be regularly rotated, added to mounting US-China tensions. The United States already has extensive military ties to Australia, including a number of military and intelligence facilities, and the new development may be increased naval cooperation and US access to a new base in the Cocos Islands for drone aircraft.[44] Some of China's defense intellectuals reportedly denounced the US buildup in Australia as evidence of the persistence of Cold War thinking in the United States, and an editorial in the official newspaper warned: "If Australia uses its military bases to help the US harm Chinese interests, then Australia itself will be caught in the crossfire."[45] Though the official Chinese response was actually fairly muted and the US move was presented as an effort to reassure traditional allies of its security commitment to Asia, clearly China was the target. Thus, the difficulty of resolving the South China Sea dispute is compounded by the fact that it is embedded in the suspicions that lately suffuse China-US relations.

Other Chinese practices have also proved troublesome in Southeast and South Asia, just as they have in some African countries. The promise of jobs for local people on Chinese engineering, railroad, and other large-scale construction sites often has not been met. Instead, Chinese workers have arrived in huge numbers—around one hundred twenty thousand by 2008.[46] Precisely in the manner of many Western companies, but in greater numbers, Chinese workers abroad keep to themselves, living in walled "little Chinas," which causes a backlash in some countries. In Vietnam, for instance, where thirty-five thousand Chinese workers are employed in a bauxite mine and other projects, complaints have been loud and long about the displacement of Vietnamese workers, the deep Chinese economic inroads that have occurred, and the fact that a country with which Vietnam was not so long ago at war is dominating the economy.[47] In the Philippines, where Beijing has promised major investments, lack of transparency apparently included kickbacks to local officials, leading to cancellation of contracts with Chinese companies.[48]

Sometimes, money talks: Chinese aid has been able to buy human-rights violations by others, such as Cambodia's deportation of twenty Uighurs to China, in direct violation of the international treaty Phnom Penh had signed that bans forcible repatriation.[49]

China's energy and environmental policies have also sometimes caused upset in Southeast Asia. It shares vital waterways with Laos, Vietnam, Cambodia, Thailand, and Burma. Ambitious Chinese dam-building plans are a major reason for the decline of fish stocks on the Mekong River, threatening the livelihood of numerous fishers. In contrast with China's suspension of plans to construct a major dam system on the Nu (Salween) River where it runs through Yunnan province—a surprise decision announced by Premier Wen Jiabao in 2004 in response, he said, to "a high level of concern in society" and the opposition of environmental groups[50]—China's dam construction along the Mekong continues apace. The affected governments have been divided on the dams and reluctant to complain too loudly, given China's economic clout.[51]

But money does not always win out, as events in Myanmar described earlier show. China's chief interests there are the security of its energy investments and border stability. But several developments are undermining those interests: ethnic warfare near the China-Myanmar border, the trade and environmental priorities of Yunnan province leaders, Obama's efforts to engage the Burmese military leadership, and Western energy investments.[52] Suddenly, in October 2011, the Myanmar government cited environmental concerns in suspending (and possibly canceling) a hydroelectric dam project on the Irrawaddy River led by a Chinese company. If the decision holds, it will affect China's plans for generating more electricity for southern China as well as its ambitious "Southwest Silk Road" project to build an oil pipeline to the Indian Ocean via Myanmar.

Moreover, when Myanmar announced the suspension, it cited public pressure, perhaps also signaling growing popular resentment of China's large role in the country's economy and its contribution to forest and species destruction.[53] It was shortly thereafter that the United States stepped into the picture with a visit from Hillary Clinton. While publicly Chinese officials said little, privately they must have chafed at the sudden Burmese shift and the likelihood of a US aid program beginning next door. (Perhaps that is why China has reportedly been forcibly repatriating Kachin fighters, who have yet to reach a peace agreement with the Myanmar government and have had to retreat into PRC territory.[54]) One Chinese commentator for a hawkish PRC publication went so far as to accuse the United States of being behind cancellation of the hydroelectric station and blocking of the oil pipeline project.[55] The very fact that Aung San Suu Kyi had to reassure Beijing of the desire to maintain good relations with a future democratic Myanmar spoke to the significance of the changeover.[56]

Meantime, China is exporting its deforestation problem, mainly to Indonesia. Having banned logging in China in 1998 following terrible flooding in the upper Yangtze River, China moved to sign contracts with Indonesia that will bring it raw wood for furniture and flooring. China will also receive palm oil, for soap products, from trees planted on the cleared land. Chinese investments in Indonesia's roads and railways will facilitate the movement of the logs.[57] Thus, at the very time Southeast Asia's tropical forests have been decimated, China is becoming a world leader in the importation of the remaining timber.

China's role in Afghanistan demonstrates its dependence on the United States to provide security in a highly unstable part of the world. In Afghanistan, the Chinese let the United States take the lead in pursuing al-Qaeda's leaders at a time of growing PRC investments in Afghanistan's resources. A Chinese state corporation, China Metallurgical Group Corporation, already had invested $3 billion in the Aynak copper deposits in Logar province near Kabul under a 2007 agreement. By 2009, as national elections approached, China was bidding for rights to Afghani iron ore, oil, and gas fields. These investments would make China the foremost foreign investor in the country, notwithstanding accusations of bribery and a sweetheart deal for the mining concern that have swirled for years. Chinese officials told the US embassy in Beijing that the PRC's views were "exactly the same" as those of the United States regarding hopes for credible and inclusive election results. These officials also expressed concern about the larger security issue posed by Islamic separatists—the East Turkestan Islamic Movement (ETIM) based in China's Xinjiang province—who might use Afghan territory for attacks in China. Here, too, US support was important: The US State Department in 2002, very likely to promote warmer relations with China, had suddenly turned its back on the ETIM and begun calling it a terrorist organization—just as the Chinese were saying. The stakes in Afghanistan were thus high enough for the Chinese that they reportedly contributed about half a billion dollars to the 2009 election and received considerable police protection around the copper mine.[58]

All this effort paid off: the Chinese firm won the bidding for mining rights with an overwhelming offer, and it promised to rely exclusively on local labor after a few years.[59] But at the same time, the Chinese complained about the precariousness of the security situation around the mines caused by "terrorist attacks" and a slow process of getting rid of mines.[60] The real lesson here is how the Chinese relied on the military power and diplomatic influence of the United States and its NATO partners to maintain the "safe climate for investment" that all foreign investors demand.

Sri Lanka was the scene of a bloody, twenty-six-year-long civil war between the majority Sinhalese and the minority Tamils that did not end until, in May 2009, the Sinhalese government forces under President Mahinda Rajapaksa brutally, and needlessly, carried out a final assault that left thousands of Tamil fighters and civilians dead. The assault led to charges of war crimes by international nongovernmental organizations (NGOs) such as the International Crisis Group, which found that the government had deliberately targeted civilians and violated promises to protect them.[61] When the United States and a few other governments finally stopped most military aid to the Sri Lankan government in 2008, citing human-rights abuses in particular, China stepped in. It built a highway, two power plants, and a port, quickly becoming Sri Lanka's major foreign benefactor; and China provided "about a billion dollars' worth of military aid, including fighter jets, air-surveillance radar, and anti-aircraft batteries."[62] China also became the biggest investor in Sri Lanka, leading the government to provide a free-trade zone for Chinese companies.

China's aid program put Sri Lanka firmly in the Chinese camp, along with Myanmar, whose military-run government at that time was condemned in a UN Security Council resolution for human-rights violations that China vetoed. These two partnerships created the strong impression that PRC aid and investments were part of a deliberate strategy to achieve a strong presence, economic and potentially military, in the Indian Ocean area—a so-called string of pearls aimed mainly at India. (Two countries that support China's disregard for human-rights issues and nonintervention joined it in assisting Sri Lanka and thumbing their noses at Western criticism: Russia, with weapons sales, and Iran, with a major credit line of more than $1 billion to purchase oil.)

The Middle East

In the Middle East as elsewhere in the developing world, realism Chinese style has been much like the West's: consistent in the quest for greater energy security, but always at the mercy of political uncertainties. Beijing has encountered some of the same problems that Western governments have found: unstable, often corrupt government partners;

inadequate infrastructure; uncollectable debt; and local opposition.[63] In Iraq, for example, China's state-owned oil company, the China National Petroleum Corporation, contracted in 2008 to begin drilling in the Al Ahdab field. Actual operations began in 2011, with Chinese oil officials anticipating that the field, though small, would give China "a foot in the door" to Iraq's huge deposits.[64] But how reliable the Iraq investment will be is open to serious doubt when we witness constant violence and political instability there, not to mention disputes among sectarian groups over oil revenues, as US forces depart.

The deeper challenge to PRC policy in the Middle East may be seen in its response to the Arab Spring of 2011. It reveals a number of qualities relevant to international leadership: the insecurity of Chinese leaders, a reactive foreign policy, and limited influence over rapidly changing political conditions. In contrast to Beijing's studied silence about unfolding events until the question of international intervention in Libya emerged, the Obama administration commented on them often and specifically. The United States was by no means consistent in espousing nonviolent change and democratization; often, in fact, Washington was behind the curve of actual events, and in the cases of Bahrain, Yemen, and Syria was notably lax in supporting popular protests. But officials were pointed in expressing US preferences: which dictators should leave their countries, and when; how the military in these countries should respond; and which of the protesters' demands were justified.[65] These pronouncements were consequential: Hosni Mubarak was forced out in Egypt; the Bahraini military stopped shooting protesters; Yemen's ruler went abroad and later stepped down; and Muammar Qaddafi faced international sanctions, NATO's bombs, and eventually death at the hands of his people.

The point is, US leaders felt they had every right to comment and act on other countries' internal affairs and to seek the removal of leaders on whom Washington had for a long time lavished military and economic aid. In those cases where the United States did not initially support regime change, strategic interests trumped supposed humanitarian concerns. Respect for sovereignty—China's calling card—was never a consideration for US leaders determined to pursue their immediate objectives.

China's leaders, by contrast, exhibited traditional insecurity: concern about the implications of the Middle East uprisings for their one-party state. China's response to the East European color revolutions in 2004/05 prefigured this response.[66] At that time, popular grievances spilled into the streets and overthrew post-Communist autocratic leaders, all fully endorsed by the United States. Chinese scholars and leaders alike became convinced that corruption needed to be seriously tackled and that ideological rectitude among CCP members required renewed attention. Once again, the bottom line for Beijing was strengthening the leadership's legitimacy and security by imposing new controls over both party and society.

When the Middle East uprisings occurred, the official press gave them minimal attention, though clearly the leadership was determined that no citizen get the idea that China could become another Egypt.[67] To make certain there would be no Jasmine Revolution (*molihua geming*) in China, internal security forces reportedly made shows of force at potential protest sites, roughed up foreign reporters, and arrested or increased surveillance of prominent human-rights advocates and lawyers, often without charges or other legal basis.[68] Churches not officially sanctioned were prevented from holding services, and work stoppages by truck and taxi drivers (to protest rising fuel costs) were disrupted. China's vast system of Internet watchdogs seemed to be doing double duty to reduce coverage of external events that might inspire political protests.

The civil war in Libya is particularly revealing of the difference between Chinese and US approaches. Here was a case of use of force against a repressive regime—arguably, a humanitarian intervention. Initially, Obama rejected military options such as a no-fly zone or direct intervention on the ground. But he also said that "all options are on the table." In the end, Obama was persuaded that obtaining Qaddafi's departure, and preventing a slaughter of rebel forces, justified using airpower. A Security Council resolution authorized enforcing a no-fly zone on humanitarian grounds; China (along with Russia, Germany, India, and a few other states) abstained, whereas most Arab League members lent support. Once military power was exercised, the Chinese press carried a number of articles criticizing the use of force, and the US role in particular, for failing to respect Libya's sovereignty, killing civilians, and neglecting possibilities of a political solution to the fighting.

Behind the scenes, three Chinese arms firms met with Qaddafi's representatives on a $200 million sale that would have violated a UN embargo that China had voted to support. The deal was never consummated, but the fact it was in negotiation shows that once again—as in Sudan and North Korea—China's respect for UN-mandated arms sanctions is paper-thin. When documents attesting to this deal were discovered, Beijing acknowledged as much, perhaps revealing a split between the pro-military defense ministry and the ministry of foreign affairs.[69]

Thus China tried to have it both ways, with a policy designed to appeal to Third World leaders opposed to a Western intervention and the protection of their sovereignty, yet also crafted to show the world that China was a responsible power willing to work within the UN system. But while Beijing may have won some plaudits in the Middle East, the bombs fell, Libya's military was largely destroyed, and Qaddafi's authority gradually reduced to his redoubt in Tripoli. By midyear even the Russians agreed with the West that Qaddafi had to go. Beijing seemed to have learned a lesson from the experience, however, when (as noted earlier) it joined Moscow in rejecting US, EU, and UN efforts to end Assad's rule in Syria or at least bring about a cease-fire.

Iran provides another instance in which the Chinese have to make tough choices when a partner is under threat. China's interests are not served by Iran's development of nuclear weapons. But neither does China want to see the United States and its allies, starting with Israel and Saudi Arabia, run roughshod over Iran, which represents an important outpost of resistance to US hegemony in the Middle East. And unlike North Korea, Iran is economically important to China as one of its top sources of oil, in which it reportedly has very substantial investments.[70] The weakness of China's options was on display in 2012 when the United States and the European Union decided to up the ante with Iran by imposing sanctions against companies seeking to buy Iranian oil through Iran's banks. The Chinese did not completely defy the sanctions: China's three principal state-owned oil companies continued to buy Iranian oil, Chinese banks reportedly routing money to Iran's banks via US-based global banks. However, Beijing also decided to slow investments in Iran and diversify its oil imports.[71] Wen Jiabao visited three Middle East oil-producing states—the first visit to the region by a PRC leader in two decades—in search of alternatives.

Latin America

China is already second only to the United States in Latin America as a trading partner. Accepting the region as being in the US backyard, China's approach to Latin America has been nonideological and "insignificant" militarily.[72] Though China has sold or transferred military-use items, including many classified as nonlethal, to countries not on friendly terms with the United States, such as Venezuela and Bolivia, China's objective seems to be to gain markets and goodwill, not bases or allies. In fact, respecting the paramount regional role of the United States seems to be one of China's Latin America policy guidelines, though this has not kept Beijing from using aid to gain diplomatic recognition ahead of Taiwan[73] or from outdoing the Inter-American Development Bank (which China joined in 2008) when it comes to making loans. As one study for the US military concludes, China does not represent a threat to US interests in Latin America, and the military side of Chinese policy there would seem to be in keeping with Beijing's legitimate security interests.[74]

In short, commerce mainly dictates PRC policy in Latin America, though one can imagine that if China's economic stake in the region were to grow a good deal larger, the PLA's role as a protector of its interests might grow too. China's principal aid projects have consisted mainly of investments to acquire oil, steel, and other commodities at low prices or to improve infrastructure such as ports and airfields. From 2002 to 2007, 36 percent of PRC aid to developing countries went to Latin America—not far behind the 44 percent assigned to Africa.[75] As in the other regions, loans have been the main feature of China's checkbook diplomacy. In 2009, for example, loans went to Venezuela ($12 billion), Ecuador ($1 billion), and Brazil ($10 billion), and Argentina was given a credit line to Chinese currency valued at $10 billion.[76] Lesser but well-targeted sums have gone to various Caribbean countries, such as a $35 million grant for a stadium in the Bahamas and $566 million in investments and loans to lease sugarcane fields and build roads in Jamaica. As has happened elsewhere, new Chinese money has been followed by a greater visibility of Chinese—laborers, shopkeepers, consultants—and by shifts of political loyalty from Taiwan to the PRC.[77]

Brazil best reflects Chinese priorities in Latin America. It is a partner in the loose group of emerging-market countries known collectively as the BRICS (Brazil, Russia, India, China, and South Africa). Not far from Rio de Janeiro, the Chinese have invested heavily in factories and infrastructure that will enable the export to China of iron ore and oil and gas equipment—valued at around $15 billion from 2002 to 2007.[78] The $10 billion Chinese loan cited in the paragraph above was made to Brazil's national oil company. In 2011, China also concluded a $7 billion deal that contracts with farmers to provide about 6 million tons of soybeans to China every year. Total PRC investment, at $20 billion in the first half of 2010 alone, enabled it to jump to first place among foreign investors in Brazil. Financing of these deals by state banks means low interest rates that undercut competitor investors.

These arrangements might seem favorable to Brazil, evidence of its successful delinking from the multilateral banks and a driving force in Brazil's new economic dynamism. But the experience has reportedly driven the two countries apart. President Luiz Inácio Lula da Silva publicly criticized China's failure to hire Brazilians to work the mines and brought antidumping charges against Chinese firms. China has become a competitor rather than a partner. Buying up Brazilian land, a practice China has tried in the Philippines and elsewhere, has rankled the Brazilian leadership and led to legislation to limit landownership by foreigners. Moreover, the pattern of the trade relationship—Chinese manufactured goods in exchange for Brazilian raw materials—follows the neocolonial pattern of previous eras, and the one we noted in Africa.[79] Similar voices of discontent may be heard in Ecuador, where some officials reportedly regard the Chinese as the "new imperialists" for driving a hard bargain to help finance a $1 billion hydroelectric plant, and even in Hugo Chavez's Venezuela, because of the low price of oil exports to China.[80]

China's Foreign Aid Program

Taken as a whole, China's economic aid program to foreign countries is also less generous than the numbers would indicate, although the latest official report suggests changing priorities. From 2002 to 2007, nearly all PRC aid—95 percent—was accounted for by government-sponsored investment and concessional (i.e., low-interest) loans. Only 5 percent went toward debt cancellation and grants. About 44 percent was for natural-resource extraction and 43 percent for infrastructure (such as public works projects); less than 2 percent, as reported by Beijing, was humanitarian assistance. One-half of China's aid, moreover, apparently was tied to purchases of Chinese goods.[81] These figures do not suggest a clear departure from the aid practices of other governments, with two major exceptions: the leading developed countries are committed to using "official development assistance" (ODA) for antipoverty purposes, and at least 25 percent of ODA must be outright grants. PRC aid, by contrast, directly serves Chinese economic and political interests—most importantly, resources for China's development, support for a one-China policy, and opening of markets for Chinese companies—and precludes sanctions when recipient governments engage in systematic repression.

Since 2009, however, Chinese aid practices may be changing. In its first official white paper on foreign aid, Beijing reported that 41 percent of total aid of $38.5 billion was in grants and 30 percent in interest-free loans.[82] The least developed countries received about 40 percent of the aid. African countries continued to be the main recipients of Chinese aid, accounting for a reported 45 percent. Asian countries were next at 32 percent. The report stressed China's adherence to the UN's

Millennium Development Goals on poverty relief, hence a focus on debt cancellation, agricultural and teacher training, and complete projects. No mention was made of military assistance or the fine line between "aid" and government-backed investment. About the only indication of the self-interested nature of China's aid program was mention of several thousand "volunteers" who have been dispatched in recent years to teach Chinese in developing countries.

Consensus or Neocolonialism?

This overview of China's activities in the developing world further clarifies that there is no hard-and-fast Chinese model or "consensus." What we see instead is the reincarnation of the "five principles of peaceful coexistence," which promise no interference by big powers in the affairs of small powers, mutual respect, equal benefit, and dialogue and consultation. These are appealing guidelines to emerging democracies and authoritarian regimes alike, especially those with a history of colonial rule, US or UN interventions, or IMF austerity programs. But that is only half the story, for we also see that China, like the United States and the rest of "the West," sometimes practices neocolonialism—such as by dumping cheap goods, exporting deforestation, starting large-scale energy projects that forcibly relocate people, taking raw materials for value-added processing back home, and displacing local businesses and labor. The practice applies equally to China's relations with authoritarian regimes such as Myanmar's and North Korea's and to its relations with democratizing governments such as Brazil's. And if "neocolonialism" seems too harsh a judgment, perhaps "dependence" will do, since in many of the countries examined here the Chinese presence is overwhelming—enough, sometimes, to cause resentment.

China's reliance on US power to protect its interests, as in Afghanistan and the Persian Gulf,[83] shows the vulnerability of a foreign policy that would have it both ways—defending state sovereignty but depending on a foreign power to protect Chinese assets. And the PRC's relationship with corrupt, even criminal regimes, as in Suriname[84] and Sudan, displays an unethical and self-interested aspect of foreign policy no different from that of the other major powers. Proponents of a so-called Beijing Consensus have to consider that China's developing-country policies often amount to old-fashioned bargains with resource-rich regimes: their land, oil, or minerals in exchange for Chinese aid without strings (that is, without having to accept IMF structural adjustment demands), construction of image-raising projects, and support of the regime in power. China is merely imitating what the West has practiced for a hundred years—trying to extract political as well as economic advantage from its financial and trading power without regard to how the local government goes about its business.

Chinese policy does provide a refuge of sorts for those governments that are unhappy with the West's aid programs and multilateral financial institutions. That enables China to have its cake and sometimes eat it, too—that is, to seemingly play the role of a responsible power within the UN system while simultaneously extracting commercial and political benefits from controversial partner governments. In the process, African and other developing countries may benefit, too; health-care clinics and office buildings are constructed, trade expands, clean technology is shared, loans flow in. But the possibility remains that reliance on China will also mean importing its destructive environmental practices and occupational diseases. After all, most of the Chinese companies doing business in developing countries are the same inefficient, heavily subsidized, state-owned enterprises that resist reform back home.[85] PRC leaders often say they want to see better behavior from Chinese businesses to avoid an anti-China backlash, but the future may be otherwise.

Notes

1. David Zweig and Bi Jianhai, "China's Global Hunt for Energy," *Foreign Affairs* 84, no. 5 (2005): 32.

2. See David Shinn's November 1, 2011, testimony before the US Senate Foreign Relations Committee, at http://allafrica.com/stories/201111021230.html.

3. See Mark Beeson, "East Asian Regionalism and the End of the Asia-Pacific: After American Hegemony"; at japanfocus.org, March 2009; and Chu Shulong, *Zhongguo waijiao zhanlue he zhengci* (China's External Strategy and Policy) (Beijing: Shishi chubanshe, 2008).

4. See Chris Alden, *China in Africa* (London: Zed Books, 2007).

5. For excellent efforts to introduce balance to analysis of China's role in Africa, see Deborah Brautigam, *The Dragon's Gift: The Real Story of China in Africa* (London: Oxford University Press, 2009); Alden, *China in Africa*; and Barry Sautman and Yan Hairong, "Trade, Investment, Power, and the China-in-Africa Discourse," *Asia-Pacific Journal*, no. 52-3-09 (December 28, 2009); at http://japanfocus.org/-Yan-Hairong/3278. Brautigam's blog, www.chinaafricarealstory.com, is also valuable for its reporting and links to actual cases involving Chinese activities in Africa.

6. Brautigam, *The Dragon's Gift*, fig. 6.2, p. 170.

7. Howard W. French and Lydia Polgreen, "Entrepreneurs from China Flourish in Africa," *New York Times*, August 18, 2007, online ed.

8. "China-Africa Trade Likely to Hit Record High in 2011," *People's Daily Online*, November 17, 2011; at http://english.peopledaily.com.cn/90883 /7647528.html; "Hu Vows More Aid for African Countries," *China Daily*, July 19,

2012; at http://usa.chinadaily.com.cn. The "record high" cited in the first source was supposed to be $250 billion in trade, but that prediction proved to be too optimistic.

9. Luo Huijun, "Africa Welcomes Chinese Investments," *People's Daily Online*, October 9, 2011; at http://english.peopledaily.com.cn/90780/7612477.html.

10. David E. Brown, *Hidden Dragon, Crouching Lion: How China's Advance in Africa Is Underestimated and Africa's Potential Unappreciated* (Carlisle, PA: Strategic Studies Institute, US Army War College, September 2012), pp. 1, 15–18. Chinese FDI may actually be as much as $40 billion, Brown points out (p. 18).

11. Bates Gill and James Reilly, "The Tenuous Hold of China Inc. on Africa," *Washington Quarterly* 30, no. 3 (2007): 37–52.

12. Brautigam, *The Dragon's Gift*, pp. 84–85.

13. Lydia Polgreen and Howard W. French, "China's Trade in Africa Carries a Price Tag," *New York Times*, August 21, 2007, online ed.; Dambisa Moyo, "Beijing, a Boon for Africa," *New York Times*, June 27, 2012, online ed.

14. At a gathering of the China-Africa Forum in Beijing, Chinese aid earned some accolades, such as from South Africa's president Jacob Zuma, who proclaimed that "we are equals." "We certainly are convinced," Zuma said, "that China's intention is different than that of Europe, which to date continues to intend to influence African countries for their sole benefit": "Hu Vows More Aid for African Countries," *China Daily*, July 19, 2012; at http://usa.chinadaily.com.cn.

15. On the same occasion (see the preceding note), President Zuma also said that Africa's "supply of raw materials, other products and technology transfer . . . is unsustainable in the long term. Africa's past economic experience with Europe dictates a need to be cautious when entering into partnerships with other economies": Leslie Hook, "Zuma Warns on Africa's Trade Ties to China," *Washington Post*, July 19, 2012, online ed.

16. Wei Liang, "China's Soft Power in Africa: Is Economic Power Sufficient?" *Asian Perspective*, vol. 36, no. 4 (2012): 678–681.

17. Jian Junbo, "China's Role in Africa," *Beijing Review*, no. 6 (February 8, 2007); at www.bjreview.com/world/txt/2007-02/05/content_55414.htm.

18. Gill and Reilly, "The Tenuous Hold of China Inc. in Africa."

19. Sharon LaFraniere and John Grobler, "China Spreads Aid in Africa, with a Catch," *New York Times*, September 21, 2009, online ed.

20. *New York Times*, November 20, 2010, and September 24, 2011, p. A4.

21. Celia W. Dugger, "South Africa Bars Dalai Lama from a Peace Conference," *New York Times*, March 23, 2009, online ed. The Nobel laureate Reverend Desmond Tutu said the South African government was "shamelessly succumbing to Chinese pressure."

22. Celia W. Dugger and David Barboza, "China May Give Up Attempt to Send Arms to Zimbabwe," *New York Times*, April 30, 2008, p. 1; David B. Kopel, Paul Gallant, and Joanne D. Eisen, "The Arms Trade Treaty: Zimbabwe, the Democratic Republic of the Congo, and the Prospects for Arms Embargoes on Human Rights Violators," *Penn State Law Review* 114, no. 3 (2010): 126–128, 136; at http://davekopel.org/2a/Foreign/Arms-Trade-Treaty.pdf.

23. Ministry of Foreign Affairs press conference, May 8, 2007, as reported by the US ambassador to China in a cable published by WikiLeaks at http://wikileaks.org/cable/2007/05/07BEIJING3063.html.

24. Adrienne Mong, "Oil-hungry China Welcomes Alleged War Criminal al-Bashir," *Behind the Wall* (NBC News); at http://behindthewall.msnbc.msn.com/_news/2011/06/28/6956369-oil-hungry-china-welcomes-alleged-war-criminal-al-bashir?chromedomain=worldblog.

25. International Criminal Court, "China's New Courtship in South Sudan," Report no. 186 (April 4, 2012); at www.crisisgroup.org/en/regions/africa/horn-of0.

26. Adam Nossiter, "Guinea Boasts of Deal with Chinese Company," *New York Times*, October 13, 2009, online ed.

27. Lydia Polgreen, "As Chinese Investment in Africa Drops, Hope Sinks," *New York Times*, March 25, 2009, online ed.

28. Loro Horta, "China Economic Engagement in Africa: Changing Approach in Mozambique," *RSIS Commentaries*, January 16, 2012; at www.rsis.edu.sg /publications/Perspective/RSIS0132012.pdf.

29. See Shimelse Ali and Nida Jafrani, "China's Growing Role in Africa: Myths and Facts," *International Economic Bulletin* (February 9, 2012); at http://carnegieendowment.org/ieb/2012/02/09/china-s-growing-role-in-africa-myths-and-facts/9j54.

30. Based on Brautigam's calculations for 2007 in *The Dragon's Gift*, p. 183.

31. These are among the conclusions of interviews of educated young Ugandans by Simon Shen and Ian Taylor, "Ugandan Youths' Perceptions of Relations with China," *Asian Perspective* 36, no. 4 (2012): 693–723.

32. "Declaration on the Conduct of Parties in the South China Sea," November 4, 2002; at www.asean.org/13163.htm.

33. The United States did not appoint a permanent envoy to ASEAN until 2008 and did not sign the TAC until 2009. It has reached agreement on free trade only with Singapore among the ASEAN-10, and only with Australia elsewhere in Asia.

34. See his speech at the United Nations Summit on September 14, 2005; at www.fmprc.gov.cn/ce/ceun/eng/zt/shnh60/t212915.htm.

35. Nick Bisley, "Biding and Hiding No Longer: A More Assertive China Rattles the Region," *Global Asia* 6, no. 4 (2011): 62–73.

36. For example, one analyst with a government think tank was quoted in the official newspaper: "Should the South China Sea and Diaoyudao be the main topic of discussion, 'what the US must do is to keep its hands out of it.'" Chen Yamei, China Research Institute for International Relations, quoted in *Renmin ribao*, September 4, 2012.

37. See Amitav Acharya, "Beyond the Chinese 'Monroe Doctrine,'" *Straits Times* (Singapore), June 20, 2011, and Mark J. Valencia, "Diplomatic Drama: The South China Sea Imbroglio," *Global Asia* 6, no. 3 (2011): 66–71.

38. Patrick M. Cronin, "Muddy Waters," *New York Times*, April 24, 2012, online ed.

39. As an example of a hawkish Chinese view, which argues that China's good-neighbor policy must be coupled with "credible commitments to the use of force," see Shao Feng, "Security Strategies for China's Maritime Domain," *Caixin*, July 13, 2012; at http://english.caixin.com/2012-07-13/100410946_all.html.

40. Yun Sun, "Studying the South China Sea: A Chinese Perspective," Center for New American Security, East and South China Seas Bulletin no. 1, January 9, 2012; at www.cnas.org/files/documents/flashpoints/CNAS_ESCS_bulletin1.pdf.

41. See Mark J. Valencia, "The South China Sea Brouhaha: Separating Substance from Atmospherics," NAPSNet, August 10, 2010.

42. See the well-informed report of the International Crisis Group, "Stirring Up the South China Sea (II): Regional Responses," July 24, 2012; at www.crisisgroup.org/~/media/Files/asia/north-east-asia/229-stirring-up-the-south-china-sea-ii-regional-responses.pdf?utm_source=chinareport&utm_medium=pdf&utm_campaign=mremail.

43. The *Impeccable* incident was described by US Admiral Dennis Blair as being the most serious since the collision of a US surveillance aircraft, the EP-3, with a Chinese jet in 2001 near Hainan. But whereas in 2001, China demanded an apology and detained the EP-3 crew on Hainan Island for several days, the *Impeccable* incident was quickly contained. Both incidents involved spying missions, but the second incident may have been more serious in that the mission focused on China's submarine capability and its economic resources within its exclusive economic zone. Yet no US apologies or regrets were extended to China, and no promises were made to stay out of its security-sensitive areas. "Common interests" with the United States were cited in the Chinese press as the reason to put the matter quickly to rest.

44. For a detailed examination, see Richard Tanter, "Back to the Bases," *Arena*, no. 117 (April–May 2012); at www.mapw.org.au/files/downloads/Arena_R.Tanter-2012.pdf.

45. Li Xiaokun and Li Lianxing, "US Base in Australia Shows 'Cold War Mentality,'" *China Daily*, November 30, 2011; at www.chinadaily.com.cn/world/2011-12/01/content_14193427.htm; Ben Packham, "China Reproaches Australia over Strengthened US Defence Ties," *Australian*, November 17, 2011; online at www.theaustralian.com.au/national-affairs/obama-in-australia/our-indispensable-alliance-barack-obama/story-fnb0o39u-1226197460882.

46. Jakobson and Knox, p. 31, citing a 2009 report of the Chinese National Bureau of Statistics.

47. Edward Wong, "China's Export of Labor Faces Scorn," *New York Times*, December 20, 2009, online ed. A prominent human-rights activist who has been involved in some of these protests, Cu Huy Ha Vu, was arrested by the Vietnamese authorities in 2011, though probably not for that reason.

48. Sharon LaFraniere and John Grobler, "China Spreads Aid in Africa, with a Catch," *New York Times*, September 21, 2009, online ed.

49. The deportees had requested asylum in Cambodia in 2009 after the Chinese police had cracked down on the Uigher population. China's aid package, with an estimated value of around $850 million, came atop previous aid to Cambodia of around $4.3 billion. See "After Expelling Uighur Asylum Seekers, Cambodia Signs Deals for Investments by China," New York Times, December 22, 2009, p. A11.

50. Jim Yardley, "China's Premier Orders Halt to a Dam Project Threatening a Lost Eden," *New York Times*, April 9, 2004, p. A6. The dams would have been built in a pristine area that is a UN World Heritage Site and is largely populated by minorities.

51. Jane Perlez, "In Life on the Mekong, China's Dams Dominate," *New York Times*, March 19, 2005, p. 1.

52. International Crisis Group, "China's Myanmar Strategy: Elections, Ethnic Politics, and Economics," September 21, 2010.

53. Thomas Fuller, "Myanmar Backs Down, Suspending Dam Project," *New York Times*, October 1, 2011, p. A4; Joshua Kurlantzick, "An Opening in Burma?" *The Nation*, January 2, 2012, pp. 34–41.

54. Human-rights organizations made this accusation, which was denied by the PRC foreign ministry. See Edward Wong, "Chinese Deny Forcing Refugees to Myanmar," *New York Times*, August 25, 2012, online ed. The Kachin Independence Army and the government had declared a cease-fire, but it expired in mid-2011. At least several thousand Kachins are said to be living in Yunnan province, China.

55. Li Xiguang (Qinghua University), "China-Myanmar Ties Challenged by US Moves," *Global Times*, November 30, 2011, reprinted in *People's Daily Online*, December 7, 2011; at http://english.peopledaily.com.cn/90780/7661052.html.

56. Steven Lee Myers, "Dissident Leader in Myanmar Endorses U.S. Overtures," *New York Times*, December 2, 2011, online ed.

57. Jane Perlez, "Forests in Southeast Asia Fall to Prosperity's Ax," *New York Times*, April 29, 2006, online ed.; David Langue, "Felling Asia's Forests," *Far Eastern Economic Review*, December 25, 2003, pp. 26–29.

58. Confidential cable of August 20, 2009; available at http://wikileaks.org/cable/2009/08/09BEIJING2404.html.

59. Michael Wines, "China Is Willing to Spend Big in Afghanistan, on Commerce," *New York Times*, December 30, 2009, p. 1.

60. US Embassy, Beijing, confidential cable of October 21, 2009; at http://wikileaks.org/cable/2009/10/09BEIJING2918.html.

61. Lydia Polgreen, "Sri Lanka Forces Blamed for Most Civilian Deaths," *New York Times*, May 16, 2009; Jon Lee Anderson, "Death of the Tiger," *New Yorker*, January 27, 2011, pp. 41–55.

62. Anderson, "Death of the Tiger," p. 48; Somini Sengupta, "Take Aid from China and Take a Pass on Human Rights," *New York Times*, March 9, 2008, online ed.

63. Even in Iran, strong economic ties have not prevented criticism of China for supporting sanctions and underpaying for oil. See Erica Downs and Suzanne Maloney, "Getting China to Sanction Iran: The Chinese-Iranian Oil Connection," *Foreign Affairs* 90, no. 2 (2011): 15–21.

64. See Edward Wong, "China Opens Oil Field in Iraq," *New York Times*, June 28, 2011, online ed.

65. For a succinct critical review of US policy, see Robert Dreyfuss, "Washington's Weak Response," *The Nation*, September 12, 2011, pp. 43–45.

66. I rely here especially on Titus C. Chen, "China's Reaction to the Color Revolutions: Adaptive Authoritarianism in Full Swing," *Asian Perspective* 34, no. 2 (2010):. 5–51.

67. In one of the few instances where think-tank intellectuals commented, it was suggested that the uprisings showed how long-standing US support of authoritarian rulers had boomeranged to China's advantage. See Mei Xinyu, "Revolutionary Tide Sees New Friends for China," *Global Times*, February 21, 2011; at http://encomment.huanqiu.com/content_comment.php?tid=625073&mid=1&cid=43.

68. Edward Wong, "Human Rights Advocates Vanish as China Intensifies Crackdown," *New York Times*, March 11, 2011, online ed.

69. Michael Wines, "Secret Bid to Arm Qaddafi Sheds Light on Tension in China Government," *New York Times*, September 11, 2011, online ed.

70. On China's huge investment (as much as $120 billion) in Iranian oil, see Michael Wines, "China's Ties with Iran Complicate Diplomacy," *New York Times*, September 30, 2009, p. A14.

71. Zhou Yan, "Iran Tensions Mean 'It's Time for China to Diversify' Crude Sources," *China Daily*, January 6, 2012; at http://english.peopledaily.com.cn/90883/7698410.html; Jessica Silver-Greenberg, "Prosecutors Link Money from China to Iran," *New York Times*, August 29, 2012, online ed.

72. Nicola Phillips, "China and Latin America: Development Challenges and Geopolitical Dilemmas," in Dittmer and Yu, eds., *China, the Developing World, and the New Global Dynamic*, pp. 177–201.

73. For example, Beijing bought $300 million in Costa Rican bonds in 2008 in return for Costa Rica's switching of diplomatic recognition from Taiwan to the PRC: *New York Times*, September 13, 2008.

74. R. Evan Ellis, *China–Latin America Military Engagement: Good Will, Good Business, and Strategic Position* (Carlisle, PA: US Army War College, Strategic Studies Institute, August 2011).

75. Lum et al., *China's Foreign Aid Activities*, tables 8 and 9, pp. 15 and 25.

76. Simon Romero and Alexei Barrionuevo, "Deals Help China Expand Its Sway in Latin America," *New York Times*, April 16, 2009, p. 1.

77. Randal C. Archibold, "China Buys Inroads in the Caribbean, Catching U.S. Notice," *New York Times*, April 7, 2012, online ed.

78. Lum et al., *China's Foreign Aid Activities*, tables 8 and 9, p. 15.

79. Alexei Barrionuevo, "China's Interest in Farmland Makes Brazil Uneasy," *New York Times*, May 26, 2011, online ed.; Phillips, "China and Latin America," p. 187.

80. John Pomfret, "China Invests Heavily in Brazil, Elsewhere in Pursuit of Political Heft," *Washington Post*, July 26, 2010, online ed.; Simon Romero and Alexei Barrionuevo, "Deals Help China Expand Sway in Latin America," *New York Times*, April 15, 2009, online ed.

81. Lum et al., *China's Foreign Aid Activity*, pp. 2–5.

82. See State Council Information Office, "China's Foreign Aid," April 2011, at http://news.xinhuanet.com/english2010/china/2011-04/21/c_13839683.htm.

83. China's ties with Iran became problematic in 2012 when the United States and the European Union imposed sanctions on companies involved with Iran's oil exports. Not only did it mean that China would have to get its oil elsewhere; Iran's threat to close the Strait of Hormuz raised the possibility of another US-supported military action to keep the strait open.

84. China has an extensive aid program to Suriname, a country of only about 500,000 people, ruled by Desi Bouterse. He is wanted by Interpol on drug charges and stands accused of authorizing the killing of numerous political opponents. See Simon Romero, "With Aid and Migrants, China Expands Its Presence in a South American Country," *New York Times*, April 10, 2011, online ed.

85. Gill and Reilly, "The Tenuous Hold of China Inc. in Africa," p. 49.

5

China's "Good Citizenship"

When the Chinese leadership chose not to devalue the yuan during the Asian financial crisis of the late 1980s, it was rightly applauded for demonstrating good citizenship. Its decision showed admirable restraint during a moment when it could have reaped huge economic benefits at the expense of its Southeast Asian neighbors. Since then, Beijing has trumpeted regional and global citizenship as a hallmark of its new foreign policy. It is now commonplace to hear Chinese leaders speak of their country as a "responsible great power." Is it? In the discussion of China's fairly consistent decision to ignore human-rights abuses in Africa and popular uprisings in the Middle East we have already seen the need to qualify the claim of responsible behavior. By examining China's relations with important Asian neighbors and with international organizations, we may be able to answer the question more fully.

Sino-Japanese relations might seem like a good place to start. Despite many years of significant economic interdependence, to the point that China has replaced the United States as Japan's number-one trade partner, history still counts heavily. Sino-Japanese relations remain fraught with suspicions based on long-standing grievances. As a result, unresolved disputes over territory and history repeatedly flare up, sometimes (as in 2005 and 2012) igniting strong public protests in China. Japanese prime ministers since Koizumi Junichiro (2001–2006) have tried to respond to some of China's sensitivities, such as by not visiting Japan's war dead at the Yasukuni Shrine in Tokyo—though this has not stopped cabinet ministers from doing so. But competing claims over Diaoyudao/Senkaku, which have potentially large oil and gas deposits, have led to confrontations at sea and prevented genuine normalization of relations. The verdict on China's relationship with Japan is clear: *zheng leng jing re*, as the Chinese say—politically cold, economically hot.

China's relations with South Korea present a more nuanced case than that of Japan. Although both countries have alliances with the United States and were once China's enemy, South Korea does not have the kind of historical record that haunts China's relations with Japan—a record that begins with Japan's expansionist policies in East Asia in the eighteenth century, when it forced the Korean kingdom to open its doors, and goes on to the invasion and occupation of China as the prelude to World War II in the Pacific. Japan's history as an enemy of China and the Republic of Korea (ROK) has in fact provided common ground for both countries. We therefore begin with developments on the Korean peninsula.

China and Korea

There was a time not long ago when Sino-Korean relations were going so well that some experts were predicting they might lead to a swing in ROK foreign policy toward China and away from the United States. That development would have been a major foreign-policy success for China, bringing to its side a US ally and putting Korean reunification in a whole new strategic light. The predictions were based mainly on China's rise to become South Korea's top trade partner, South Korea's rapid ascent to become one of the leading foreign investors in and trade partners of China, and the decision of successive ROK presidents—Kim Dae Jung and Roh Moo Hyun—to seek to engage North Korea rather than pressure it over the North's nuclear-weapons program, a position favored by China and opposed by the United States. Roh even went so far as to suggest that South Korea might play a "balancer" role in Northeast Asia, which some people in Washington took to mean a distancing from the United States.

But political developments in and around the Korean peninsula are volatile, and predictions of a deep China-ROK partnership have proven incorrect. For even though leaders of both countries periodically upgraded characterization of their relationship—in 2008 it was declared a "strategic cooperative partnership"—to the point of having regular military talks and a hotline linking the two countries' militaries (much to North Korea's chagrin, we may imagine), cracks began to appear. When a conservative, Lee Myung Bak, assumed the South Korean presidency in 2008, policy toward North Korea toughened and the ROK-US alliance strengthened. Now, a once tension-free PRC-ROK relationship is marked by resentment and mistrust, even as leaders of the two countries foresee reaching a free-trade agreement and pushing bilateral trade over the $300 billion mark.

As is now clear, politics ultimately talks more loudly than economics in China's relations with Korea, just as it does in China's relations with Japan and some other countries. *Renmin ribao*, the official daily, made that point when it reported at the start of 2012 that the China-Korea relationship was becoming worrisome. Despite their tight commercial interdependence and some important common interests—paramount among them the determination to avoid another war on the Korean peninsula, to seek a "soft landing" for North Korea in the event of its implosion so as to avoid civil war and a refugee crisis, to resolve the North Korea nuclear issue by negotiations, and to keep nuclear weapons off the peninsula—the Sino-Korean honeymoon is over. Jae Ho Chung has concluded that as "the overall level of interdependence has risen, sources of friction between South Korea and China have also amplified."[1]

Among the actual or potential sources of friction is each side's dual policy. China has long had a "two-Koreas" policy: while it wants to further develop its economic relationship with Seoul, it also wants to keep North Korea afloat for as long as possible with political support and food and energy assistance. Politically, China has consistently upheld North Korea's sovereign right to develop nuclear power and has only partially applied UN sanctions. Economically, China has in effect subsidized the North's large trade deficit, even while selling it goods on commercial rather than "friendship" terms. China has also established a major stake in North Korea's mineral sector. The ROK government had long hoped that Beijing might use its influence with North Korea to bring about complete and verifiable elimination of the North's nuclear weapons and long-range rocket tests, counting, for example, on the fact that well over half the North's overall trade is with China. But Seoul has been consistently disappointed with China's unwillingness to use its presumed leverage with the DPRK.

The North's nuclear-weapon and missile tests have clearly discomfited Beijing, but not to the point of abandoning them. In 2010, for instance, China's support of the DPRK was challenged in an exceptional way: North Korea apparently attacked and sank a South Korean corvette, *Cheonan*, with forty-six sailors killed; it later carried out an artillery barrage against Yeonpyeong Island, also with some loss of life on the South's side, and revealed that it had an advanced uranium-enrichment facility in addition to a plutonium bomb program. China neither joined in demanding an apology from the North nor in fully carrying out sanctions against it voted by the UN Security Council.[2] These events capped a period in which disputes had emerged between China and the ROK over trade and investment practices. Then, in 2012, when rumors circulated of an impending third North Korean nuclear-weapon test, Beijing very publicly expressed its opposition. But at the same time it reportedly began building a massive highway and rail network near the border with North Korea, presumably to facilitate coal imports.[3]

As mentioned earlier, the Chinese were never going to abandon Kim Jong Il, and they are not about to dump Kim Jong Un, his son and successor. Korean reunification is not a Chinese priority, especially if it means (as Beijing probably assumes) eventual reunification under a pro-US government. Nor are the Chinese going to respect international law by allowing North Koreans who manage to escape over the border into China to remain there. Chinese police crackdowns on North Korean refugees and defectors occur regularly. (Four South Koreans who have worked with North Korean defectors in China charged in 2012 that they were illegally detained and tortured by the police.)[4] Even history intrudes into the Sino–South Korean relationship. Koreans discovered that China had a "Northeast Project" that claimed that land once within the ancient Korean kingdom of Koguryo belonged to China. South Koreans' opinion of China, which until 2004 had been more positive than it was of the United States, reversed course. The United States is now again much more popular than the PRC in South Korea.

Meantime, the ROK has its own dual policy. It consists of strengthening the alliance with the United States while making the most of its burgeoning economic ties with China. This situation once was of little concern to China, but more recently the Chinese have begun to wonder if the ROK-US alliance might be oriented to contain it if US-China relations worsen. The Koreans also worry about their trade dependence on China—despite the fact that they consistently run a substantial surplus in trade.

Chinese opinion of South Korea has likewise become more negative as some of their expectations have also been dashed. The Chinese seem to have expected more Korean gratitude for absorbing a constant trade imbalance and for helping keep North Korea from creating even more trouble. They evidently hoped the ROK would reset its foreign policy to achieve greater balance, essentially neutralizing the alliance with the United States as a prospective anti-China force. As South Korea, with strong US support, has become more militarily active on the international stage, for example in combating piracy and assisting the US military missions in Iraq and Afghanistan, some Chinese worry about the implications for the Korean peninsula after reunification. A sizable Korean-Chinese minority lives in areas adjacent to North Korea, raising the prospect of Korean irredentism.

The bottom line of the China-Korea story may be that you can't buy love. Neither close economic ties nor a "China fever," in which Korean tourism to China exceeded that to the United States and learning Chinese for a time became more popular than learning English, has enabled China to displace or rival the United States in Korean policy-making. Beijing, meanwhile, is saddled with an unpredictable, militantly nationalistic ally in the North and the burden that comes from being a new economic heavyweight in the South.

China and India

For some time now, India's rise has been mentioned in the same breath with China's. Since they are the countries with the world's largest populations, with India set to surpass China in about another decade, a comparison of the two makes sense. When we do compare them, we see two sets of contradictory indicators, one strategic and the other developmental. Officially, China and India have a "strategic and cooperative partnership" that began in 2005. Accordingly, they have rapidly increasing trade, with China as India's leading partner, regular high-level diplomatic contacts, agreements on confidence-building measures (CBMs) along their border, and a shared stance via the BRICS on global environmental and economic issues. They also have some common international policies, such as agreeing to continue importing Iranian oil in defiance of US and EU sanctions. Yet the two countries have thus far failed to overcome the bitter legacy of their 1962 border war. As a result, their common border has yet to be defined or demarcated, making military moves by either side hazardous. India's long-range missile development is clearly aimed at deterring China, not Pakistan. In recent years, some Chinese specialists have been concerned about India's increasing military and nuclear-energy cooperation with the United States, while India worries about an increasing Chinese military presence in the Indian Ocean under a "string of pearls" strategy.

The second developmental set of contradictions lies in the components of their rise. In a word, India is well behind China in economic growth and human development. As Table 5.1 shows, India trails China in size of the economy, public health, life expectancy, education, and gender equality, among other categories. India also compares poorly with China in terms of urbanization, rate of population growth, and reduction of child malnutrition.[5] Among the few factors in which China is at a disadvantage relative to India are the aging of its population and (arguably) the extent of environmental problems, both of which cut into China's real economic growth.[6]

Table 5.1 China and India

	China	India
Size of economy		
-GDP ($trillion)	$9.09	$1.73
-Per capita (PPP-adjusted)	$6,809[a]	$2,993
Merchandise trade (exports+imports, 2010)	$2.973 trillion	$547 billion
Foreign direct investment (FDI, 2010)	Outflow: $245.7 billion (2009) Inflow (utilized): $105 billion[b]	Outflow: $18.3 billion (2008) Inflow: $22.9 billion
Human Development Indicator rank (2011)	101	134
Education		
-Spending (% of GDP)	2.5	3.1
-Adult literacy (%)	94	62.8
-Universities in top 500	8	0
Gender inequality (2011)[c]	0.209	0.617
Carbon emissions per capita	4.96T	1.5T
Ecological footprint of consumption (global hectares per capita, 2007)[d]	2.2	8.9
Natural resource depletion (% of GNI)	3.1	4.2
Public Health		
-Spending (% of GDP, 2009)	1.9	1.1
-Infant mortality rate (per 1,000 births)	16.5	50
-Doctors (per 1,000 people)	1.5	—
-Hospital beds (per 1,000 people)	2.5	0.9
Life expectancy	73.5	65.4
Internet users (2011)	477 million	100 million

Sources: Derek Scissors, "The United States vs. China—Which Economy Is Bigger, Which Is Better," April 14, 2011; at www.heritage.org/research/reports/2011/04/the-united-states-vs -china-which-economy-is-bigger-which-is-better; WTO, *International Trade Statistics, 2010*; at www.wto.org/english/res_e/statis_e/its2011_e/its11_world_trade_dev_e.pdf, table 1.8; US-China Business Council; at www.uschina.org/statistics/fdi_cumulative.html; "Measuring China," *Global Asia* 5, no. 2 (2010): 10–11; UN Development Programme, *Human Development Report, 2011: Sustainability and Equity: A Better Future for All* (New York: Palgrave Macmillan, 2011); at www.beta.undp.org/content/dam/undp/library /corporate/HDR/2011%20Global%20HDR/English/HDR_2011_EN_Complete.pdf; "Not There Yet: India vs. US & China," *Global Asia* 6, no. 1 (2011): 18–19; World Bank, *World Development Indicators*; at www.google.com/publicdata; World Bank at http://devdata .worldbank.org/AAG/ind_aag.pdf (February 25, 2011); UNDP 2011; at http://hdrstats.undp.org /en/indicators/66006.html and www.hdr.undp.org/en/statistics; Internet World Stats, "Usage and Population Statistics"; at www.internetworldstats.com/stats14.htm.

Notes: a. Other sources put the figure lower. For example, the US-China Economic and Security Commission study (*2011 Report to Congress*, November 2011, p. 21) uses a projected $5.87 trillion GDP for 2011. b. In 2009, the United States ranked fifth with $3.6 billion invested, behind Hong Kong, Taiwan, Japan, and Singapore. c. The lower the value, the better the rating. Norway ranks first at 0.083. d. The UNDP defines "ecological footprint" as the "amount of biologically productive land and sea area that a country requires to produce the resources it consumes and to absorb the waste it generates."

The politics of food in India is a concrete example of its troubles in meeting human-security needs. Despite having huge and growing rice and wheat surpluses that are larger than China's, sacks of food sit rotting in the open in India while one-fifth of the population goes hungry. The reason comes down to politics: corrupt officials up and down the food distribution chain steal food for their own profit. Only about 40 percent of the food in government warehouses ever reaches Indian homes. The poor, who are supposed to receive rice and wheat at subsidized prices, rarely see them.[7]

No matter how you slice it, the fact is that China is much more important to India than India is to China. Whether measured in terms of tourists, media attention, development model, or simply individual interest, China looms very large in India's sights, whereas India is a sideshow for Chinese citizens and leaders.[8] Though Indians can be rightly proud of their democratic traditions and their stark contrast with China's authoritarian system, they see themselves as racing to catch up with China. The Chinese are not concerned with that race, however; their race is with the West, much as Japan's drive to modernize looked to the West for comparison, not to its East Asian neighbors.

In mid-August 2011, an Indian activist, Anna Hazare, brought the government to a standstill with a fast against official corruption. His one-man crusade quickly mushroomed into a nationwide protest against a host of other social ills, such as unemployment and poor social services—all this despite consistent economic growth in the range of 7 to 9 percent in recent years. It was the sort of protest movement that would never be tolerated in China. Yet there was little confidence, so far justified, that the force of public opinion in a democratically organized country would translate into sweeping policy changes. India's much ballyhooed rise runs up against political barriers every bit as formidable as those that undercut China's rise. Increasing inequality, agricultural problems, and corruption among elites are among the factors that have kept India's human development low. Unlike China, as the World Bank has consistently found, India is a classic case of increasing economic growth and declining poverty *rates*, but rising *numbers* of people living in poverty, especially in rural areas. While India's officials and some academics boast of the country's privatization of the economy and improved business climate, even predicting that India will become the world's third-largest economy by 2025, Indian critics point to neglect of human development in favor of conspicuous consumption.[9] Anna Hazare's protest will surely be followed by others.

The significance of this comparison for our purposes is that it points up the extraordinary accomplishments of China's post-1978 economic reforms in a country that is so large and geographically diverse. Yet as good as China's rise looks relative to India's and therefore also to its standing among developing countries, that rise has been accompanied by serious social, economic, and political problems. I explore these in the next chapter.

Global Citizenship

Proclaiming that one's country is a responsible great power is one thing; actually being one is another. Besides, Chinese and Western leaders have very different notions of what "responsibility" at any level means. Westerners—a good example is Robert Zoellick, who, as deputy secretary of state under Bush in 2005, sought to upgrade US-China relations by beseeching China to be a "responsible stakeholder" in the international system—tend to see responsibility hierarchically. In his view, a "responsible stakeholder" acts in accordance with global norms—established international rules and regulations; in short, a higher authority. Speaking in Beijing, Zoellick invited China to join the United States in supporting US-EU-Japan policy preferences, such as tough sanctions on Iran and North Korea. Zoellick said China could demonstrate that it deserved to be in the ranks of the great powers if it lent such support. To the Chinese, however, responsibility is mainly owed to oneself, not to a higher power. Being responsible means faithfully meeting Chinese priorities, a definition reaffirmed when the CCP's official news service accused Washington in 2011 of "dangerously irresponsible" behavior in its financial policies and urged the United States to adopt "responsible policies and measures"—an interesting turning of the tables.[10] Only if the interest of the international community (meaning the major powers led by the United States) happens to coincide with China's best interest will China act "responsibly" or urge such responsibility on others. That is what it did in the Asian financial crisis and what it urged on the United States in 2011.

As I have argued, China approaches international relations from a defensive posture, the goal being to protect itself from more powerful states so as to give its version of socialist development under one-party rule ample opportunity to move ahead. If China were devoted to causes of the sort that preoccupy US administrations, it would be constantly preaching (as Mao did) the advantages of socialism, collectivism, party-state unity, and a worldwide united front against Western hegemony. But that is no longer how Beijing conducts foreign relations, though China's more jingoistic media does urge that "China should unite with all possible forces" in order to deal with US attempts to contain it.[11]

We can expect China to demand a greater voice on global management and regulation issues such as occur in trade, finance, and climate change. Nevertheless, China is unlikely to be so insistent on accommodation to its preferences as to cause a serious rift with the United States and its chief partners. There is no evidence, for example, that China is seeking to bandwagon with other dissatisfied states to "balance" US power.[12] Biding time is more appealing than crisis management. But China is *actively* biding its time: it is taking advantage of the West's neglect and mistakes and creating opportunities of its own. It seems to have a mini/max foreign-policy strategy: minimum input to gain maximum influence.

China has quite a few "strategic partnerships," but—again unlike the United States—no security alliances. To make up for that gap, the PRC has been working within or supporting international organizations not dominated by the United States and the West. The ARF under ASEAN is one example; the China-Africa Forum is another. A third is the Shanghai Cooperation Organization (SCO), which has held joint military exercises, mainly involving Chinese and Russian units. As a group (which includes Kazakhstan, Tajikistan, Kyrgyzstan, and Uzbekistan), the SCO has sometimes adopted common policies, for example urging the United States to withdraw from bases in Uzbekistan and denouncing US missile-defense plans for central Europe. But the SCO has shown no interest in forming a military alliance. Its emphasis is on counterterrorism, which really means dealing with ethnic minorities in common borderlands that seek greater autonomy or separation. Nor have China and Russia developed a genuinely strategic relationship, though they do sometimes share common policy positions, such as on Iran, North Korea, and US intervention in the Middle East.

A fourth international group with active PRC participation is the BRICS, which is a useful vehicle for China in calling for restructuring of the IMF within "a new global monetary and financial architecture."[13] But each of the BRICS has its own interests, which means clashing views and different ways of demonstrating international activism. We saw one example in Brazil's concerns about Chinese land purchases and terms of trade. China-India rivalry is likely to endure for some time, as mentioned earlier. Policy differences between Russia and China are fairly routine: one example is over Russian arms sales to India; others include the generally critical PRC response to Russia's intervention in Georgia and Russia's decision to call for the ouster of Libya's Qaddafi.

Diverse positions among the BRICS may be detected over global environmental issues and relations with the United States, Japan, and Europe. Even when the BRICS were in agreement, such as their initial opposition to a UN Security Council vote to establish a NATO no-fly zone over Libya, they proved powerless to stop it and did nothing more than abstain from the vote on the enabling resolution. All these circumstances undercut any notion that the BRICS represent a unified front, at least outside their bilateral and trilateral relations.[14] Even their common demand for restructuring the global financial architecture accepts the ground rules of a world economic order based on the US dollar, though Russia's Prime Minister Putin was even more critical of the United States than was China in 2011 for nearly defaulting on its debt.

China does not have the capacity to exercise *global* leadership. Its diplomacy is certainly *international* in scope, but it is not equivalent to initiating and actively guiding global developments in new directions. China's leaders understand the difference: they know they do not have the authority to convene a Middle East peace conference, persuade UN organs to accept China's version of human rights, or become the deal maker or path breaker in a new global compact on, say, the environment, energy, labor, international law, or nuclear weapons. Aside from its important role as convener of the Six Party Talks on North Korea, Beijing has generally eschewed mediating disputes or engaging in the kind of shuttle diplomacy that helps create the give-and-take necessary for reaching agreement.

Moreover, China's international diplomacy can be exceedingly clumsy, such as when Beijing threatened to retaliate against countries that planned to be represented at the Nobel ceremony honoring Liu Xiaobo or when (as described earlier) it intervened twice to prevent the Dalai Lama from visiting South Africa. Another case was when it imposed restrictions on key exports (such as raw materials and raw earths) during a territorial dispute with Japan in apparent violation of WTO rules.[15] When China has substantial interests at stake, such as oil, it will happily do business with dictators. And there are quite a few, as we have seen: four in Africa (Sudan, Zimbabwe, Guinea, and the DRC); three in the Middle East (Syria, Iran, and Libya under Qaddafi); and two in East Asia (Myanmar and North Korea). The usual Chinese excuse that it refuses to violate the principle of state sovereignty falls flat, for in every one of these cases China's support—political, economic, and military—involves or did involve the repression of innocent people and even protection of regimes guilty of crimes against humanity.

China has won support among those governments that share its rather narrow perspective on "rights"—dictators who welcome China's defense of state sovereignty as a way to deflect criticisms of their oppressiveness and cultural relativists in Asia who argue that "Asian values" put defense and definitions of human rights in the hands of the state, not individuals. China's argument on human rights—that it has successfully promoted one valuable right, that of subsistence—is valid; but the argument vanishes when we turn to Chinese practices at home. The central government has imposed virtual martial law on Tibet since the 2008 demonstrations in Lhasa. In the words of the Dalai Lama, Tibet has become a "hell on earth"—so much so that in a twelve-month period in 2011 and 2012, nearly thirty Tibetan Buddhist nuns, monks, and herders self-immolated to protest Chinese policies.[16] Tibetans protesting in western Sichuan province in January 2012 saw a security cordon imposed on the area by soldiers and police. A party-state that leads the world in executions;[17] that harvests organs for transplant from executed prisoners;[18] whose police and security forces have been sharply criticized by the UN Office of the High Commissioner for Human Rights for "widespread" use of torture[19] and for other inhumane treatment of political, religious, and ethnic dissidents; and that usually bars international NGOs and other groups seeking to monitor China's observance of human rights can hardly qualify as a model of good governance, much less be a candidate for regional or global leadership.

Notes

1. Jae Ho Chung, "Korean Views of Korea-China Relations: Evolving Perceptions and Upcoming Challenges," *Asian Perspective* 36, no. 2 (2012): 219–236.

2. In accordance with Security Council resolutions, China has taken some mild steps to limit North Korean trade in illicit goods. But China has not intercepted and boarded North Korean vessels. Illegal North Korean shipments of ballistic-missile technology to Iran, reported by a UN committee that included a Chinese expert, apparently were delivered by air through China. See Dan Bilefsky, "China Delays Report Suggesting North Korea Violated Sanctions," *New York Times*, May 14, 2011, online ed.

3. "China in Huge Infrastructure Projects Near N. Korea Border," *Chosun Ilbo* (Seoul), July 20, 2012; at http://english.chosun.com/site/data/html_dir /2012/07/12/2012071201118.html. According to this report, China will spend more than $10 billion on the project by 2015, and an additional purpose might be military—"to secure easy access for Chinese troops in case of an emergency in the North."

4. Evan Ramstad, "South Korean Activist Presses Seoul, Beijing," *Wall Street Journal*, August 6, 2012; at http://online.wsj.com/article /SB10000872396390443517104577572662205363598.html?mod=googlenews_wsj.

5. See Rajiv Kumar, "International Role and Respect? Not Without Economic Prosperity," *Global Asia* 6, no. 1 (2011): 30–35; Sharon LaFraniere, "Unicef Cites China's Gains in Fighting Child Hunger," *New York Times*, May 3, 2006, p. A7.

6. Sonia Luthra, "An Interview with Nicholas Eberstadt," National Bureau of Asian Research, December 29, 2011; at www.nbr.org/research/activity.aspx?id=195; Christopher Flavin and Gary Gardner, "China, India, and the New World Order," in Linda Starke, ed., *State of the World, 2006* (New York: W. W. Norton, 2006), p. 7.

7. Vikas Bajaj, "As Grain Piles Up, India's Poor Still Go Hungry," *New York Times*, June 7, 2012, online ed.

8. Vikas Bajij, "India Measures Itself Against a China That Doesn't Notice," *New York Times*, August 31, 2011, online ed.

9. The arguments for India's rise are made by Jyotiraditya M. Scindia (India's minister of state commerce and industry), "India Engages the World: The View from New Delhi," *Global Asia* 6, no. 1 (2011): 12–16, and Anil K. Gupta, "India in 2025: What Kind of a Superpower?" *Global Asia* 6, no. 1 (2011): 20–23. The views of critics may be found in Celia W. Dugger, "Rich-Poor Gap Endangers India, President Warns," *International Herald Tribune*, January 26, 2000, and Pankaj Mishra, "The Myth of the New India," *New York Times*, July 6, 2006, p. A23.

10. Bettina Wassener, "China Urges U.S. to Take Responsible Action on Debt," *New York Times*, July 14, 2011, online ed.

11. "Pentagon Plan Changes Game in Asia," *Global Times*; at http://english.peopledaily.com.cn/90780/7697683.html.

12. See Peter Van Ness, "China's Response to the Bush Doctrine," *World Policy Journal* 21, no. 4 (2004–2005): 38–47.

13. See the BRICS statement of March 14, 2009, prior to the G-20 meeting in Britain; at www.g20.utoronto.ca/2009/2009-bric090314.html.

14. See Vidya Nadkami, *Strategic Partnerships in Asia: Balancing Without Alliances* (London: Routledge, 2010).

15. In a case brought by the United States, the European Union, and Mexico, the WTO ruled against China in July 2011 on restrictions Beijing imposed on nine industrial raw materials. Another case, brought by the EU, makes a similar argument concerning China's restrictions on the export of raw earth elements. Stephen Castle, "W.T.O. Says Chinese Limits on Raw Material Exports Break Global Trade Rules," *New York Times*, July 6, 2011, p. B3.

16. Edward Wong, "Dalai Lama Says China Has Turned Tibet into a 'Hell on Earth,'" *New York Times*, March 11, 2009. The same article cites a Human Rights Watch report, based on official Chinese accounts, that since the Tibetan uprising of March 2008, "there have been thousands of arbitrary arrests, and more than 100 trials pushed through the judicial system." The European Union has also been highly critical of China's policies in Tibet: in March 2009, it called on Beijing to "open a constructive dialogue" with Tibet on autonomy, release imprisoned Tibetans, and open the country to foreign reporters and human-rights groups. Agence France-Presse (Strasbourg), "EU Lawmakers Urge China to Discuss Real Autonomy with Tibet," *NAPSNet*, March 13, 2009. Information on the self-immolations is from the Tibet Justice Center; www.tibetjustice.org.

17. Amnesty International has reported (in its publication, *World View* [Summer 2008]: 8), that in 2007 there were more than 1,860 executions in China. Pakistan was second with 307, and the United States was fifth with more than 100.

18. A Chinese official promised in 2012 that this practice would stop in a few years.

19. The investigation was conducted by Manfred Nowak, the special rapporteur of the UN Commission on Human Rights. See Joseph Kahn, "Torture Is 'Widespread' in China, U.N. Investigator Says," *New York Times*, December 3, 2005, online ed.

6

Feet of Clay

Wukan, on the Guangdong (Canton) coast, is a village of about twenty thousand people. In another era it would never have been the setting for public protests, but for about three months in late 2011, villagers confronted local authorities over illegal land grabs and corruption—uncompensated sales of as much as 60 percent of the village's territory over an eighteen-year period, orchestrated by "elected" village committee members who had been in office for many years and had paid a good deal of money to get in position to reap the rewards of controlling the village budget. Villagers were largely in the dark about these sales.[1]

The dispute escalated when the police detained and probably tortured one of the protest leaders, leading to a police cordon around the village. Villagers demonstrated with signs such as "The people of unjust Wukan!" They hoped Beijing would intervene and punish the police and local government officials, but instead the officials denied that torture had occurred and accused the protest leaders of being hoodlums. No mention was made of the illegal confiscations that had led to the protests.[2] The standoff ended when provincial officials met with village leaders, agreed to release villagers who had been detained, and removed the local officials. A new village council was elected that included several activists, and one of the protest leaders became council head. But the land issue and the allegations of torture remain unresolved.

The Wukan incident tells us something about the best and the worst of what is happening in rural China, and for that matter in the rest of China. Local officials were eventually punished and apparently fair elections were carried out, vindicating the protesters and lending support to official claims that grassroots political reform is a reality. Yet the incident also showed that official corruption and unfair treatment of ordinary people are a constant problem, that protesting is dangerous, and that the pattern of blaming the victim is always available to those in power. Mass protests are becoming more and more common in China, and the fact that the outcome in Wukan is not at all typical points to the underside of China's rise: the many sources of insecurity.

First, the Good News

The Chinese like to say that a country's foreign policy reflects its domestic circumstances. Internal security is a critical component of that idea: for a country to be truly secure from external threat, it must first be secure within. Applying this perspective to China reveals much that is praiseworthy about the country's rise. Most notably, it has dramatically alleviated poverty for some 600 million people. Whether one accepts the Chinese government's definition of absolute poverty or the World Bank's, the reduction in rural poverty since the start of the economic reforms has been extraordinary—so much so that "China alone has accounted for over 75% of poverty reduction in the developing world over the last 30 years."[3] Progress in some aspects of human development, as measured annually by the United Nations Development Program, is likewise very impressive, such as life expectancy, literacy, female inequality, and immunization coverage (see Table 5.1). China typically falls in the middle ranks of 187 countries surveyed when the various human-development indicators are averaged—101st in 2011, ahead of Thailand (at 103), South Africa (at 123), and India (at 134), but well behind Russia (at 66) and Brazil (at 84).

The Chinese party-state has institutionalized leadership transition, greatly reducing the chance of a succession crisis and ensuring that a new generation of younger, better-educated people will take the reins of power by 2017. (The removal of Bo Xilai mentioned earlier was a huge embarrassment to the leadership, however, as it threatened to unhinge the smooth transition to a new leadership.) With the retirement in 2012 of most members of China's two top decisionmaking institutions—the twenty-five-member party politburo and its nine-member (now seven) standing committee—a substantial turnover of leading personnel took place that will continue in five years at the next party congress. Social controls have loosened, allowing for greater freedom of expression and movement than ever before. Grassroots democracy has gained a small toehold in village elections that sometimes actually do result in the election of nonparty leaders. A few townships have experimented with a consultative form of decisionmaking in an effort to promote popular choice of projects for government funding. An onerous system of taxes and fees imposed on farmers has been abolished, and in those farming areas with good leadership, productive land, and other assets, quality-of-life opportunities have greatly improved.[4] State-run and state-subsidized institutions employ modern social-science techniques in their research.

As the world's second-largest economy—having surpassed Japan and attained around 60 percent of the size of the US economy—China has truly become something of an economic growth miracle. A principal reason is the extensive privatization of the economy. At the same time, adroit economic planning by the government has so far enabled China to avoid the costly recessions and financial woes that have plagued the capitalist world. The country continues to pile up trade surpluses, becoming one of the top three exporters. China has become a global leader in the manufacture and export of wind turbines and solar panels, backed by government subsidies in land and credit that may be in violation of WTO rules.[5] (We should pause to note that both the United States and the European Union have been found guilty by the WTO of subsidizing their aircraft industries, among others.) China's investment in clean energy has also vaulted it to first rank in hydropower and biofuels. Under the 863 Program, named for its start in March 1986, China's goal is to have renewable energy comprise 10 percent of total energy consumption by 2020.

Human Underdevelopment

Notwithstanding the above, when China's internal problems are objectively examined, we find serious weaknesses—weaknesses that often are freely acknowledged by Chinese sources that, to their credit, now provide hard data in support of critical analysis. In human development it is still some distance from the most developed countries in a number of basic-needs categories. As one prominent Chinese economist of international reputation has written, China, while surpassing Japan in GDP in 2010, still must look to Japan as a model in terms of social equality, environmental protection, and innovation.[6] In life expectancy, educational quality, and infant mortality, China trails far behind Japan.

China is particularly lagging in public health. It is well behind South Korea, Japan, and the United States when it comes to health insurance, hospital beds, public-health spending, work-safety regulations, and number of physicians relative to population. People living in central and western China are even more disadvantaged in access to health care. Environmental pollution, now including smoking and auto accidents along with severe air pollution, is a major factor in China's declining public health. Air-pollution levels in nearly all the major cities far exceed World Health Organization (WHO) guidelines. Every year, several hundred thousand people die prematurely from illnesses caused by particulate matter in the air, the WHO has found. (For these and other comparisons with the United States, see Table 6.1, which repeats the information on China in Table 5.1.)

Despite increasing incomes and personal savings, people in China are worried about their health care and thus do not spend as much as they might ordinarily in order to guard against sudden illness. This situation puts a new perspective on China's economic growth. As Yanzhong Huang of Seton Hall University has written,

> Still preoccupied with GDP growth, local governments, which [run the health insurance plans and] are supposed to finance about 70 percent of all public health spending, have few incentives to spend much on health care. As a result, not only does China's domestic demand continue to be suppressed, but the burden of the costs of disease continues to rise, canceling out the gains from economic growth. Between 2003 and 2010, while China's GDP increased by 193 percent, the economic burden of disease increased by 197 percent.[7]

China's demographic profile offers further grounds for future uncertainties. While it has made great strides in lengthening life expectancy (now about seventy-one years, on average), its rapidly aging population—by 2035 nearly one-quarter (roughly 390 million people) will be sixty or more years old[8]—China no longer has the social safety net it once could count on. On the other end of the demographic scale, the one-child-per-family policy has been *too* successful: the working population of young people will soon begin shrinking as birthrates remain low while the population of seniors continues to expand. This situation creates three major problems.[9] One is a labor shortage, even in the major industrial cities that attract rural migrants. Second, the government's burden to support its seniors will increase at a staggering rate, forcing either reductions in spending that affect young people seeking jobs or decreases in spending on education and training. While the government plans for the overwhelming majority of the aged to be cared for at home, young people are less and less likely to be able to spend time with them, raising the issue of state or private nursing-home care. It is a daunting challenge common to many other countries: how the working 50 percent of the population will be able to support seniors and children who constitute the other 50 percent.[10]

Third, the traditional Chinese family's preference for males over females has created a large gender imbalance in births (117 to 100, according to China's 2000 census), leading to a big gap between young men seeking marriage and young women available to marry. China may

Table 6.1 The United States and China: Society and Environment

	United States	China
Human Development Indicator rank (2011)	4	101

Education
  -Spending (% of GDP)
  -Adult literacy (%)
  -Universities in top 500
	5.5
	99
	168
		2.5
		94
		8

Gender inequality (2011)[a]	0.299	0.209
Carbon emissions per capita -Total (2007)	19.34T 5.8 million kT	4.96T 6.53 million kT

Ecological footprint of
  consumption (global hectares
  per capita, 2007)
	8.0	2.2

Natural resource depletion (% of GNI)	0.7	3.1

Public Health
  -Spending (% of GDP, 2009)
  -Infant mortality rate (per 1,000 births)
  -Doctors (per 1,000 people)
  -Hospital beds (per 1,000 people)
	7.1
	6.1
	2.3
	3.3
		1.9
		16.5
		1.5
		2.5

Life expectancy	78.5	73.5
Internet users (2011)	245 million	477 million

Sources: "Measuring China," *Global Asia* 5, no. 2 (2010): 10–11; UNDP 2011; *Global Asia* 6, no. 1 (2011): 18–19; World Bank, *World Development Indicators*; at www.google.com /publicdata; UNDP 2011; at http://hdrstats.undp.org/en/indicators/66006.html; UNDP 2011; at www.hdr.undp.org/en/statistics; Internet World Stats, "Usage and Population Statistics"; at www.internetworldstats.com/stats14.htm.
Note: a. Lower value indicates higher rating.

have to overhaul the one-child-per-family policy as more affluent couples want a second child, hopefully a girl; but, in common with most developed countries, people now understand the economic good sense of family planning. Strange as it may seem when talking about China, a declining population may sap the country's strength.[11]

China's educational record is a good indicator of how far it has come and how far behind it remains. The number of Chinese science and technology graduates surpasses that of every other country, and high school students in Shanghai rank first globally in internationally recognized tests. The Chinese government has been quite successful, moreover, in attracting scientists and other talented people living abroad to return home. China is also receiving increasingly large numbers of foreign students, an estimated 120,000 now, including around 14,000 from the United States. With money to burn and concern about China's weakness in soft power, China has invested in globalizing its language and culture: the education ministry provides substantial seed money for a worldwide network of Confucius Institutes that host teachers from the PRC, give local teachers training in teaching Chinese, fund speakers on many China-related subjects, and donate textbooks for students from kindergarten to college. (In 2010, the Chinese press reported that there were 316 Confucius Institutes in ninety-four countries, including around seventy in the United States.)

Yet China is hardly a global educational leader. Only eight Chinese universities rank among the world's top five hundred. Government educational spending is low—it was only 2 percent of GDP in 2006, well below the official target of 4 percent. Going abroad, especially to the United States, is still the key to advanced learning for young Chinese who can afford it: about 160,000 undergraduate and graduate students were enrolled in US institutions in the 2009/2010 academic year, the largest contingent (22 percent) of all foreign students.[12] Most returnees to China, it turns out, are not among the top-notch scholars and scientists—rating as *hai dai* (seaweed) rather than *hai gui* (sea turtles).[13] Nowadays, those Chinese students who do not go to the United States can attend US university branches and programs at home. New York University, for example, has announced the establishment of a four-year degree-granting campus in Shanghai that the university expects will eventually have three thousand students. For the great majority of Chinese students who obtain degrees, the growing problem is finding a job. "Not having a job is a perfect recipe for social unrest," writes one observer.[14] China's leaders are surely aware that many (perhaps most) of the young protesters in the Middle East were highly educated but had lost hope of finding meaningful work.

This last circumstance reflects the relative attractiveness of China and the United States, not only to international students but also to people seeking work. The United States continues to absorb far more immigrants than any other country, as reflected in the percentage of the population composed of foreign-born persons (13 percent), their actual number (about 38 million), and the millions of undocumented workers. Needless to say, China has no migrant workers, and even though there is actually a shortage of labor in industrialized coastal cities, it is hard to imagine the Chinese authorities importing workers or looking the other way if a person seeking work illegally crosses the border. (As noted earlier, China is a net exporter of labor.) Other than Taiwan businessmen, hardly anyone voluntarily moves to China, and anyone who does has a very difficult time being accepted for residency.[15] A sad case in point is that of the North Korean refugees in China mentioned earlier who have been subject to forced repatriation.

As daunting as all of these problems are, they pale in comparison with environmental damage—China's Achilles' heel.[16] The immediate environmental issues are water shortages and drought, floods, air and water pollution, yellow dust, acid rain, deforestation, and desertification. All of them exact a huge toll on public health, safety, and agricultural and industrial production. Hundreds of thousands of deaths annually are attributable to environmental degradation. The predicted costs of dealing with these problems are astronomical—somewhere between 8 percent and 12 percent of GDP annually.[17] What such figures mean goes beyond government budgeting: they tell us that China's real economic growth rate is far lower than is reported. "If environmental damage were fully factored into the state's account books, China's economic growth rate would probably be halved," Wang Yuqing, former deputy director of the state environmental protection ministry, warned in March [2012]. He estimated environmental damage last year at about 2.5 trillion yuan (US400 billion), or 5 to 6 percent of China's GDP."[18]

While air and water quality have improved, "the overall environmental situation is still very grave," said a senior environmental protection official in his ministry's 2010 report.[19] The situation is likely to get much worse. Already, sixteen of the world's twenty most polluted cities are in China; yet the country remains dependent on dirty coal for 70 to 80 percent of its electricity, and China will soon surpass the United States in the number of cars on the road.[20] If the Chinese government's plan transpires to have half the population living in cities by 2030—about 32 percent do now—urban managers could easily be overwhelmed by pollution and attendant public health issues.[21]

When it comes to China's environmental problems, most foreign media attention has focused on carbon dioxide emissions, which since 2006 have surpassed those of the United States on a total, though not per person, basis.[22] But water is the greater crisis, with respect to both availability and pollution. Reduced access to drinkable water is a consequence of urban growth, an enormous increase in usage by people and industrial and agricultural producers, wastage, underpricing, and poor government management. Consider the drought that hit China's southwestern region in the summer of 2011. By Chinese accounts, 14 million people were left short of drinking water and millions of acres of farmland were parched. Yet the government is implementing an extraordinary—and extraordinarily expensive—"south to north" transfer of water that seems likely eventually to drain the south of water. Social tensions are simmering over this project as farmers in the south come to understand their bleak future. As for pollution, various studies inside and outside China report that drinkable water is as little as 30 percent of the water supply in most urban and rural areas.

The long-term dangers of these environmental problems are even more troubling, for both China and—given China's size—the world. A water crisis translates into lowering of the water table, reduced food production, loss of productive land, rising food prices, and increased migration to cities, where water availability is already threatened.[23] Pollution increases public-health costs and reduces economic growth and opportunity. As dirty industries move to rural areas, the 2010 environmental report cited previously said, pollution in the countryside is becoming a major problem. So is the threat to biodiversity. A two-year-long survey of water pollution that China's environmental protection agency issued in the same year examined around 6 million pollution sources. For the first time the survey included agricultural effluents, resulting in a much grimmer picture of water pollution and its implications for farmers than had previously been reported.[24]

The ministry of environmental protection, though sensitive to these matters, often finds itself powerless against prodevelopment forces that operate through larger, better-funded government agencies headed by officials close to the top leaders. Local-level leaders may be an even bigger obstacle: they often have close financial or political ties to heads of polluting industries and therefore have no interest in environmental-impact assessments, broad public participation in decisionmaking, or other responses that might result in eliminating or cutting back questionable projects. Market-based approaches, such as raising the price of water, meet popular resistance, suggesting that public education as to the real cost of water pollution has yet to take root. Natural resources, in a word, do not yet have high social value.

China's environmental NGOs, such as the local Greenpeace and World Wildlife Federation offices, and environmental activists such as Ma Jun have occasionally been effective at delaying large-scale energy projects and naming and shaming polluting industries. (Ma Jun's Institute of Public and Environmental Affairs produces a map that gives current figures on water pollution, air quality, and solid waste discharge in each of China's provinces.) Chinese citizens sometimes take matters into their own hands, such as by doing their own monitoring of city air pollution and "tweeting" the results, since the government has refused to publish them. But in general, activists are up against powerful local and bureaucratic forces that put "development" and "growth" ahead of any other objective.[25]

As Ma Jun has said, supply-side thinking leads to more "massive engineering projects" in response to energy needs rather than to an emphasis on conservation. These projects are precisely the kinds that help generate social instability, the very thing the PRC leadership fears most. China's citizens have demonstrated, literally, that they will not easily tolerate tainted food, lead poisoning, schools that collapse during earthquakes, buildings without fire protection, and forced resettlement to make way for dams. (The infamous Three Gorges Dam on the Yangtze River, the centerpiece of China's hydropower push, has displaced over 1.1 million people and caused considerable environmental damage, even as it has provided electricity to millions more. Another dam slated for construction on the Yangtze, Xiaonanhai, which like Three Gorges will be very expensive once built, will endanger numerous rare fish species and displace some four hundred thousand people. But the dam has powerful political support that outweighs the opposition of Chinese NGOs and scientists.)[26] At the same time, many of these problems raise costs for the international community as well, as for example with rising food prices, climate change, and the spillover into bordering countries of China's acid rain, deforestation, and overapplication of pesticides.

Public and occupational safety has become a highly visible issue. China leads the world in mine accidents, building construction codes are routinely violated, tainted food is a recurring problem, and unsafe buses are routinely used to shuttle children. Child trafficking has emerged in response to the one-child-per-family policy. Official cover-ups of these problems have angered citizens as well as tarnished China's reputation. Consumerism has taken a backseat to capital accumulation that will finance bank lending; in fact, China ranks last among the major economies in consumer spending as a proportion of GNP. The frequent stories about Chinese who can now buy brand-name products obscure the greater reality that ordinary Chinese put their money into low-interest bank accounts for lack of higher-priced goods they can afford. But doing so only helps underwrite low-interest state bank loans to the biggest enterprises.

Internal migration in search of employment is a serious problem: at least 150 million migrant workers (Premier Wen Jiabao, in the speech quoted earlier, said 200 million) crowd cities looking for work, a major factor in the extraordinary shift in population that is occurring from countryside to cities. As in so many other countries, migrant workers are treated shabbily in China. Though they perform the menial tasks that enable many businesses to function and the rich to enjoy life, China's migrant population is constantly subject to police harassment, eviction from housing and schools, and forced return to rural areas. They also count for a largely unreported component of the unemployment rolls, making China's jobless rate much higher than officials report.

The Economy: Not All That It Seems

Is China's awesome economic growth sustainable? This is a subject of constant debate among specialists inside and outside the country.[27] Much depends on which aspect of growth the analyst considers most crucial. China has experienced an extraordinary growth rate of GDP since the early 1980s, marked by very large state investments, which is why many analysts rather facilely predict that China will overtake the United States as the largest economy sometime in the 2020s. But these assessments often project upward from the present, thereby failing to take into account the long list of problem areas discussed here that, cumulatively, will eat into China's ability to keep throwing money into the economy.

Publications outside China focus on *market* socialism, the official categorization of the country's economy. But it is a serious error to believe that China's economy is actually capitalist—not when a few state-run institutions control banking, telecommunications, oil, and other leading sectors. Here we look at banking, where four banks dominate loans and capital, so much so that Premier Wen, speaking in 2012, sounded like a muckraker in saying that "we have to break up [the banks'] monopoly" if private capital is to have any chance of competing.[28]

China has already been through periods of breakneck construction and cowboy financing that have led to the accumulation of nonperforming loans, bank failures and lack of transparency in the banking system, real-estate bubbles, and serious inflation, the last always a hot button for political leaders. A repeat performance is entirely possible. Local governments that are competing to replicate the massive public-works projects of Beijing and Shanghai have a level of debt so high—over $2 trillion, perhaps more—that banks and the central government may again face a financial crisis.[29] Of course, it is entirely possible that the construction projects—subways, parks, sewer systems—will produce revenue sufficient to offset the debt. The central government may be successful at reining in local government spending, though that is far from ensured. Private entrepreneurs chafe at the favoritism shown by the government and the banks to state-owned enterprises (SOEs). SOEs and other parts of the state-run sector of the economy received nearly one-half of government stimulus funds when the 2008 recession hit China,[30] and in 2009 SOEs received 85 percent of bank loans.[31] Chinese justifiably say "*guo jin min tui*": the state advances, the private sector retreats.

On the international side we need to consider foreign aid, overseas investments, and trade. The total US foreign-aid program, military and economic, dwarfs China's (see Table 3.1).[32] China's outward direct investment has risen substantially in recent years. But at around $245 billion cumulatively (in 2010), its investments are minuscule in comparison with US and other Western FDI, which is measured in the trillions of dollars in actual value and year-by-year investments. And the Chinese generally are seeking mergers rather than full ownership of overseas companies.[33] "Going global" is becoming more commonplace for Chinese enterprises; but few of them can invest large sums (defined as more than $100 million), and when they do, they are attracted by the same conditions that Western firms seek, namely, market size, access to technology, and safety of investment.[34]

Even China's enviable trade record has a major downside. China is a world leader in exports, currently valued at about $1.5 trillion (compared with the United States at more than $2 trillion in exported goods). The export-led development model that China, along with many other East Asian countries, has adapted from Japan works well when consumer and worker interests are suppressed and the international market is favorable. South Korea, for example, became a major trading state starting in the 1980s through a collusive partnership between the state's political and banking leaders and the giant industrial conglomerates known as *chaebol*. This iron triangle prevented the organization of independent unions and kept wages and other work conditions below international standards. Meantime, military-led governments directed bank loans to the largest *chaebol*, which in turn funneled huge sums of money into presidential slush funds. As workers gained political strength and the middle class and religious groups rallied against the repressive state, the Korean model became unsustainable. China may be susceptible to the same kinds of developments—rising consumer demand, worker organizing, and increasing competition from abroad.

China's energy capacity and use have exploded. One expert cites annual average growth of 11 percent in electricity generation from 2006 to 2011, about equal to GDP average annual growth over the same period. Unfortunately, highly polluting coal dominates in electricity production, with hydro (16 percent), nuclear (under 2 percent), and wind power (just over 1 percent) accounting for not quite one-fifth of the total.[35] China's leaders are clearly riveted on a post-coal future that embraces greatly increased oil and natural gas imports now and considerable reliance on conservation technologies and nonfossil fuels down the road. China is developing a large network of wind and nuclear power stations—fourteen nuclear plants are already on line and another twenty-six are under construction[36]—and it has set ambitious targets for energy conservation, as noted earlier.

Still, China's energy security path may be less secure than would appear. One reason is that China has chosen to rely for oil and gas imports on regimes with questionable durability. As mentioned, it must also depend on others, notably the United States, to secure the sea-lanes and gas pipelines that bring the energy to China. Having fully embraced an automobile culture, China's dependence is sure to increase no matter how successful it is at conserving energy and building more nuclear power plants. Nor is nuclear energy a next-best option, not only for safety reasons—the nuclear industry is shorthanded in terms of both engineers and safety personnel[37]—but also because Chinese who live near nuclear power plants are becoming aware of the risks, especially after the Fukushima Daiichi tragedy in Japan in March 2011. And they are starting to protest.[38] Yet despite pausing to conduct safety inspections of plants under construction after Fukushima, China's approvals of new construction resumed in July 2012.[39] Thus, China's energy picture may be inherently unstable and much less likely than the United States to achieve energy independence.

In China's case, rising consumer demand and improving wages may soon compel the leadership to address the internal market and stop focusing investments on big state-run enterprises. Premier Wen's final report of early 2012 promised just that—but so have previous such reports. As Zhou Tianyong, a professor at the Central Party School in Beijing, has written in *Where Is China Headed?*: "Which way will we go down?" "If we choose the right route we can avoid falling into a development trap; if we choose the wrong one, we may fall into a 'China trap' of social and political turmoil, slow economic growth, enduring lack of prosperity, and weak and declining national competitiveness." By the "China trap" he was referring to a pattern of economic growth that "privileges industry, big corporations, big capital and big projects."[40]

Social Instability

No one knows better than China's leaders and intellectuals the depth of its internal problems. Internal stability, we have observed, has been the central concern of China's leaders ever since the country achieved a shaky unity early in the twentieth century. Foreign policy reflects this concern: all Chinese leaders have embraced the notion that if the country is disunited and weak, foreign powers will take advantage. *Nei luan wai huan*—where there is chaos within there is calamity without—was the cry of the May Fourth movement in 1919, at the birth of Chinese nationalism. Achieving political stability and dynamic economic growth are the antidotes to chaos. This has nothing to do with Marxism; it is an interpretation of China's modern history as one of political and economic disintegration that enabled victimization by the West and Japan.

Thus, whether during the years of Mao's confrontations with the United States and the Soviet Union or on the eve of the initial economic reforms under Deng or in the assaults on Tibetans and other ethnic groups in the lead-up to the 2008 Olympic Games, the imposition of domestic order and resistance to foreign criticism or pressure have consistently framed Beijing's international outlook.[41] The leadership's response to the global economic downturn that began in 2008 and to US pressure for currency revaluation was no different: the first thought was how economic policy changes would affect social stability, and the second thought was how to respond to pressure from the United States to change its currency value. The social contract was on the line in the first instance, and China's identity in the second. Failure to deliver growth, prosperity, and employment, and failure to show foreign powers that China "will not be bullied," risk protests, including violent ones, and then possibly questioning of the regime's legitimacy. Likewise, failure to protect the public interest, such as by ignoring factories that dump hazardous waste into the water supply, is increasingly likely to arouse the public's wrath.

No wonder China's reported public-security budget, around $111 billion in 2012 for all levels of government, is approximately the same size as the official defense budget. Laid-off industrial workers, ethnic minorities—Tibetans, Uighurs, Mongolians—and migrant farmworkers are among the many disempowered groups demanding their rights. Ordinary citizens want remedial action for instances of gross incompetence—as witness demonstrations in the aftermath of the Sichuan earthquake, various mining accidents, and fires. With rising land values, illegal seizures of farmland have become a major source of public anger. As happened in Wukan, corrupt local officials in cahoots with police and courts seek to convert land to industrial parks, apartments, factory sites for foreign firms, or golf courses, often with little compensation. (Homeowners in cities face comparable worries from uncompensated demolitions ordered by bureaucrats linked to land developers.) According to one survey published in a state-supported magazine, public anger over these injustices is spreading across China.[42]

Weak civil society, moreover, helps ensure that a rapidly growing economy will incur high current and future costs. Since there are no officially accepted channels for venting grievances other than petitions to authority figures that are easily ignored (and that are sometimes dangerous to submit), protests are the alternative. These are becoming commonplace—the official designation of them is "mass incidents"—as farmers, city dwellers, ethnic minorities, environmental refugees (people displaced by dam projects), and laid-off industrial workers sound off. Each year the official figure on all these incidents rises sharply—to more than 125,000 in 2010, according to one leaked report[43]—though the figure includes protests of all sizes and types, whether violent or not. People have become more demanding of their government, independent investigative reports by journalists challenge the censors, the cultural moorings of Chinese society have been upset by rapid social and economic changes, and the central government's ability to buy off diverse constituencies is not unlimited. "Popular resistance and economic imbalances are now moving China toward another major crisis," one prominent Chinese economist has written.[44]

Official corruption is extensive; money laundering, illegal sales of state assets, and embezzlement are frequently cited instances.[45] Gaps in income and living standards are widening between rich and poor, between urban and rural dwellers, and between coastal and interior populations. If hidden wealth is taken into account, the rich-poor divide is probably one of the world's largest.[46] Getting rich is no longer taboo; but not too many people will be able to achieve wealth, for income inequality in China is now the same as in the United States: both have a Gini coefficient of 0.47. Personal income has not advanced as fast as GDP. Urban incomes on average are a worrisome 3.5 times as large as rural incomes.[47] Industrial strikes are increasing in frequency as workers have little faith that Communist Party–controlled unions can protect their interests. Threats to public health are increasingly grounds for protests; they have become particularly common when a town's water supply is threatened by industry. In 2011 and 2012, for instance, such protests occurred in Shifang, Sichuan province, against a copper refinery; in Dalian, Liaoning province, against a petrochemical plant; in Qidong, near Shanghai, against a waste-discharge plant; at a solar energy plant in Jiaxing, Zhejiang province; and in Ningpo, south of Shanghai, against a planned expansion of a petrochemical plant. All five incidents prompted government promises to close the offending plants, though not all the promises have been kept.[48]

To be sure, none of these sources of unrest threatens the Chinese party-state. It maintains the ability to quash protests, using the People's Armed Police (a division of the PLA) as well as the regular military when necessary. The state's internal security apparatus annually arrests more than one thousand people—mainly ethnic minorities—for "endangering state security." Few political prisoners are ever heard from again.[49] Protests by Muslim (Hui), Tibetan, and other minorities are invariably characterized as separatist and terrorist acts rather than quests for greater cultural and political autonomy, a distinction that owes much to the vocabulary of the US "war on terror." It is easy to understand why, to the Chinese authorities, the term *national security* chiefly means *domestic security*. The fact that the number of "incidents" keeps rising puts the maintenance of order at the top of their priorities. Thus, while the leadership takes pride in having maintained "social stability" for the past thirty years, preserving another thirty years of *that* kind of stability is uncertain.

The Limits of "Reform"

Thanks to the economic reforms, the Chinese people have greater personal space than ever before in terms of mobility, interpersonal communication (China has more netizens than anywhere else, and more microblog, or *weibo*, users), and opportunities over the Internet to express their patriotism or their discontent over social issues. They are using these, often getting around the Internet policing system by the time-honored Chinese device of using homonyms—words that have the same sound but different tones and meaning—to disguise criticisms of authority and avoid banned words. For example, *hexie* can mean either harmonious, as in "harmonious society," or river crab, a stand-in for *repression*. It's just one phrase in a large resistance vocabulary that Internet users have developed.[50] The surveillance system (officially called the Golden Shield Project, but popularly known as the Great Firewall) is under the ministry of public security and is *thought* to employ—no one really knows—more than thirty thousand people.

On the whole, the Great Firewall is exceptionally effective, and the Internet system, from servers to customers and cafés, is tightly regulated. Twitter and Facebook have been effectively blocked. Everyone is aware of the political subjects that must be avoided, such as criticizing the one-party system.[51] True, the Internet police have not been able to stop young people from getting out a message of disgust and dismay at the government's consistent failure to tell the truth—whether about tainted food, HIV/AIDS, SARS, polluted runoff from factories, abuses of authority, or unsafe buildings and railways. Sometimes hostile public opinion has reversed an injustice following an effort to cover it up. State officials have occasionally been stopped from imposing new Internet controls, as in 2009 when they tried to require that all new computers carry censoring software.[52] Late in 2011, however, they issued new regulations for Beijing that require *weibo* users to register their real names and demand that companies that host *weibo* obtain a license. Blogging in China has thus become a tug-of-war between the regulators and the public.

Among the Chinese elite, there is a source of insecurity even deeper than the mounting protests and the bloggers. The great wall that the leaders have erected to sustain the one-party state and keep the people from being infected by liberal political ideals has had a long-standing impact on people's psyches. In a nutshell, it is an emptiness of values and self-confidence that extends to doubts, rarely articulated, about the political system's legitimacy.[53] Squarely confronting history carries too high a price in terms of the presumed social reaction. Thus, "forbidden zones" of public discussion remain: the antirightist movement of 1957 against educated people; the famine during the Great Leap Forward (1958–1962); Mao's "erroneous policies" during the Cultural Revolution from 1966 to 1976; the Tiananmen crackdown on June 4, 1989 (referred to as "May 35" by microbloggers to get around the censors). Thus also the immature peevishness that often characterizes China's reaction to criticism from abroad. Kicking out a US reporter for Al Jazeera, announcing (in May 2012) a campaign against foreigners illegally in the country or "carrying out illegal activity," bashing foreigners in the press who criticize China, canceling foreign cultural events—these actions go backward in time to previous antiforeign episodes. The fact that this lashing out is happening simultaneously with China's extraordinary economic successes suggests that just below the surface lies self-doubt, an inability to deal with the corruption and human-rights problems that bedevil the leadership.

Materialism has filled the gap left by the Maoist era of antimarket asceticism[54]—a poor substitute, which may explain the leadership's appeals to nationalism by hosting the Olympics, conducting anti–Dalai Lama campaigns (and trying to foist a handpicked Panchen Lama on Tibetan Buddhists as an alternative successor to the Dalai Lama), and preventing Liu Xiaobo's acceptance of the Nobel Peace Prize in 2010. No wonder some astute, and courageous, Chinese commentators have warned of the risks of overemphasizing social stability while failing to respond adequately to ordinary people's insecurity and legitimate claims of violations of their rights.[55]

Trouble is, Chinese leaders face a huge dilemma as they seek to maintain the party-state system and sustain high-powered economic growth. They see the strains that such growth produces on the political system, and they surely are aware that pervasive social controls cannot forever keep people's grievances under wraps. Yet, having witnessed what happened in the Soviet Union and Eastern Europe, and later in the Middle East, China's leaders are evidently also convinced that they open up the party-state system at their peril. The editor of a Chinese journal is quoted as saying: "Mao used to say that 'revolution is not a dinner party.' But right now revolution is precisely a dinner party." He was referring to ongoing debate in intellectual circles and among some members of the party elite about political reform—a debate that seems to go nowhere beyond dinner conversation, not only because the top leaders aren't interested in political reform, but also because a consensus is lacking about what and how to reform.[56]

Chinese leaders from Deng to Hu have all spoken of the need for "political reform," and Xi Jinping hinted at it when he invoked the "Chinese dream" on becoming the new leader. But none of them has ever favored a competitive, transparent, accountable political system. "Political reform" to them meant a more efficient and productive system—less bureaucratic and centralized, more flexible and less ideologically dogmatic, staffed by younger and more professional people—that was devoted to strengthening the party-state system and the economy. The last thing party leaders want, or will tolerate, is "chaos" (*luan*), which to them means another Tiananmen protest movement. So far they have succeeded in preventing both political liberalization and the emergence of a Chinese Mikhail Gorbachev. But they have not prevented the emergence of many sources of social fractioning that might one day coalesce in a civil-society movement.

Sustaining the "people's democratic dictatorship," as both Mao and Deng called it, is likely to be increasingly difficult for party leaders in such turbulent circumstances. All the more so as the top ranks of the party, state, military, and business are heavily populated by so-called princelings (*taizi dang*), the offspring of senior leaders and revolutionary heroes. Hu Jintao, Wen Jiabao, Xi Jinping, and the unfortunate Bo Xilai are examples: the children of Hu and Wen are prominent in business, while Xi is the son of a former vice premier and guerrilla leader, and Bo the son of one of the Communist Party's "eight elders." In fact, seven of the twenty-five members of the party politburo in 2011 were princelings—a big increase over previous politburo memberships.[57]

As a group, the princelings represent a privileged class akin to the *nomenklatura* of Soviet days. Unlike their Soviet counterparts, however, many princelings have positioned themselves in the world of high finance and leadership of state corporations, and are thus able to channel and earn for themselves enormous amounts of money.[58] Families and friends of the top leaders have been especially fortunate. Their hands, and money, can be found in every conceivable industry that has been at the forefront of China's rise, from minerals to mobile phones. The trend seems to be that the further up the chain of command a man rises, the more his relatives take advantage—and bring friends and associates with them. The leaders themselves may keep a safe distance from the wealth, which is measured in the multimillions and even billions of dollars. But their wives, children, and assorted relatives have no such scruples.[59]

The children of princelings also benefit by being sent to the best schools in China and abroad, often to Harvard and other elite US universities. Of the nine members of the politburo standing committee in early

This cartoon by Cao Yi, published in Southern Weekly (Nanfang zhoumo), *depicts a banker (left panel) sucking profits from his bank's cloud. The ordinary fellow on the right holds a wilting plant, marked "corporate profits," that desperately needs rain; http://behindthewall.msnbc.msn.com/_news/2012/02/17/10431649-chinese -cartoonist-shows-that-bank-resentment-is-universal?email=html.*

2012, at least five had children who were studying or had studied in the United States.[60] Considering that China's top leaders now need to demonstrate their legitimacy more than ever before, the prominence of princelings represents another source of public resentment about the fairness of the system. The cartoonist in the work above may well have had them in mind.

The Soft-Power Side

Commentators on soft power in Asia tend to fix on business and financial strength, both of which China has in abundance. But soft power really embraces a great deal more, including the attractiveness of a country's culture, institutions, policies, and ability to effectively project positive images, such as through acts of generosity or internal changes. Ultimately, soft power lies in the persuasiveness of a country's communication to the world.[61] China's soft power certainly has enjoyed successes, such as the Confucius Institutes, the Beijing Olympics in 2008 and the Shanghai Expo in 2010, and its diplomacy in Africa, well publicized by Chinese television and radio broadcasts that compete with US and EU media.[62] Yet China cannot match the global impact of all the sources, business and nonbusiness, that collectively transmit US and other Western cultural values and political preferences; for example, multinational corporations and the advertisers of their products, media and information agencies, governmental and nongovernmental aid and trade officials, the investment-promoting programs of the major international financial institutions, philanthropic organizations, labor and educational outreach programs, and of course the Internet.

Scientific and business innovation and protection of intellectual property are also important aspects of global soft-power reach. China's leaders have ambitious plans for innovation as marked by the number of patent applications—about 2 million—projected by 2015. About one-half of these would be for inventions.[63] Whether quantity will be matched by quality is another matter, of course. And that may depend on whether China can create a risk-taking research environment similar to, say, corporations such as Microsoft or Intel. But even without it, one report suggests that China is forging ahead with developing the next generation of the Internet—Internet Protocol version 6 (IPv6)—that will build on its world leadership in computer and consumer electronics production.[64] China's achievements in supercomputing and space technology show its tremendous scientific potential. At the same time, China must dramatically improve its protection of copyrights, its process for awarding patents, and its prevention of design theft if it wants to have continued access to others' technologies.

Chinese leaders openly worry these days about cultural power. They believe China is losing the cultural battle with the West. Here again, insecurity rears its head. In October 2011, the Central Committee called for a return to "core socialist values" so as to "build our country into a socialist culture superpower."[65] Hu Jintao, sounding very much like Chairman Mao, warned that "international hostile forces are intensifying the strategic plot of westernizing and dividing China, and ideological and cultural fields are the focal areas of their long-term infiltration."[66] Rather than address the issue of censorship, which many Chinese intellectuals believe is responsible for China's weak international cultural influence, Hu saw the need for an "ideological struggle." No doubt the guardians of China's "cultural security," as it is being called, are delighted. China's playwrights, poets, and novelists must be rolling their eyes in dismay; they have seen it all before.

By now it should be apparent to readers that the admiration China has drawn for its dramatic economic growth and poverty reduction does not extend to the values and methods embedded in China's achievements. "Harmonious society" *might* represent a value worth exporting but for the fact that it is not taken seriously in China itself. Charter 08, a document signed by more than three hundred Chinese intellectuals in 2008, called for the party's acceptance of universal values such as "freedom, equality, and human rights" (see Appendix, document 3). The protest advocated implanting democratic government based on the rule of law and economic and ethnic equality. Two of the document's leading authors, including Liu Xiaobo, were arrested. Such fearfulness was on view when the Nobel Prize for literature was awarded in 2012 to Mo Yan, an outstanding but not overtly critical novelist. The party establishment lavished praise on him and said the award demonstrated that "mainstream" Chinese writers were finally getting some recognition from the West. But it would not allow the press to report Mo's modest "hope" for the release of Liu Xiaobo from prison.

As Wang Jisi has written (see Appendix, document 1),

> under an extraordinarily powerful Party leadership and with omnipresent government intervention in social life, few people can confidently define what the Chinese value system is, or whether a coherent value system exists besides "getting rich," "enjoying life" and "patriotism."

Symbolizing this dilemma over values, in January 2011 a huge bronze statue of Confucius that had been prominently unveiled in front of Beijing's National Museum was removed in the dead of night after about only four months on view. This icon of social harmony evidently could not survive an inner-party ideological struggle over the proper symbol of obedience to authority. Later in the year, a two-year-old child was run down, twice, in the southern city of Foshan. Neither the drivers nor any passersby stopped to help. One longtime activist explained their response this way: "All the traditional values of Chinese society were thrown out the window to make way for Mao and the rest of the party leadership. But that died long ago, and there was nothing to replace it except a materialistic hunger." Millions of Chinese commented on blog sites, most of them very critical of their seemingly uncaring culture.[67]

China's 1982 state constitution is loaded with guarantees of fundamental freedoms and civil rights. Some rights, such as equality for women and protections for children, go beyond the rights guaranteed in the US Constitution. But despite some reforms in criminal procedure, rule *by* law has not replaced the rule *of* law. "State security" often trumps individual rights, as numerous crackdowns on religious, ethnic, and labor protesters show. The consequences of resistance can be profound: arbitrary arrests without trial, long-term imprisonment in the "work and reform" (*laogai*) system, lack of access to legal help or family. Lawyers who defend the powerless, such as Ni Yulan and, most famously, Chen Guangcheng, are just as likely themselves to wind up in court, and sometimes in prison where they suffer unspeakable cruelties.[68] On the other hand, as the trial of Gu Kailai (the wife of Bo Xilai who poisoned a British business associate) showed, the rich and powerful can literally get away with premeditated murder. She was found guilty, but received a suspended sentence that most likely will make her eligible for release some years from now.

To further hem lawyers in, the state now requires that new lawyers take an oath of loyalty to "uphold the leadership of the Communist Party of China and the socialist system" as well as the constitution and the law. The contradiction here is obvious: as one lawyer said, "We all know that the party's interference is often the reason why the law can't be implemented."[69] Here is another holdover from the Mao era that Deng Xiaoping fully supported: adhering to the "four cardinal principles" (Marxism–Leninism–Mao Zedong Thought, Communist Party leadership, socialism, and the people's democratic dictatorship) precisely *in order to* carry out economic reforms. As Chen Guangcheng said after arriving in the United States: "The fundamental problem that the Chinese government must face is the lawlessness of officials. China does not lack laws, it lacks the rule of law. For this reason the officials who for many years handled my case openly flouted the nation's laws through all kinds of means."[70]

Censorship of speech and press is also systematic. Notwithstanding greater opportunities for independent reporting (since publications below top level no longer are government subsidized), restrictions remain imposing. Some Chinese intellectuals and former directors of media organs have been courageous enough to challenge censorship of publications. In 2010, for instance, twenty-three of them (including Li Rui, Mao Zedong's former personal secretary) signed a protest letter to the Standing Committee of the National People's Congress that cited the unconstitutional actions of the Central Propaganda Department—an "invisible black hand," they called it—and demanded enforcement of freedom of speech as guaranteed in article 35 of China's state constitution. The signers called for dismantlement of the entire censorship system and its replacement with a "system of legal responsibility," which would take press freedom out of the hands of both party and state (see Appendix, document 4).

China's intellectuals have spoken as a group in protest of official policies on other occasions, though their criticisms range from cosmopolitan to nativist.[71] But the real story of emerging freedom of speech in China belongs to the *weibo* writers. These microbloggers have become fearless commentators on China's corruption, cover-ups of official misdeeds, and poor public safety record. Many of them have acquired large numbers of followers.[72] When, for instance, a very expensive new high-speed train system suffered a costly wreck in mid-2011 with considerable loss of life, bloggers were quick to raise questions about the government's response. Some charged a cover-up; others wondered why safety was being sacrificed to economic development; and still others implied, contrary to official explanations, that a corrupt railway system was ultimately responsible for the wreck. Hu Jintao's personal visit to the scene of the accident hardly quieted the Internet chatter, especially as it was followed by a news blackout that forbade further reporting. Months later a government investigation blamed a number of named railway and other officials, and technical failures, for the accident.

Communist Party leaders are worried about the bad press that crackdowns on free speech get, as the new regulations on Beijing-based microblogs in 2011 showed. This approach smacked of Maoism rather than cosmopolitanism—cracking down rather than opening up. For the unpleasant reality is that Chinese artists, writers, and bloggers still feel under the gun, afraid to speak out on touchy issues and inclined to self-censorship as a result. As one outspoken novelist and blogger said, in a speech that he was not, in fact, permitted to give on accepting an official award:

It is hardly news that in this world there are some things that can be written about and some that cannot; some things can be said yet other things can only be thought. Our mother tongue has been cut into two parts: one safe, and the other risky. . . . Why is contemporary China short of works that speak directly? Because we writers cannot speak directly, or rather we can only speak in an indirect way. Why does contemporary China lack good works that critique our current situation? Because our current situation may not be critiqued. We have not only lost the right to criticize, but the courage to do so. Why is modern China lacking in great writers? Because all the great writers are castrated while still in the nursery.[73]

China's Quandary

To conclude, I must emphasize that China is not yet a country that has established a way of life that might be envied and emulated by others. This may be the essential test of its soft power, particularly in the realm of civil society. Rapid economic growth raises eyebrows worldwide, but does not easily translate into transmittable ideas and values. Alexis de Tocqueville once wrote that the most dangerous time for a bad government is when it starts to reform itself. China's experience may validate that comment: the economic reforms—and, to a much lesser extent, political changes—have unleashed the anger of previously repressed groups as well as ordinary citizens who have been wronged by a system dominated by powerful interest groups.

One Chinese foreign-policy intellectual well-known for his realist and nationalist views has written that the *moral* dimension of China's foreign policy keeps it from rivaling the United States. Citing his study of the Chinese classics, he concluded that only by establishing "humane authority" at home can China create a greater attractiveness abroad. "This means China must shift its priorities away from economic development to establishing a harmonious society free of today's huge gaps between rich and poor. It needs to replace money worship with traditional morality and weed out political corruption in favor of social justice and fairness."[74] In short, China's party-state must overcome its own deficiencies, chief among them being establishing legitimacy on a firmer basis than mere economic performance, before it can hope to be an acknowledged global leader.

China in many ways is still an inward-looking country, a bystander on many important international issues, a newcomer on others, and an imitator of the power politics of the West in still others. Michael Walzer has written that countries with wealth and power have a special responsibility in world affairs; namely, that they "contribute disproportionately to the common good or, better, that they contribute in proportion to their disproportionate wealth."[75] The United States can certainly do better in this regard; it gives more foreign aid by amount than any other country, for instance, but as a percentage of national wealth its aid program is among the world's stingiest. China is stingier still: it now has enormous foreign reserves that could be devoted to human development and human security elsewhere, yet it chooses to hide behind the label of "developing country" so as to avoid commitments one would expect of a powerful state.

Perhaps it is not unfair to say that, at present, China needs the world more than the world needs China. That is, China needs the United States and other countries to keep oil lanes open, terrorism contained, Japan's nationalism and its military confined, markets liberalized, the Korean peninsula denuclearized, Taiwan pressed not to declare independence, and the value of US T-bills and government-backed securities kept strong. In a word, China is a net consumer of public goods, not a purveyor of them. For the world, the main goal is simply to help China stay focused on "peace and development."

Notes

1. Michael Wines, "A Village in Revolt Could be a Harbinger for China," *New York Times*, December 25, 2011, online ed.

2. Ed Flanagan, "Villagers Defiant as Government Creates New Narrative," NBC, "Behind the Wall"; at http://behindthewall.msnbc.msn.com/_news/2011/12/15/9471648-villagers-defiant-as-government-creates-new-narrative.

3. World Health Organization report, "China: Country Health Information Profiles," p. 68; at www.wpro.who.int/countries/chn/2010/chn.htm; hereafter, cited as WHO-China.

4. See Minzi Su, *China's Rural Development Policy: Exploring the "New Socialist Countryside"* (Boulder, CO: Lynne Rienner Publishers, 2009).

5. Keith Bradsher, "On Clean Energy, China Breaks Rules," *New York Times*, September 8, 2010, online ed.

6. Justin Lin, "China Scores Silver Ahead of Japan in GDP Olympiad," *East Asia Forum*, September 5, 2010; at http://www.eastasiaforum.org/2010/09/05/china-scores-silver-ahead-of-japan-in-gdp-olympiad/.

7. See www.nytimes.com/roomfordebate/2011/11/01/is-china-facing-a-health-care-crisis/chinas-health-costs-outstrip-gdp-growth.

8. WHO-China, p. 66.

9. See Dali L. Yang, "China's Looming Labor Shortage," *Far Eastern Economic Review* (January–February 2005): 19–24.

10. Didi Kirsten Tatlow, "Rise in China's Aging Poses Challenge to Beijing," *New York Times*, September 10, 2012, online ed.

11. Li Jianmin, "China's Lopsided Population Pyramid," *China Security* 3, no. 2 (2007): 54–65; Sharon LaFraniere, "As China Ages, Birthrate Policy May Be Difficult to Reverse," April 7, 2011, p. 1.

12. Institute of International Education press release, November 14, 2011; at www.iie.org/en/Who-We-Are/News-and-Events/Press-Center/Press-Releases/2011/2011-11-14-Open-Doors-Study-Abroad.

13. David Zweig, "China Learns Education Lessons," *Far Eastern Economic Review* (July–August 2006): 37–39.

14. See the blog forum, "Educated and Fearing the Future in China"; at http://roomfordebate.blogs.nytimes.com/2010/03/07/educated-and-fearing-the-future-in-china/?scp=3-b&sq=Chinese+students+and+jobs&st=nyt.

15. "A Ponzi Scheme That Works," *Economist*, December 19, 2009, p. 41.

16. Among the many excellent sources on China's environmental problems, see Elizabeth Economy, *The River Runs Black: The Environmental Challenge to China's Future* (Ithaca, NY: Cornell University Press, 2004), and her "The Great Leap Backward? The Costs of China's Environmental Crisis," *Foreign Affairs* 86, no. 5 (2007): 38–59.

17. Economy, "The Great Leap Backward?" p. 46.

18. Jonathan Watts, "China's Green Power Experiment: Whither the Environment?" *Asia-Pacific Journal* 10, no. 3 (2012); online at http://japanfocus.org/-Robert-Marks/3791?utm_source=July+9%2C+2012&utm_campaign=China%27s+Connectivity+Revolution&utm_medium=email.

19. Ian Johnson, "China Faces 'Very Grave' Environmental Situation, Officials Say," *New York Times*, June 3, 2011, online ed.

20. Economy, "The Great Leap Backward?" pp. 39–40.

21. WHO-China, p. 66.

22. Elisabeth Rosenthal, "China Increases Lead as Biggest Carbon Dioxide Emitter," *New York Times*, June 14, 2008, online ed. In 2007, US per-person carbon dioxide emissions were 19.4 pounds, compared with 5.1 pounds for the average Chinese. But by volume, Chinese emissions were about 14 percent higher than US emissions.

23. See, for example, the story of Shijiazhuang in north China: Jim Yardley, "Beneath Booming Cities, China's Future Is Drying Up," *New York Times*, September 28, 2007, online ed.

24. See Jonathan Ansfield and Keith Bradsher, "China Report Shows More Pollution in Waterways," *New York Times*, February 9, 2010, online ed.

25. See his interview at a Carnegie Council forum, "Tackling Sustainability in China"; at www.policyinnovations.org/ideas/audio/data/000625?sourceDoc=000059.

26. The dam's estimated cost is $3.8 billion. Bo Xilai, as party secretary of Chongqing, was a principal backer. Opponents include Friends of Nature and The Nature Conservancy. Michael Wines, "China Proceeds on Plan for Disputed Yangtze Dam," *New York Times*, December 30, 2011, p. A8.

27. See, for instance, Derek Scissors, "The United States vs. China—Which Economy Is Bigger, Which Is Better," April 14, 2011, at www.heritage.org/research/reports/2011/04/the-united-states-vs-china-which-economy-is-bigger-which-is-better.

28. David Barboza, "Wen Calls China Banks Too Powerful," *New York Times*, April 4, 2012, p. B1.

29. Wuhan, a city of about 9 million people southwest of Shanghai, is a good example. It is in the midst of an enormous building spree that has produced a huge public debt, with loans going mainly to special investment corporations rather than directly to local governments. This process creates off-the-books financing that is highly risky. See David Barboza, "China's Cities Piling Up Debt to Fuel Boom," *New York Times*, July 7, 2011, p. 1.

30. See Albert Yee, "China's Macroeconomic Response to the Global Recession: Ideational Sources and Substantive Contents," *Asian Perspective* 36, no. 1 (2012): table 1, p. 15.

31. U.S.-China Economic and Security Review Commission 2011, p. 41.

32. In 2010, the United States once again led all countries in total arms deals—$21.3 billion, or 52.7 percent—and in arms sales to developing countries, $14.9 billion, or 48.6 percent of the total. Russia was second by a large margin in both categories: Thom Shanker, "Global Arms Sales Dropped Sharply in 2010, Congressional Study Finds," *New York Times*, September 24, 2011, p. A10, reporting on the most recent annual report of the Congressional Research Service. In overseas development assistance, the United States donated about $28.8 billion in 2009; http://stats.oecd.org/qwids/#?x=2&y=6&f=3:51,4:1,1:24,5:3,7:1&q=3:51+4:1+1:2,2 5,24+5:3+7:1+2:1+6:2005,2006,2007,2008,2009,2010. But the United States ranked last among the twenty-two richest countries in aid as a percentage of GNP. See www.gatesfoundation.org/annual-letter/2010/Pages/rich-countries-foreign-aid.aspx.

33. Nargiza Salidjanova, "Going Out: An Overview of China's Outward Foreign Direct Investment," U.S.-China Economic and Security Review Commission, Staff Research Report, March 30, 2011, pp. 1–3; at www.uscc.gov /researchpapers/2011/GoingOut.pdf.

34. Lucian Cernat and Kate Parplies, "Chinese Foreign Investment: What's Happening Behind the Headlines?" July 16, 2010; at http://www.voxeu.org /index.php?q=node/5301.

35. Xu Yi-chong, "Nuclear Power in China: How It Really Works," *Global Asia* 7, no. 1 (2012): 32–43.

36. Liu Xuegang, "China's Nuclear Energy Development and Spent Fuel Management Plans," Nautilus Institute report, October 16, 2012, at http://nautilus.org/napsnet/napsnet-special-reports/chinas-nuclear-energy -development-and-spent-fuel-management-plans/?utm_source =NAPSNet&utm_campaign=379467cb48-Special_Report_October_16 _201210_15_2012&utm_medium=email. By 2020, according to this source, nuclear power plants will generate an estimated 4 percent of China's electricity.

37. Xu, "Nuclear Power in China: How It Really Works."

38. Leslie Hook, "China Nuclear Protest Builds Steam," *Financial Times*, February 28, 2012; "China Defrosts Nuclear Plans, Though Issues Remain," *China Digital Times*, March 22, 2012; at http://chinadigitaltimes.net/2012/03/china-defrosts-nuclear-plans-though-issues-remain/?utm_source=feedburner&utm _medium=feed&utm_campaign=Feed%3A+chinadigitaltimes%2FbKzO+%28China +Digital+Times+%28CDT%29%29.

39. According to Liu Xuegang ("China's Nuclear Energy Development and Spent Fuel Management Plans"), "the near-term influences of the Fukushima nuclear accident on China's nuclear plans have been (1) a pause in the approval of new plants and (2) the suspension of the start of construction of four approved units."

40. Quoted by Alan Wheatley, "In China's Success, a Need for Change," *New York Times*, August 30, 2010, online ed.

41. "A unique feature of Chinese leaders' understanding of their country's history," writes Wang Jisi, "is their persistent sensitivity to domestic disorder caused by foreign threats": "China's Search for a Grand Strategy," p. 69.

42. Reuters, "Chinese Land Grab Disputes Spread West, Hit New High," October 30, 2011; at www.reuters.com/article/2011/10/31/us-china-unrest-idUSTRE79U0B620111031. On land seizures and other sources of farmers' discontent, see He Qinglian, "The Relationship between Chinese Peasants' Right to

Subsistence and China's Social Stability," *China Rights Forum*, no. 1; at www.hrichina.org/crf/issue/2009.01.

43. Jeremy Page, "Wave of Unrest Rocks China," *Wall Street Journal*, June 14, 2011, p. 1.

44. Yang Yao, deputy dean of the National School of Development in Beijing, who adds: "Strong and privileged interest groups and commercialized local governments are blocking equal distribution of the benefits of economic growth throughout society, thereby rendering futile the CCP's strategy of trading economic growth for people's consent to its absolute rule." "The End of the Beijing Consensus," February 2, 2010; at www.foreignaffairs.com/print/65914?page=show. See also Joseph Fewsmith, "Now for the Hard Part: Into the Next Decade," *Global Asia* 5, no. 2 (2010): 16–21.

45. For example, an audit by China's National Audit Office of state-run enterprises and government departments found that in the first eleven months of 2009, corrupt behavior had cost the government about $35 billion, as well as led to the prosecution of more than one thousand officials: David Barboza, "China Finds Huge Fraud by Officials," *New York Times*, December 29, 2009, p. 1. Disciplinary measures are reportedly being widely used. In 2010, Chinese sources say, there were 146,500 cases of punishment meted out to party officials, of which about 5,000 were at county level or above. Around 800 prosecutions occurred.

46. A report by Credit Suisse, published in China, points to enormous wealth, mostly illegal, that rich families have been able to hide—and that therefore is not considered in official figures on household income. When this so-called gray income is figured in for all households, the top 10 percent of households have more than twenty-five times the wealth of the bottom 10 percent. See Bloomberg News, "Study Tallies Hidden Income of China's Wealthy," in *New York Times*, August 12, 2010, online ed.

47. On some of these points, see Yasheng Hwang, "Rethinking the Beijing Consensus," *Asia Policy* (National Bureau of Asian Research), no. 11 (January, 2011): 1–26.

48. See, for example, Andrew Jacobs, "Protests in China Against Refinery Reach Third Day," *New York Times*, October 28, 2012, online ed.

49. See the testimony before the US House Committee on Foreign Affairs of John Kamm of the Dui Hua Foundation, "Separate and Unequal: State Security Detainees in China," November 3, 2011 (www.duihua.org). Those arrested are almost always indicted and imprisoned. The figure of one thousand does not include people arrested for protesting or engaging in religious activities.

50. For other examples, see Mark McDonald, "Watch Your Language! (In Chinese They Really Do)"; at http://rendezvous.blogs.nytimes.com /2012/03/13/watch-your-language-and-in-china-they-do/.

51. On the different kinds of issues discussed on the Internet that the Chinese government either allows or forbids, see Eunju Chi, "The Chinese Government's Responses to Use of the Internet," *Asian Perspective* 36, no. 3 (2012): 387–409.

52. See the *Guardian* story, "China Backs Down over Controversial Censorship Software"; carried by WikiLeaks at http://wikileaks.org/wiki/China_backs _down_over_controversial_censorship_software.

53. As Perry Link writes, the new China "inwardly lives with an unsure view of itself. People sense, even if they do not want to talk about it, that their country's current system is grounded partly in fraud, cannot be relied upon to treat people fairly, and might not hold up. Insecurity, the new national mood, extends from laid-off migrant laborers to the men at the top of the Communist Party. The socialist slogans that the government touts are widely seen as mere panoply that covers a lawless

crony capitalism in which officials themselves are primary players": "China: From Famine to Oslo," *New York Review of Books*, January 13, 2011; at www .nybooks.com/articles/archives/2011/jan/13/china-famine-oslo/.

54. Dali L. Yang, "Total Recall," *The National Interest Online*, March 5, 2008; at www.nationalinterest.org/PrinterFriendly.aspx?id=16996.

55. See, for example, Yu Jianrong, "The Unbearable Cost," *Caijing wang*, January 19, 2011; at http://english.caing.com/ajax/print.html.

56. Michael Wines, "As China Talks of Change, Fear Rises on Risks," *New York Times*, July 18, 2012, p. 1.

57. "Princelings and the Goon State," *Economist*, April 14, 2011; at www .economist.com/node/18561005. On previous princeling representation in China's party politburo, see Cheng Li, "China's Most Powerful 'Princelings': How Many Will Enter the New Politburo?" Brookings Institution paper, October 17, 2007; at www.brookings.edu/articles/2007/1017china.aspx.

58. Rick Carew, "China's 'Princelings' and the PE," *Wall Street Journal*, February 1, 2010; at http://blogs.wsj.com/deals/2010/02/01/chinas-princelings-and -the-pe/.

59. Some well-researched stories on this subject have appeared in the Western press—and been suppressed by Chinese censors. Concerning Xi Jinping, see Bloomberg News, "Xi Jinping Millionaire Relations Reveal Fortunes of Elite," at http://www.bloomberg.com/news/2012-06-29/xi-jinping-millionaire-relations- reveal-fortunes-of-elite.html. On Wen Jiabao, see David Barboza, "Billions in Hidden Riches for Family of Chinese Leader," *New York Times*, October 25, 2012, online ed.

60. Andrew Higgins and Maureen Fan, "Chinese Communist Leaders Denounce U.S. Values but Send Children to U.S. Colleges," *Washington Post*, May 18, 2012, online ed.

61. See Jean-Marc F. Blanchard and Fujia Lu, "Thinking Hard About Soft Power: A Review and Critique of the Literature on China and Soft Power," *Asian Perspective* 36, no. 4 (2012): 565–590.

62. See Andrew Jacobs, "Pursuing Soft Power, China Puts Stamp on Africa's News," *New York Times*, August 16, 2012, online ed. For an overview, see the spe- cial issue on "China's Soft Power" in *China Rights Forum*, no. 4 (2009).

63. Steve Lohr, "When Innovation, Too, Is Made in China," *New York Times*, January 1, 2011, online ed.

64. David Barboza and John Markoff, "Power in Numbers: China Aims for High-Tech Primacy," *New York Times*, December 5, 2011, online ed.

65. Michael Wines, "China Tries to Add Cultural Clout to Economic Muscle," *New York Times*, November 8, 2011, p. A8.

66. Edward Wong, "China's President Lashes Out at Western Culture," *New York Times*, January 4, 2012, p. A7.

67. Michael Wines, "Bystanders' Neglect of Injured Toddler Sets Off Soul- Searching on Web Sites in China," *New York Times*, October 18, 2011, online ed.

68. Ni Yulan represented people evicted from their homes to make way for the Beijing Olympics in 2008. She has been imprisoned three times and is unable to walk as a result of beatings by the authorities. Chen Guangcheng was beaten, imprisoned, and placed under house arrest for advocating on behalf of women who underwent forced abortions and sterilizations. Helped by a network of supporters, he escaped from his rural home and sought asylum at the US embassy in Beijing. After considerable wrangling over his fate, China agreed to allow Chen and his family to leave for study in the United States, a decision that almost certainly ensures he will never return to China.

69. Edward Wong, "Chinese Lawyers Chafe at New Oath to Communist Party," *New York Times*, March 22, 2012, online ed.

70. Chen Guangcheng, "China's Unlawfulness" (Zhongguo de bufa), *New York Times*, May 29, 2012. This is the Chinese version supplied along with the English version ("How China Flouts Its Laws") on the same date.

71. For example, when the crackdown on Tibetan dissent occurred in 2008, more than a dozen journalists, scholars, and others circulated a petition that urged the government to stop its "one sided" anti-Tibetan propaganda, which the group said was harming China's international image: Howard W. French, "Intellectuals in China Condemn Crackdown," *New York Times*, March 24, 2008, p. A10. On the other hand, China's so-called New Left has been critical of the CCP's full-out embrace of globalization and the income and other inequalities that are believed to stem from it.

72. Evan Osnos, "The Han Dynasty," *New Yorker*, July 4, 2011, pp. 51–59.

73. Murong Xuecun (aka Hao Qun), speech of November 19, 2010, on being awarded the 2010 People's Literature Prize; at www.vintage-books .co.jk/books/International_writing/China/%5C.

74. Yan Xuetong, "How China Can Defeat America."

75. Walzer, "On Humanitarianism: Is Helping Others Charity, or Duty, or Both?" *Foreign Affairs* 90, no. 4 (2011): 77.

7

The United States by Default?

Focusing on US leadership is by no means meant to suggest that it has been benign or all that successful. Nor should it be inferred that the Washington Consensus model is worthy of continuation, since there is scant evidence that its emphasis on export-led growth has helped promote human security. (What the WC *has* often promoted in developing-country economies are increased government indebtedness, reduced social welfare, and a multitude of opportunities for multinational corporations.)

As I have written elsewhere,[1] US policy in East Asia has been lacking in many ways: its encouragement of Japanese "normalcy," especially during the years when Koizumi Junichiro was prime minister (2001–2006), has fed China-Japan rivalry, most recently by seeming to side with Japan in the controversy over Diaoyudao;[2] its long-standing reluctance to deal directly with North Korea contributed to the North's insecurity and consequent development of nuclear weapons and long-range missiles; its penchant for acting unilaterally has alienated ordinarily friendly countries and publics; its discouragement of an all-Asian monetary fund after the 1997 financial crisis was shortsighted; and its continued reliance on security alliances from the Cold War era has put the United States at a disadvantage when it comes to working cooperatively with Asian multilateral groups. Globally, the United States has often not led by example. During the eight years of the George W. Bush administration, the conduct of the United States approached that of an international outlaw—disregarding the United Nations on Iraq and other issues, secretly condoning and carrying out the torture of prisoners, and rejecting international treaties that would have advanced arms control and environmental protection.

The Costs of Exceptionalism

Especially pertinent to the question of global leadership is the exceptional cost of US exceptionalism. That cost is usually measured in two ways: in terms of guns-versus-butter—that is, the economic and social problems underfinanced at home in order to pay for US global involvements; and the costs of overseas military bases, foreign-aid programs, arms sales, and other measures of support to help protect allies, enhance military capabilities and access, and (supposedly) help stabilize friendly regimes. As John Ruggie has observed, US *exempt*ionalism adds a third cost: the damage to the nation's reputation and political influence from the insistence that the United States is not beholden to certain international laws or the jurisdiction of certain international institutions.[3] From US objections to the automatic jurisdiction of the International Court of Justice in the 1950s to withdrawal from the treaty that created the International Criminal Court and flouting of UN conventions on torture and intervention in the early 2000s, the United States has a long history of putting its own interests above the rule of law that it so earnestly preaches to other countries.

President Dwight D. Eisenhower warned many years ago that excessive military spending was a "theft" from the people of money better spent at home. President Obama returned to that theme in 2011 when, in announcing plans for a gradual drawdown of US troops in Afghanistan, he acknowledged that "over the last decade, we have spent a trillion dollars on war, at a time of rising debt and hard economic times." It was time, he said, to "focus on nation building here at home."[4] US mayors, meeting around the same time, passed a resolution urging the president and Congress to "bring these war dollars home to meet vital human needs."[5] But how much money will actually be freed for domestic spending, and for which purposes, remain far from certain. Pentagon spending will be cut, but in ways that will not amount to a major shift either in weapons development or in international missions. In the same Afghanistan speech, in fact, Obama again invoked the special US role in the world, saying for example that "we must remember that what sets America apart is not solely our power—it is the principles upon which our union was founded. . . . We protect our own freedom and prosperity by extending it to others."

US involvement in overseas wars is the other major component of the costly military equation. While China has been busy becoming richer, the United States has been bogged down in Middle East conflicts. "Leadership" has come to mean interventionism, a dead-end road that has been enormously costly, yet has failed to provide real security or improve the US image abroad, especially in the Middle East. A very conservative estimate is that the wars in Iraq and Afghanistan cost about $1.2 trillion between September 11, 2001, and early 2011;[6] other estimates place the figure at three times that amount, the difference depending on what else besides actual appropriations by Congress are counted (such as veterans' benefits and interest on the accumulating debt).[7] The war in Afghanistan alone, in which just over one hundred thousand US troops were fighting, was costing about $10 billion a month in 2011.[8] Deadlines announced for ending US combat involvement in both wars—by the end of 2012 for Iraq and 2014 for Afghanistan—do not actually mean that US involvement there will completely cease. US bases dot the maps of both countries and others in the Middle East. Military training programs and economic assistance will continue. US private security contractors, who wound up outnumbering US troops in Iraq, will probably still have plenty of work to do. One can only imagine the pleasure the Chinese government derives from watching the United States deplete its financial and other resources in one conflict after another, though the fact of fixed US bases in countries bordering China is an irritant to Beijing.

As US combat troops are withdrawn from the Middle East, the United States is deepening its involvement along China's periphery. US officials now describe Asia as the new strategic "pivot point," a development that is said to have heightened PRC leaders' "sense of threat."[9] The deployments in Australia, actual and potential, coincide with an announced "broadening" of US security ties with the Philippines and are in addition to the solid US alliance relationships with Japan, South Korea, and Thailand and naval and air access points in Singapore and several other locations in Central and Southeast Asia. China has no match for these assets. Some Asian countries may accommodate China more than usual because of its economic clout, but they are clearly hedging their bets by favoring a more robust US military presence in the region. Closer ties with China do not mean reduced US influence in or access to Asia, however; the reverse seems to be happening. If anything, the most troublesome problems for the United States will arise from its own decisions, such as partnership with Pakistan despite that country's questionable commitment to fighting the Taliban and al-Qaeda, provocative naval patrolling near or in China's territorial waters, continued arms sales to Taiwan, and efforts to retain a security presence in Afghanistan and Iraq.

Neglect at Home

US claims to exemplary international status are further undermined by failures on the home front, very much in keeping with Eisenhower's warning. For starters, the United States faces enormous debt: In 2012, the US national (public) debt exceeded $15 trillion. Interest on the debt was approaching $200 billion a year, a surefire cause of social conflict over how to cut budgets in critical areas such as education, health care, and defense. A country's debt-to-GDP ratio is often considered the best single indicator of an economy's health. While several other countries, led by Japan, have a larger debt-to-GDP ratio than the United States—234 percent compared with 110 percent for the United States—the US ratio is a troubling sign. (We cannot reliably compare China's debt-to-GDP ratio because the usual estimates—anywhere from 18 to 33 percent—are widely considered far from the reality.) The bipartisan National Commission on Fiscal Responsibility and Reform put the issue in crisis terms when it reported that "our nation is on an unsustainable fiscal path. . . . We face staggering deficits. . . . Since the last time our budget was balanced in 2001, the federal debt has increased dramatically. . . . We have arrived at the moment of truth, and neither political party is without blame."[10]

Many state governments have huge budget shortfalls that have led to ugly conflicts with working people over pensions, health insurance, and other social benefits once thought to be dependable safety nets. At the federal level, US government revenue these days annually falls well short—by over $1 trillion—of expenditures. Unemployment has reached crisis proportions: about 15 percent of the workforce when discouraged workers are counted. White-collar as well as blue-collar crime, drugs, gun-related violence, denial of health care to as many as 50 million people, and illegal immigration that stands at around 12 million people are just some of the other problems that divide the country.

The richest country in the world is actually among the most unequal. The income gaps between rich and poor in the United States, and between the rich and middle classes, are larger than in any other industrialized country. These gaps are growing each year, as is the one between racial groups, now at a historic high.[11] In 2009, the income of the top 20 percent of Americans, with earnings of $100,000 or more, was nearly fifteen times higher than the income of the bottom 20 percent. The poorest of the poor, earning 50 percent below the poverty line, was the highest on record, with 21 percent of children living in poverty.[12]

Among many social consequences is the so-called achievement gap: the rich-poor divide in the United States has created a large and growing gap in reading proficiency, completion of college, and prospects of future success. Overall, as the Census Bureau reported in 2011, poverty and joblessness are at record highs: more than 46 million people (about 15 percent of the population) are living below the official poverty line; an astounding 48 million people of working age are not working at all, and just under 50 percent of the population lack health care coverage.[13] In fact, the United States, in company with Mexico and Turkey and in contrast with France and Sweden, has both relatively low social spending per person and a high poverty rate.[14] It therefore comes as no surprise to find that the prison population is huge and the rate of incarceration higher than in any developed country. This reality has created an absurd budgetary situation: "The U.S. spends almost two-and-a-half times as much per prisoner as per public school pupil."[15]

As one astute observer of the US scene has written, inequality has poisoned the country in many ways. "Like an odorless gas, it pervades every corner of the United States and saps the strength of the country's democracy." Government, under both parties, "has consistently favored the rich" over the last thirty years, thanks in no small part to "organized money and the conservative movement." The restraints on gross inequality that once existed—in congressional legislation, the tax code, even self-restraint on Wall Street—are now gone, replaced by unbridled greed and an enormous expansion of lobbies.[16] And as inequality grows, social mobility seems to be declining. The meritocracy that great wealth creates, Chris Hayes observes, no longer accommodates newcomers.[17] Cynicism about the country's future is widespread. As the comedian George Carlin once said, "The American dream: You have to be asleep to believe it."

Yet no great public outrage has occurred over the fact that the heads of major corporations and financial firms are paid extraordinary amounts of money even after poor economic performances and an economy in recession; over the fact that no leader of these companies has been charged with a crime, much less jailed, for violating the public trust in the 2008–2009 financial crisis; nor over the fact that many giant corporations pay little or no federal taxes, and in some instances (for example, the oil and nuclear energy industries) receive huge federal subsidies while earning enormous profits.[18] Even when public opinion has been focused on economic issues, it has been ignored. In the 2011 tug-of-war between Republican and Democratic members of Congress over raising the debt ceiling and reducing the budget deficit, polls clearly showed a two-to-one public preference for both budget cuts and tax increases on the wealthy. When a deal was finally struck, only budget cuts survived thanks to conservatives who practiced what liberals called extortion: they would only vote to raise the debt ceiling if they were promised massive cuts in the federal budget—cuts that would have a dire impact on middle- and low-income people and would have no prospect of making a significant dent in unemployment.

The influence of private capital, both individual and corporate, over the political process has reached extraordinary proportions. Money drives the system, as numerous commentators have pointed out for many years. Every general election pushes the cost of political campaigns a billion dollars higher. It was around $8 billion in 2008. Roughly speaking, it now takes as much as $10 million to win a US Senate seat and $1 million to win a seat in the House of Representatives.[19] Due to the Supreme Court's 2010 decision in the *Citizens United* case, corporations (and unions) have virtually no restrictions on contributions to federal election campaigns. The power of corporate money in elections at all levels—in 2010, business political action committees (PACs) alone donated $72 million to candidates,[20] and so-called super PACs, which can funnel even larger funds to particular candidates while maintaining the fiction that they are independent of them—and in the formulation of legislation is only one way in which government has become dysfunctional. (Labor unions and public-interest groups also donate through PACs, but the amounts are a tiny percentage of what business groups and very rich individuals give.

As many retiring national politicians have said, civility has vanished from political debate. Cutthroat tactics now dominate. The Christian right's ultraconservative voice in politics is far stronger than its numbers warrant. The aim of the opposition party has become blocking every initiative of the ruling party and undermining the president, regardless of the merits of the issues in debate. It is the kind of politics that makes for good theater but leads to paralysis—a self-consuming process that was once thought to be the exclusive province of banana republics.

Notes

1. See, for example, Gurtov, "The Bush Doctrine in Asia," in David P. Forsythe, Patrice C. McMahon, and Andrew Wedeman, eds., *American Foreign Policy in a Globalized World* (New York: Routledge, 2006), pp. 287–311; and Gurtov, *Superpower on Crusade: The Bush Doctrine in US Foreign Policy* (Boulder, CO: Lynne Rienner Publishers, 2006).

2. See the blunt criticism of Chen Jian, formerly China's ambassador to Japan and a UN undersecretary general: Jane Perlez and Keith Bradsher, "Ex-Envoy Says U.S. Stirs China-Japan Tensions," *New York Times*, October 30, 2012, online ed.

3. John Gerard Ruggie, "Doctrinal Unilateralism and Its Limits: America and Global Governance in the New Century," in Forsythe et al., eds., *American Foreign Policy in a Globalized World*, pp. 31–50.

4. Text in *New York Times*, June 23, 2011, online ed.

5. See *The Nation*, July 18–25, 2011, p. 5.

6. Amy Belasco, "The Cost of Iraq, Afghanistan, and Other Global War on Terror Operations Since 9/11," Congressional Research Service Report RL33110, March 29, 2011; at www.fas.org/sgp/crs/natsec/RL33110.pdf.

7. For an estimate of around $3 trillion in total war costs (as of 2008), see Linda J. Bilmes and Joseph E. Stiglitz, "The Iraq War Will Cost Us $3 Trillion, and Much More," *Washington Post*, March 9, 2008, online ed.

8. Elisabeth Bumiller and Brian Knowlton, "Ambassadorial Nominee Warns of Risk If the U.S. Abandons Afghanistan," *New York Times*, June 8, 2011, online ed.

9. Wang Jisi and Lieberthal, "Addressing U.S.-China Strategic Distrust," p. 10.

10. The National Commission on Fiscal Responsibility and Reform, "The Moment of Truth: Report of the National Commission on Fiscal Responsibility and Reform" (Washington, DC: White House, December 2010), p. 10.

11. A Pew Foundation study found that Hispanic, black, and Asian households (in that order) suffered far more than whites in the recession, leading to a historically unprecedented disparity in wealth. Sabina Tavernise, "Recession Study Finds Hispanics Hit the Hardest," *New York Times*, July 26, 2011, p. 1.

12. CBS News, "Income Gap Between Rich, Poor the Widest Ever," September 28, 2010; at www.cbsnews.com/stories/2010/09/28/national/main6907321.shtml.

13. Sabrina Tavernise, "Soaring Poverty Casts Spotlight on 'Lost Decade,'" *New York Times*, September 13, 2011, online ed.

14. See the 2008 OECD study on income inequality and related graphs at www.oecd.org/document/0,3746,en_2649_33933_41530009_1_1_1_1,00.html.

15. From a 2011 report of the Children's Defense Fund, quoted by Charles M. Blow, "Failing Forward," *New York Times*, August 27, 2011, p. A19.

16. George Packer, "The Broken Contract: Inequality and American Decline," *Foreign Affairs* 90, no. 6 (2011): 20–31.

17. Christopher Hayes, *Twilight of the Elites: America After Meritocracy* (New York: Crown, 2012).

18. US businesses often complain that they are the most taxed of any business community in the world. But while it is true that the statutory tax rate (including local, state, and federal taxes) for US businesses is higher (at 39.2 percent in 2010) than anywhere except Japan, the *effective* tax rate puts US businesses on average in the middle of the pack: see *New York Times*, May 3, 2011, p. B9. The main reason is that US businesses, especially those with branches overseas, have several accounting tricks to lower their tax obligations, including shifting production to low-tax countries, tax shelters, and subsidies. As a result, corporations account for less and less of the US government's revenue—only about 9 percent in 2010.

19. Ezra Klein, "Research Desk Responds: Mo' Money, Mo' Politics," *Washington Post*, June 24, 2010; at http://voices.washingtonpost.com/ezra-klein/2010/06/research_desk_responds_mo_mone_1.html.

20. Brody Mullins and Alicia Mundy, "Corporate Political Giving Swings Toward the GOP," *Wall Street Journal*, September 21, 2010; online at http://online.wsj.com/article/SB10001424052748703989304575503933125159928.html.

8

Whose Century?

A fairly common view of China these days is that its global leadership is only a matter of time. As I have been arguing, however, despite China's increasingly large footprint in both the developed and the developing worlds, it is in no position to lead either one, now or in the foreseeable future.

For one thing, China's record as a "responsible great power" is at best a mixed one. On the positive side we see active engagement in multilateral diplomacy, support of UN peacekeeping operations, beneficial aid programs in Africa, leadership in the G-20, and brokering of nuclear talks with North Korea. But the negative side is imposing, such as its hardline stance in territorial disputes with East Asian neighbors; its support of repressive regimes; its deployment of missiles that can threaten Taiwan; its weak support of global governance when it comes to UN sanctions, climate change, and arms control; and its violation of international trading rules. Second, China cannot lead while being dependent on US and other Western markets and by relying on US power to protect sea-lanes and keep energy-rich regions and countries secure.

Third, what some may call a Beijing Consensus hardly amounts to an effort to construct an alternative, China-dominated world. The PRC seems to be attracting countries that, for diverse reasons, find the Chinese approach to economic development and the notion of strict adherence to sovereignty to their liking. But the Third World honeymoon with China has soured in some places and in others may have no more lasting appeal than the Washington Consensus. Fourth, and perhaps most important, the Chinese leadership's conduct of domestic affairs, while laudable from a macroeconomic point of view, hardly constitutes a model for other countries concerned about human development and human security in their fullest senses.

How well this checkered record plays out in terms of international influence is hard to say, in part because sudden developments—such as China's currently uncompromising behavior in nearby territorial disputes and its defensive response to the Middle East uprisings—can quickly make any analysis outdated. Another factor complicating prediction is the inevitable uncertainty about China's development and national-security policies. What if China becomes the world's largest economy? What if, on the other hand, China's economy goes south, causing massive unemployment and strikes? What if China works out some kind of unification formula with Taiwan or, in emulation of Taiwan's successful democratization, which has included five consecutive multiparty presidential elections, creates a more representative political system? Or will China be even more difficult to govern than it is now and simultaneously become truculent in international affairs—including deploying a blue-water navy, seeking bases around its periphery, and putting new pressure on Taiwan and Southeast Asia?

We can only pose questions about the future, not answer them. But one thing is certain: as China's leaders consider the country's role in the world, they confront a dilemma that is not going to go away in the foreseeable future. As a rising power whose claims on the international system are increasingly large, it must embrace increased global responsibilities or face limits on the benefits of globalization that China now enjoys.

This begs the question: What would China have to do to replace or stand shoulder to shoulder with the United States as a global leader? China would have to be a truly open-market country, be willing to run persistent trade deficits for the sake of its friends, remove barriers to extensive foreign investment and their in-country sales, have a fully convertible currency that rivals the dollar, and allow all currencies to be brought into the country. It would have to allow civil society to flourish, particularly by removing obstacles to the rule of law. It would have to abandon or at least sharply modify the model of low consumption/high savings in favor of the very (US) model its leaders have criticized as globally irresponsible—high consumption/low savings. Further, China would have to have a network of military access points, even if it eschews bases, so that it can deploy force when necessary to maintain strategic stability and safeguard oil tankers. It would therefore have to dramatically increase its military spending to be able to satisfy the PLA's appetite for new weapons, and it would have to find and subsidize allies. In short, China would have to be prepared to provide guns and butter—be willing to meet the needs of both international partners and domestic interest groups. To state the obvious, this is a menu well beyond what Chinese leaders now and for the foreseeable future seem willing or able to provide.

And why should they? Just as China's leaders seem to have learned from the Soviet Union's demise about the costs and limits of power, so may they privately now be convinced by the US example that the burdens of leadership outweigh its benefits. Common to both cases are global ambitions and huge military burdens. China's new generation of leaders seems determined not to follow these paths. Contrary to Western observers who are convinced that the more China grows economically, the more ambitious its leaders will be, Chinese leaders may be quite comfortable avoiding a race to the top with the United States. Indeed, as Chas Freeman has pointed out, PRC leaders apparently have decided on a path of "affordable security"—focusing on defense of China's near seas rather than on developing a huge naval force, and developing cyber warfare to disable US high-tech weapons rather than seeking to acquire the same. In this way, Freeman observes, China is reversing the Cold War pattern in which the United States sought to spend the Soviets into the ground. Now we may be in the Soviets' shoes and China in ours.[1] Instead of winding up like Russia or the United States, the Chinese may be thinking as follows: The United States is deeply in debt, beholden to unreliable governments, and fighting costly and controversial battles in distant lands. Let's preserve our assets for other purposes, such as long-term energy security.

In the heyday of China's rift with the Soviet Union, Mao referred to the Russians as "teachers by negative example." Chinese leaders may regard politics in the United States similarly today. As much as CCP leaders fear their country's infection by Western-style democracy, they are probably cheered by signs of dysfunction in the democracies. One study of Chinese commentaries on the Occupy Wall Street (OWS) phenomenon has observed, for example, that most of them avoided the income-gap issue and focused instead on the decaying of the US political system. OWS, in these Chinese critiques, revealed both that the US system is unworkable and that its politicians are unable to agree on remedies for the system's ills.[2] One can imagine that other well-publicized US political problems, such as increased voting restrictions, the nasty debate over universal health care, and the power of PAC money give Chinese party leaders further ammunition to trumpet their brand of socialism. As they search for ways to reform their own system without fundamentally changing it, these critiques provide justification for avoiding democratization—and silencing those in China who advocate it.

Yet the fact remains that China has unfulfilled international ambitions with powerful internal implications, starting with Taiwan, and that the one country capable of thwarting those ambitions is the United States. Will China at some time in the near future decide that it can no longer postpone unification with Taiwan and no longer tolerate US support of a one-China, one-Taiwan policy? Will China raise the ante the next time a naval or air incident occurs with the United States over violations (as the Chinese see it) of their coastline? It is not out of the question that China will throw caution to the wind in defense (again, as they see it) of their sovereign rights. If the Chinese leadership reaches that point, however, it would also have to consider the daunting array of domestic problems it faces. Internal unrest and social dislocations require stability at home, which means keeping state resources focused on homeland security rather than on external disputes.

Do these internal problems threaten to break China apart? The notion of China's disintegration has its adherents, and Chinese leaders themselves clearly worry about how long they can keep the lid on unrest and control the pace of political change. Some of the usual sources of a breakdown—angry military officers, an underground revolutionary group, a prodemocracy clique within the Communist Party, and a foreign invader—are hard to find in today's China, however. On the other hand, there are plenty of dissatisfied social groups that conceivably could, in combination, cause unrest on a much wider scale than currently: migrant workers, students upset over official corruption and jobs, the unemployed, farmers, ethnic minorities, environmental refugees. Most likely in light of the communication technology now available, the unrest would reverse the Maoist revolutionary formula: the cities would spark trouble in the countryside. Here again, the likelihood of a dramatic uprising seems very small; there are simply far too many factors that will keep China together, not least its increasing prosperity, than will bring about either its collapse or its sudden rush to democratize.[3] But the challenges posed by increasingly upset citizens will, I and some other China scholars have been arguing, force its leaders to stay focused on internal affairs.

If history is any guide, the conflict between an unsatisfied international agenda and a costly, and mounting, domestic agenda will be resolved in a Chinese foreign policy that, for some time to come, will remain fundamentally defensive and reactive: it will protect borders and territorial interests, preserve policy independence, and seek international acceptance as a necessary player at the table.

Nationalism is, of course, as elsewhere, a powerful force in China. It can have unpredictable effects, and defensiveness has its limits. Even taking all the constraints on China's international activism into account may not be sufficient to deter China from militarily confronting the

United States or a US ally if it perceives that its fundamental interests are being threatened. But the primacy of national interests applies to all other countries, too. The related but different idea here is national pride or xenophobia, which to some observers is the principal driving force in Chinese foreign policy. That view overlooks, or underestimates, not only the internal problems already enumerated but also China's enmeshment in economic globalization and the extent to which "the concept of global governance has entered Chinese consciousness and discourse."[4]

Analyses of decisionmaking in China support the above view. It is more consensual, more influenced by bureaucratic self-interest and expertise, and more decentralized than ever before. China wants more international influence and accommodation, but it will accede to foreign pressure on occasion. Image, reputation, and public opinion shape policies to a degree unheard of twenty years ago. Still, in the end Chinese policy remains essentially realist on international issues: What's in it for China and the security of its elite? The national interest is not going to be sacrificed for the sake of scientific opinion or international reputation.[5] China will not accept intrusive measures or pressures that compromise its definition of sovereignty or freedom of action, and any concessions to the "international community" or to the United States that China does make will carry a high bill.

Not China's . . . and Not America's

Just because the new century will not belong to China does not mean it will (or should) belong to the United States. US leaders may continue to talk as though the country is exceptional and destined now as always to lead. They may continue to act as though unilateralism in world affairs is sometimes unavoidable, and in ways that neutralize would-be challengers. And they may remain by far the world's leading military power, arms seller, and donor of development aid. But in many other countries, certainly including China, these claims and circumstances are refuted by other political and economic realities of the sort delineated in the preceding chapter.

It might fairly be said that one thing the United States and China have in common is that their economies are becoming increasingly *unsustainable*, and in similar ways. Market socialism and free-market capitalism alike accept degrading of the environment and waste of natural resources as necessary costs for the sake of "development." Both systems suffer from widening income and wealth gaps. And both face serious sources of social instability due to race, ethnicity, gender, and class. Neither system thus can seriously claim to have found a sure path to either social justice or equitable, environmentally friendly economic growth.

Indicative of the depths to which US politics has sunk are the issues that draw attention and provoke division. One might imagine that in the world's number-one power, secure employment, war and peace, environmental protection, the welfare of children, and education would be most on people's minds. But political debate in the United States today tends regularly to elevate the trivial. Abortion, gay marriage, the president's birthplace, and religion—these were among the dominant issues in the presidential election campaign in 2012. Jobs and health care were properly given great attention; but climate change, foreign policy outside the Middle East (such as China!), gun control, and campaign financing hardly got any. Perhaps worst of all was the lack of civil discourse, rational argument, and a spirit of compromise across the political spectrum.

The legitimacy of government itself is up for discussion. As the budget crisis deepened in 2011 and headed toward a deadline over the national debt, many in the United States took the position that it would be better to close down the government than raise the taxes necessary for government to function. In Minnesota, a standoff over how to deal with a $5 billion revenue shortfall did lead to a shutdown of all but the most critical government services. Several California cities filed for bankruptcy. All this occurred as opinion polls showed a particularly low regard for Congress: polls in mid-2011 put public confidence in Congress at only about 13 percent, compared with nearly 70 percent confidence in the military. "Government" is unpopular in ways it never was before—hardly the kind of situation that would give credibility to calls for emulating US democracy abroad.

Domestic political divisions in the United States have also impacted US leadership abroad. Infuriatingly ill-informed debate and narrow nationalism have prevented the United States from taking the lead on climate change, protection of the global commons, and international criminal law. Movements with enormous amounts of money at their disposal, such as the Tea Party and far-right groups generally, can wield enough power to (for example) bend science to their will, as in the case of denying the importance or even the existence of global warming. Nor did Obama's much-touted early emphasis on engagement bear fruit— not because it was the wrong approach but because it wasn't tried determinedly enough, such as with Iran and North Korea, in good part because of predictable opposition to engagement in Congress. In the Middle East, the hesitant and inconsistent US alignment with popular demands for the removal of dictators foreclosed an opportunity to take credit for positive political change. Powerful political and strategic interests, notably support for Israel and counterterrorism, trumped professed US concerns about human rights and democratic ideals.

The lack of signature achievements in international affairs may account for the US public's changing view of the country's unique place in the world. In a 2011 poll, 53 percent said the United States was only one of the greatest countries, whereas 38 percent said it "stands above all other countries in the world." Least convinced of US greatness were young people (ages 18 to 29), by 59 percent to 27 percent, and college graduates, by 58 percent to 34 percent.[6]

What sets the United States apart from China, notwithstanding these serious leadership deficits, are the capacity for renewal and innovation, openness to dissent, and the strength of civil society. Recent US social history is dominated by movements to extend or reaffirm individual and group liberties, in sharp contrast with Chinese social movements that amount to reinforced controls. Though international awards have their biases, the fact is that the United States leads the rest of the world in Nobel Prizes by a large margin, particularly in the sciences.[7] (Chinese scientific researchers are, however, catching up thanks to rapidly rising government funding of research.) Both the US public and private sectors have usually shown the ability to rise to challenges, such as in biomedical research. Where they do not, as in the federal response to Hurricane Katrina in the New Orleans area, the criticism can be unrelenting. Whistleblowing is a fine art, and is legally protected, though in the area of national security there seem to be more exceptions than ever before.[8] China's response to crises is often to cover them up and make exemplary punishments that protect higher-ups. China's critics and protesters must always be careful not to aim too high or tread into the forbidden zones.

In the United States, the opportunities for critical dialogue and the ability of individuals to make a difference remain large. Ideas for dramatically reforming the economy, the financial world, and the political system fill public forums. The underground economy, cooperatives, and farmers' markets exemplify the range of efforts to disconnect from the corporate-dominated economy. The two-party political system is always being challenged, whether by liberal reformers or far-right ideologues, and at local levels the major parties often are insignificant. Thanks to the Internet, the public is bombarded by information and opinion even as the number of newspapers is declining—though the scope of mainstream opinion is narrowing, as just a few news conglomerates spread their net. Technology is gradually transforming political debate in the

United States, for good or for ill, whereas in China information technology is the enemy of officials, who are determined to eradicate news and views they find threatening.

In China, the notion of civil society is still new and not well tolerated by political leaders: NGOs must register with the state, independent unions do not exist, opposition political groups are suppressed, and (as discussed earlier) news and information outlets are always subject to censorship and elimination. The United States, on the other hand, is not just a participant society, it is an *advocacy* society. The number of NGOs, nonprofit organizations, and other civil-society groups—unions, business and professional associations, neighborhood groups, lobbies—is countless. Every conceivable interest seems to have its own organization and publication. Many seek to influence public policy at some level, such that no official is immune from criticism or scrutiny. Public protests, large and small, are a constant, and civil-rights movements have been responsible for major social reform legislation with respect, for example, to environmental protection, women's and children's rights, workplace safety, and immigration. The Occupy Wall Street protest movement that started in the fall of 2011 in New York City quickly spread to other cities—the kind of unpredictable populist outburst against "the system" that the United States is known for and China is not.

For all these differences, US politics today is clearly dysfunctional, and this reality has led to vigorous debate about the country's future. Yet at times the debate really seems to be about its past. There is a yearning for an earlier time, perhaps idealized, when the middle class could expect decent improvements in the quality of life, social welfare for the needy was almost universally supported, civility and sensibility were apparent in government, education was a high priority, and consultation with allies was seriously practiced. Today's critics often urge moderation, practicality, and common sense on US leaders, contending that economic and social problems can be fairly easily resolved if only the leaders would stop acting like spoiled children. The trouble is, such advice is supplied by a small group of intellectuals and policy wonks, not by ambitious politicians and their advisers, for whom the political game is zero-sum. A new social compact is clearly necessary—between government and business, business and labor, and Democrats and Republicans in Congress, for starters. It's "politics as theater," Fareed Zakaria laments: "A can-do country is now saddled with a do-nothing political process, designed for partisan battle rather than problem solving."[9] Exactly—and with no clue as to how to break the pattern.

Notes

1. Chas W. Freeman Jr., "Beijing, Washington, and the Shifting Balance of Prestige: Remarks to the China Maritime Studies Institute," Newport, RI, May 10, 2011.

2. See Christopher A. Ford, "'Occupy Wall Street' and Communist China's Emerging 'Neo-Kong' Discourse of Antidemocratic Legitimacy," Hudson Institute Briefing Paper, Washington, DC, May 2012; at www.hudson.org/files /publications/CFord-OccupyWallStreet-053112.pdf.

3. See the excellent review of selected writing on China's political future by Andrew J. Nathan, "Present at the Stagnation: Is China's Development Stalled?" *Foreign Affairs* 85, no. 4 (2006): 177–182. Nathan's own projection is "resilient authoritarianism," which is mine as well.

4. Wang and Rosenau, "China and Global Governance," p. 11.

5. See, for instance, Elizabeth Economy in Lampton, ed., *The Making of China's Foreign and Security Policy*, pp. 230–253.

6. Pew Research Center, June 30, 2011; at http://pewresearch.org/pubs/2045 /america-global-standing-most-say-among-greatest-but-not-single-greatest-nation.

7. See www.aneki.com/countries2.php?t=Countries_with_the_Most_Nobel _Prize_Winners&table=table_nobel&places=2=*=*&order=asc&orderby=table _nobel.value&decimals=—&dependency=independent&number=all&cntdn =asc&r=-199-201-202-203-204&c=&measures=Country-Number%20of %20Laureates&units=—&file=nobel.

8. Journalists are being prosecuted for disclosing classified information given to them. In the WikiLeaks case, where hundreds of thousands of classified US documents on foreign affairs were released to the press, the US Army private (Bradley Manning) who was said to be responsible for the leak was jailed while awaiting trial—900 days as of November 2012—and the founder of the WikiLeaks organization is threatened with trial for treason if he is ever returned to the United States.

9. Fareed Zakaria, "The Future of American Power: How America Can Survive the Rise of the Rest," *Foreign Affairs* 87, no. 3 (2008): 41.

9

Toward Sino-US Reengagement

At a summit meeting in 1996, President Jiang Zemin asked Bill Clinton: "Are you trying to contain China or not?" Clinton said, "No, no, I'm trying to engage, I don't want to contain you." But Clinton said he also told Jiang: "The greatest threat to our security that you present is that all of your people will want to get rich in exactly the same way we got rich. And unless we try to triple the automobile mileage and to reduce greenhouse gas emissions, if you all get rich in that way we won't be breathing very well . . . and you will do irrevocable damage to the global environment." So Clinton expressed the hope the two countries might collaborate on this issue. Clinton said it seemed Jiang "hadn't thought about it [US-China relations] just like that before."[1]

Mixed Messages

Responsible leadership in our time should mean finding common ground between adversaries on policies and ideas that serve the global community as well as the countries immediately affected. As the Clinton-Jiang exchange shows, this will not be easy. Relations between China and the United States run hot and cold, defenses are always up when leaders meet, and mutual perceptions tend to shift abruptly. There is every reason to expect, moreover, that the pattern of cooperation and friction, tension and friendliness, will continue in the foreseeable future. In China some of the same key policy advisers who uphold the virtues of US-China cooperation also believe the United States is China's biggest problem.[2] In a country where policy wonks can now debate publicly and get published abroad, and where think tanks proliferate, Chinese opinion on Sino-US relations is about as wide-ranging as it is in the United States. But nationalism is the common coin among Chinese analysts, and among the Chinese public. Favorable Chinese opinion of the United States fell from 58 percent to 44 percent from 2010 to 2011, presumably in response to the downturn in relations.[3] More than 50 percent of Chinese surveyed by the Pew Research Center over the last several years believe that "eventually" China will replace the United States as the world's leading power.[4] The Chinese surveyed—probably in the major cities rather than in the countryside—are extremely satisfied with "the way things are going" in China; more than 80 percent have said so every year from 2006 to 2011.[5]

China deplores US "interference" in its internal affairs, referring to Taiwan and Tibet, whenever Washington sells weapons to Taiwan, long a top US arms customer,[6] or gives official attention to the Dalai Lama and repression in Tibet. Chinese officials and experts also react angrily when the United States criticizes China's human-rights situation. As mentioned earlier, China is also critical of US financial policies, its global military deployments, and its uses of force. Yet virtually all speeches and writings by highly placed Chinese emphasize the overriding importance of positive PRC-US relations and the necessity of cooperating to deal with issues of mutual concern. (See Appendix, document 5.) Indeed, when it comes to maintaining positive relations with the United States, the PRC leadership is often out ahead of the Chinese public and media, which are highly sensitive to "China bashing," "Western bias," and other instances of perceived offense to national pride.[7]

For their part, US officials consistently reassure China that they wish it peace, prosperity, and stability. Publicly, just as Bill Clinton told Jiang Zemin, they reject equally the notion that China's rise threatens the United States and that the United States seeks to contain China.[8] But with equal consistency, US officials deplore limits on religious and personal freedom in China, the absence of military transparency, failure to respect intellectual property rights, and China's skirting of international trade rules. These criticisms stem from what is politically advantageous to say at election time as well as from genuine concern. References since 2011 by senior US officials to a "pivot point" in Asia policy have added to the inconsistency of US statements about China.[9] Obama's harder line in China policy, which included deployment of a missile-defense radar system in Japan and trade complaints against China filed with the WTO, raised the question whether engagement with China was dead.[10] His reelection affords an opportunity to reaffirm that policy direction.

US public-opinion surveys show that by substantial margins, the US population wants strong ties with China, believes China's economic threat exceeds its military threat (in fact, one-half of those surveyed believe China now has the world's strongest economy), and wants the US administration to get tougher with China on trade issues.[11] While many US people surveyed in 2011 have unfavorable views of China's government (48 percent), they are very positive about the Chinese people (82 percent).[12] A 2012 opinion poll that included policy experts as well as the general public worried about China's economic power too. Yet when asked about global leadership, majorities among both groups favored a shared leadership role between the United States and China.[13] Conservative critics, as previously mentioned, are far more jingoistic than the public or most experts, contending that China is fast becoming a military rival in East Asia and is gaining influence there at US expense. Contrary views in US academic circles, suggesting Chinese assertiveness rather than aggressiveness in support of its territorial claims, probably do not register as strongly with the Chinese as do expressions of alarm about China's ambitions. The US message to China is thus as mixed and inconsistent as is China's message to the United States.

Finding Common Ground

Whenever top officials of the two countries meet, these issues invariably come up and are politely debated, but without either side changing its position. Yet at the same time, both sides agree on the need for a common approach to major global issues. They also agree that China's prosperity is a good thing for the world, though in US circles prosperity links to democracy and freedom—goals the Chinese leaders have always rejected. Still, for all their differences, China and the United States need each other and therefore need to expand their cooperative agenda. That agenda includes reducing military spending, deployments, and arms transfers, while increasing transparency about them as well as about military objectives; combating global climate change; finding common ground on trade openness and currency rates; sharing energy-saving technologies; providing grassroots assistance to reduce poverty in the poorest countries; and reining in governments such as Syria's, North Korea's, and Iran's that defy agreed-upon international norms.

With an eye on the future, US-China dialogue should be able to advance mutual interests on issues such as energy resources, computer security, and a potential arms race in space.[14] Even on issues that seemingly are immune to a common position, such as North Korea's nuclear weapons and missile programs, consistent high-level US-PRC diplomatic engagement may lead to deeper understanding if not immediately to joint action. David M. Lampton's advice for the conduct of US-China relations is sound:

> to work together with China and other partners to maintain a stable major power equilibrium in the region; to work in concert with the region and China to maintain and develop the security and human infrastructure necessary for economic and human development; and to address the transnational issues that are the existential challenges of this century—food, energy, climate, proliferation, resource availability (not least of which is water), and sustainable economic growth.[15]

In fact, largely behind the scenes, US-China cooperation is happening in a wide range of fields. The United States and China have more points of direct, official contact (Track I) than ever before—around sixty of them, in fact, at both the bilateral and working-group levels (see Appendix, document 6). Many of these contacts take place in the context of two overarching forums: the US-China Strategic and Economic Dialogue, which in 2011 for the first time included discussion of military and defense issues as well as the more usual economic and financial issues; and Asia-Pacific Consultations, which began in 2010 and in 2011 involved bilateral talks on US arms sales to Taiwan and China's currency valuation. US-PRC civilian nuclear cooperation has been ongoing since 1998. The US government, either through the Department of State or the Congress, supports legal training and programs that seek to advance democracy in China. Funding amounted to about $110 million from 1999 to 2006.[16]

Military-to-military contacts between the PRC and the United States have gone on for well over a decade, though they have been suspended several times over unanticipated incidents, such as the mistaken NATO bombing of China's embassy in Belgrade, Yugoslavia, in 1999, and the collision of US and Chinese aircraft near Hainan Island in 2001. Top US military leaders stress the importance of military-to-military contacts to deal with common problems such as terrorism and piracy.[17] Chiefs of staff and defense secretaries of both countries' militaries have exchanged visits a number of times in recent years.[18] The essential issue is confidence building, such that China's inevitable steps forward in military modernization—such as aircraft carriers and warships—will not be taken as signifying hostile intent, and US alliance building and deployments in the Pacific will not be taken to mean the renewal of containment of China. The two countries' very different military doctrines for deterring each other, especially over Taiwan, are a recipe for misperception and miscalculation.[19] Naval matters in particular need frank discussion if confrontations at sea are to be avoided.

Track II (mixed official and unofficial) and Track III (unofficial) activities may have the greatest lasting value. Chinese and US scholars, businesspeople, and officials acting in an unofficial capacity meet all the time for exchanges of view in informal settings. Track III features the work of US NGOs in China, which may make the greatest contribution of all to mutual understanding. The reason is simple: NGOs are non-governmental by definition (though some do accept US government funds), do not have an ideological ax to grind, and present a positive example to China's GONGOs—government-organized NGOs. "China Development Brief" lists two hundred international NGOs active in China. Many of them are based in the United States.[20] Environmental Defense, the Natural Resources Defense Council, and Greenpeace China, for example, work on water quality, sustainable development, and air pollution. The Ford Foundation funds rule-of-law and civil-society projects. Education is the focus of the Committee on Scholarly Communication with China and the Institute of International Education. Children's issues are the concern of World Vision International, and health care engages the Bill and Melinda Gates Foundation and Project HOPE. Little mass-media attention is devoted to these initiatives, yet they meet real needs while also providing important building blocks of mutual confidence

Commercial relations, too, are prominent Track III activities. China's trade with the United States, both overall and in terms of exports, ranks first in the world. Total trade was about $456 billion in 2010, a sizable proportion of China's total world trade of nearly $3 trillion.[21] Total US direct investments in China were $60.5 billion by 2010, fifth in rank. Chinese investments in the United States are growing rapidly; in 2010 they came to about $4.9 billion, including around $1 billion in New York real estate alone.[22] The changing US government position on Chinese acquisitions of US companies may help improve the investment climate. Whereas one of China's national oil companies was prevented from acquiring a US oil company (Unocal) in 2005, in 2012 the three main Chinese banks were allowed to purchase a US bank (the Bank of East Asia in New York) and expand branch operations in two US cities.

People-to-people exchanges play a vital role in China-US relations. Of course, "getting to know you" may sometimes create or harden negative views. But a positive outcome from personal interactions seems to be the safer assumption. With so many US and Chinese students, scholars, government officials, and specialists visiting each other's countries, a strong constituency is emerging in favor of mutual understanding and conflict avoidance. Of particular relevance is the growing number of

Chinese foreign-policy officials and academics who have Western fel-lowships and degrees and significant travel abroad.[23] Many Chinese sci-entists have returned home after being trained at US institutions, and if the era of Tiananmen protests is any guide, scientists are likely to be leaders in China's democratization. They reflect a new cosmopolitanism among PRC specialists, but we should be mindful that cosmopolitanism competes with an abiding nationalism when it comes to assessing inter-national issues. Two writers have described this situation in terms of a "dual identity"—pride over recent national achievements coexisting with lingering insecurity stemming from China's "century of humilia-tion."[24]

Learning from the Past

This duality certainly plays a large part in US relations with China. We might recall that during the Cold War, Track III bridge-building efforts also occurred in US-USSR relations, though by no means to the extent we see today in US-China relations. And while war did not occur then, serious confrontations did—in Berlin and Cuba, for instance. The Cold War mentality is still around, moreover—consider the remarks in 2006 of Admiral William Fallon when he served as commander of US Pacific forces[25]—and it is not confined to the defense establishments of the United States and China. Moreover, as happened during the Cold War, one side's advances in arms are interpreted by the stronger side as evi-dence of ill intent. During the Cold War the Soviet Union was constantly playing catch-up, recognizing the military reality that for all its bigger nuclear weapons, the United States fielded better arms at every level—more reliable, accurate, and technically better—than it did. Various Chinese spokesmen in and outside the PLA have said the same. Yet sus-picions are rife in the Pentagon and among conservative politicians that China is quietly preparing eventually to challenge US military predomi-nance in the Pacific and even beyond.

The PLA is certainly modernizing its weapons, and in ways that can be interpreted as being primarily aimed at neutralizing long-standing US advantages. Aircraft carriers, antiship weapons, and advanced sub-marines are all in development. Stealth technology may erode certain US advantages. US officials insist on knowing the purpose of China's weapons modernization as well as China's military plans in general. The Chinese counter in two ways: first, that the Americans need not worry, since China cannot possibly match the huge US advantage in naval and airpower; second, that US deployments and military assistance programs all along the arc of the Asia-Pacific are possibly as directed at China as the United States believes China's weapons are directed at US interests.

To advance intelligent, objective discussion of US policy toward China, here are ten points that may be worth remembering.

First, history deeply informs the relationship. US support of Chiang Kai-shek's government during China's civil war; the post-1949 embargo and nonrecognition policy toward China; the Korean War, leading to US defense of Taiwan and intervention in Vietnam; the crises in the Taiwan Strait in the 1950s and early 1960s; China's perception of US-Soviet "collusion and contention" in the 1970s; US consideration of an attack on China's nuclear weapons complex in the early 1960s—all these may be long forgotten in Washington but surely not in Beijing. As one Chinese scholar put it to me many years ago, "China's memory is too long; America's is too short."

Second, both China and the United States are guilty of inconsistent strategies and actions toward one another. This has allowed for numerous instances of miscommunication and, as in the Korean War, fatal miscalculation. So far, such disastrous collisions have been avoided in the post–Cold War period. But tense moments have occurred, and signal the need for closer consultations: US boarding of the Chinese ship *Yinhe* in 1993 in a mistaken search for missile parts supposedly destined for Iran, China's missile tests near Taiwan in 1996, the Belgrade bombing incident in 1999, the EP-3 aerial incident near Hainan in 2001, China's confrontation of the USS *Intrepid* in 2009, and US-ROK joint naval exercises in the Yellow Sea in 2010.

Third, asymmetries of power have been a constant shaping force in the relationship. The United States is capable of significantly influencing China's economy, diplomacy, and culture. China cannot do the same to the United States. Wang Jisi has written that "the tremendous gap between the two countries in national power and international status and the fundamental differences between their political systems and ideology have prevented the United States from viewing China as a peer."[26]

Fourth, different ambitions and levels of strategic interest—global (US) vs. regional (PRC)—have also contributed to mistrust. The United States has a grand strategy and the means to carry it out; China doesn't. US leaders identify their country as a global leader; China may aspire to that status, but is a long way from reaching it.

Fifth, structural differences have also been part of the problem: a rising power confronts the predominant power. Exacerbating this difference is the fact that conflicts between China and the US have centered on areas of security sensitivity to China, namely Korea, Taiwan,

Vietnam, and Tibet, which are a reminder of another difference: as the Chinese see it, national integration is incomplete, hence their periodic concern about foreign (i.e., US) meddling in their "internal" affairs and along their borders. (One can only imagine the US government's response to Chinese efforts to influence Florida's electoral process, or to the sighting of a Chinese warship off the Pacific coast.)

Sixth, domestic politics—leadership struggles in China, US election campaigns, bureaucratic disputes and interests in both countries, budget battles, nationalistic rallying cries on both sides—have intruded into and distorted the relationship. Neither country has been very good at taking this factor into account in assessing the other's policymaking. Increased exchanges among politicians, military officers, and cultural officials at various levels might help to correct these distortions. For instance, the US cultural presence in China is surprisingly weak, the number of US consulates there is small, and since 9/11 Chinese seeking visas have been delayed or denied on questionable grounds. Correcting these deficiencies may be important for letting younger Chinese know that the United States takes their interest in it seriously.

Seventh, each country has its own view of what a "responsible" foreign policy should mean, as noted earlier. These days the Chinese find US handling of its economy, its arms sales to Taiwan, and its efforts to influence China's domestic politics irresponsible. US officials counter that China's unwillingness to pressure North Korea and Iran on nuclear weapons, provide fair business opportunities for US firms, and end human-rights abuses are irresponsible. Needless to say, this huge gap in positions is not conducive to a positive future.

Eighth, China's priorities include recognition of its emergence as a key player on all international issues, and achievement of its economic development goals so as to maintain its political system and internal unity. The United States, while rightly calling for improvement in human rights and other matters in China (and while improving its own domestic circumstances), should reposition itself as a partner with China in making globalization work for everyone. The key arena for such partnership is not just the bilateral relationship, for as Chinese leaders have emphasized for some time, *multilateral diplomacy* is now an accepted and important channel for dialogue on economic and security issues.

Ninth, rather than think overly much about the ways China can threaten US interests, we might consider what the Chinese believe most threatens them. The difference in perspective is huge—focusing on the Chinese leadership's fears for the exposure of its weaknesses instead of on how China is plotting to extend its power. What most seem to concern PRC leaders are, internally, the prospect of organized, large-scale social protests such as occurred in June 1989, and externally, a direct conflict with the United States. Either one would most likely derail China's economic reforms and potentially plunge the country into chaos. As President Clinton once remarked, that outcome would not be beneficial to the United States: "As we focus on the potential challenge that a strong China could present to the United States in the future, let us not forget the risk of a weak China, beset by internal conflicts, social dislocation and criminal activity, becoming a vast zone of instability in Asia."[27]

Tenth, regularizing the Sino-US military relationship should be a priority for the civilian and military leaderships of both countries; failure to do so could easily lead to another Cold War. With the US-Soviet case in mind, Chinese and US officials ought to be focusing on confidence building. Neither country can really afford arms racing, though both are in a position to finance one if required. The Americans will have to accept, however, that China's military modernization will continue, if only because the PLA will keep lobbying for it as a deserved benefit of China's prosperity. Self-righteous US statements about China's military spending should stop. The Chinese, meantime, will do well to respond positively to the US desire for increased military-to-military contacts, while the United States should be mindful of Chinese anxieties when it comes to conducting intelligence missions along the China coast, strengthening forces and military access points around China's rim, and making another arms sale to Taiwan.

Notes

1. As told by Thomas L. Friedman, "Gardening with Beijing," *New York Times*, April 17, 1996, online ed.

2. Wang Jisi, "China's Search for Stability with America," *Foreign Affairs* 84, no. 5 (2005): 39–60. As Wang writes (p. 46), "The Chinese-U.S. relationship remains beset by more profound differences than any other bilateral relationship between major powers in the world today. . . . It is not a relationship of confrontation and rivalry for primacy, as the U.S.-Soviet relationship was during the Cold War, but it does contain some of the same characteristics."

3. "Opinion of the United States"; at www.pewglobal.org/database/?indicator=1&country=45. The Pew sample for these surveys of Chinese opinion is around three thousand people.

4. "World's Leading Superpower"; at www.pewglobal.org/database/?indicator=33&country=45.

5. "Satisfaction with Country's Direction"; at www.pewglobal.org/database/?indicator=3&country=45.

6. US arms exports include about $7.5 billion in arms and military services delivered to Taiwan from 2002 to 2009, making Taiwan the fourth-largest US cus-

tomer during those years. Weapons deals in recent years have included advanced F-16 jets, several types of missiles (such as antiship and air defense), and helicopters. Taiwan officers regularly receive training in the United States. See Shirley A. Kan, "Taiwan: Major U.S. Arms Sales Since 1990," CRS Report RL30957, August 2, 2011; at www.fas.org/sgp/crs/weapons/RL30957.pdf.

7. Qingshan Tan, "The Change of Public Opinion on US-China Relations," *Asian Perspective* 35, no. 2 (2011): 211–237.

8. See, for instance, Hillary Rodham Clinton's speech of January 14, 2011, calling for a "positive, cooperative, and comprehensive relationship with China"; at www.state.gov/secretary/rm/2011/01/154653.htm.

9. See Stephen Glain, "By Choosing Arms over Diplomacy, America Errs in Asia," *New York Times*, December 15, 2011, online ed.

10. Mark Landler, "Obama's Journey to Tougher Tack on a Rising China," *New York Times*, September 21, 2012, online ed.

11. Pew Research Center, January 12, 2011; at http://pewresearch.org /pubs/1855/china-poll-americans-want-closer-ties-but-tougher-trade-policy.

12. "Indiana University Professors Release Survey Results About Americans' Views of China," March 13, 2011; at http://newsinfo.iu.edu/news/page/normal /17450.html.

13. "U.S. Public, Experts Differ on China Policies," Pew Research Center, September 18, 2012, at www.pewglobal.org/2012/09/18/u-s-public-experts-differ -on-china-policies/.

14. See the special issue of *Asian Perspective* 35, no. 4 (2011), "Avoiding an Arms Race in Space," edited by Peter Van Ness.

15. Lampton, *Power Constrained*, p. 11. For a comprehensive assessment of the need to improve U.S.-China relations and how to do it, see Kenneth Lieberthal and Wang Jisi, "Addressing U.S.-China Strategic Distrust," John L. Thornton China Center, Brookings Institution, no. 4 (March 2012). This is the English version of the report cited in n. 4 of Chapter 2.

16. Thomas Lum, "U.S.-Funded Assistance Programs in China," CRS Report no. RS22663, May 18, 2007.

17. Voice of America, "Security Strategy in Asia," citing a speech by Admiral Mike Mullen, chairman of the Joint Chiefs of Staff, August 11, 2011; at www.voanews.com/policy/editorials/asia/Security-Strategy-In-Asia-127538538. html. See also Mike Mullen, "A Step Toward Trust with China," *New York Times*, July 25, 2011, online ed. Mullen wrote the op-ed article following an exchange of visits with his counterpart, General Chen Bingde.

18. For a review of these contacts, see Shirley A. Kan, "U.S.-China Military Contacts: Issues for Congress," CRS Report 32496, July 26, 2011; at www.fas.org/sgp/crs/natsec/RL32496.pdf.

19. See Christopher P. Twomey, *The Military Lens: Doctrinal Difference and Deterrence Failure in Sino-American Relations* (Ithaca, NY: Cornell University Press, 2010).

20. At www.chinadevelopmentbrief.com/dingo/.

21. Statistics from the U.S.-China Business Council; at www.uschina.org /statistics/tradetable.html.

22. Hong Kong, Taiwan, Japan, and Singapore ranked higher. U.S.-China Economic and Security Review Commission 2011, pp. 3–4. On New York investments, see Kirk Semple, "As Investors, Chinese Turn to New York," *New York Times*, August 11, 2011, online ed.

23. Jakobson and Knox, "New Foreign Policy Actors in China," Stockholm International Peace Research Institute (SIPRI) Policy Paper no. 26, September 2010, pp. 22–23.

24. Ibid., p. 21.

25. "[China] isn't a clone of the Soviet Union. However, there are institutions of our government that seem to act in a manner that has just transferred whatever we thought the Soviet Union was, and we have moved it into China and we kind of do things in the same manner, which I think is incorrect." Michael R. Gordon, "To Build Trust, U.S. Navy Holds a Drill with China," *New York Times*, September 23, 2006, online ed.

26. Wang Jisi, "China's Search for Stability with America."

27. Text in NAPSNet, April 8, 1999.

10

Reassessing the China Challenge

When the Chinese Communists assumed power in 1949, Mao Zedong made a speech in which he wondered why some colleagues looked to the imperialist West as teachers when the teachers had always committed aggression against their pupils. Throughout the Cold War years the theme of "imperialism versus China" predominated in relations with the United States. Now that Mao is gone and China has been building markets instead of Maoism, one would think the "threat" theme would disappear. But it hasn't. Instead, many in the United States view China as having gone from being a largely military and ideological threat under Mao to being an even greater threat, economic as well as military. Chinese leaders have good reason to wonder what they must do to satisfy Western critics. Clearly, some Chinese have decided it is wrong to try. They are among the strongly nationalistic Chinese who see the "US challenge" as their country's main problem.

Disentangling the "Challenge"

Examining the "China challenge" usually invites ideas on how to defeat or deflect it. But in the United States, the task could be altered to consideration of China as a mirror of US strengths and weaknesses. China's disregard of fundamental civil liberties, its heavy-handed approach to ensuring political stability, its cozying up to dictators in Third World countries, and its poor environmental record are surely among the negatives. But China's hardworking people, its huge savings, its highly limited military involvement (including arms shipments) outside the country, and the proactive role of government in stimulating the economy and promoting nonmilitary research—these are just some aspects of contemporary China that the United States might learn from. The "number one nation" may also want to ponder how well China's leaders have handled being "number two."

Most critically, the United States must avoid believing that the "China challenge" is *the* reason, or even *a* reason, for declining US economic power and global influence.[1] Yes, there are commercial inequities in the relationship, but neither righting the trade imbalance nor getting the Chinese to revalue their currency will erase the US deficit. US decline is largely self-inflicted, the consequence of profligate military spending, imperial overreach, a deeply flawed financial system and political process, and widening inequalities between social classes. Indeed, none other than the former chairman of the Joint Chiefs of Staff, Admiral Mike Mullen, said that "the continually increasing [US] debt is the biggest threat we have to our national security." As he pointed out, the interest on the debt equaled the US military budget for 2011.[2]

US domestic problems are reversible, yet highly unlikely to be reversed anytime soon. The same holds for China. As mentioned at the outset of this study, the China challenge is mainly *to* China, not *from* it—the myriad economic, political, environmental, and social problems that the post-1978 reforms have unleashed.

The idea that modern China has never been more secure than it is today is true, but incomplete. It is more secure *from external threat* than ever before, but PRC leaders may be *less* secure than ever before. They must cope with large-scale and costly domestic problems well into the future, and as time goes on these problems will attract increasing public criticism and calls for change. Party leaders will do what comes naturally by trying to quell dissent, but they will find that repression is increasingly dysfunctional. Complicating their approach is that some domestic problems, such as ethnic minority unrest and energy needs, cross into the domain of international security. And so long as the PRC leadership's agenda of completing national unification remains unfulfilled— with Taiwan a well-established democracy, Tibet under the gun, and many Hong Kong citizens expressing dissatisfaction with rule from Beijing—Chinese leaders must be careful not to further alienate the populations there.

The insecurity of Chinese leaders can be an opportunity for the United States to adjust to the idea of not being the dominant world power, of needing to pare down national interests and priorities, and of sharing global responsibilities. Many in the current generation of US leaders will resist such adjustments, of course. To them, any concession of authority to other countries or international institutions is anathema, whether it means incorporating international legal opinion into US law, engaging in multilateral military operations without being in charge, or accepting internationally negotiated limits on pollution. But narrow nationalism is part of the problem of our times. We have to recognize that the era of US hegemony is over. As a report of the US National Intelligence Council concluded, the United States by 2025 will probably still be the most powerful country, but it will have to share the stage with other influential actors, China among them.[3] The opinion poll mentioned earlier of the US public and policy experts supports the idea of a shared leadership role with China. Only if we follow that advice can we have some confidence that the United States will remain globally influential in the most important ways—as a work-in-progress, but also as a "shining example" with respect to democratic governance, cultural inclusiveness, social justice, and individual initiative.

The argument of what I have called America Firsters—that US decline does not mean the demise of the Western-based international order and that China will have to continue to abide by the West's economic and commercial rules—borders on wishful thinking. True, China's so-called development model adheres, though not consistently, to globalization's rules and institutions when it comes to trade and financial liberalization. At the same time, however, the Chinese have provided developing countries with an alternative to the West's requirement of structural adjustment and high indebtedness. China, in short, only partially embraces liberal internationalism, and as its influence and economic power continue to expand, we can expect that it will seek to modify the rules of the IMF and the World Bank while simultaneously, within the BRICS and other groups, creating a strong lobby for its own policy preferences. Chinese nationalism is not going to be overwhelmed by internationalism; the tortured history of China's relations with the West ensures that.

Contrary to the view of some political scientists, the world does not have to rely on a hegemonic power to operate peacefully and productively. Leadership can, and should, be a shared responsibility. So far as Asia is concerned, that means a US-China relationship that is cooperative and mutually respectful, but not aimed (as the China Duopolists propose) at putting the two countries in a controlling position over regional affairs. The benefits of US-China cooperation should be self-evident; for example, in space exploration, international financial stability, an Asia not squeezed by two competing giants, environmental protection, and prevention of cyber attacks. US cooperation with China will not be possible on all issues: the "war on terror" was an example of misplaced and exaggerated common interest, and a common policy on dictatorships will always be very difficult to craft. But as we witness more frequent national and regional crises that have global implications and major human consequences—the Chernobyl nuclear plant meltdown of 1986, the Asian financial crisis of 1997–1998, Southeast Asia's tsunami in 2008, the US financial crisis of 2008–2010, Japan's nuclear plant disasters of 2011, mass hunger and civil wars in developing countries—we come to understand the imperative of a cooperative approach to real security. In fact, a cooperative US-China relationship would have a crucial additional payoff: the opportunity for the United States to shift attention and resources away from China and into impoverished, crisis-prone areas of the world.

Thus, the Engagers are right; they *have* to be. So long as China remains a competitive rather than an aggressive country—a circumstance that serious US engagement with it will help determine—it represents no threat and, to the contrary, a potential partner in many enterprises of mutual benefit. The United States cannot afford to be in a conflict-prone relationship with China, and the reverse is equally if not more true. Neither seeking actively to contain China nor pretending that US (or Western) superiority will endure indefinitely is an effective idea in a world that is increasingly integrated economically and ecologically. Nor will worrying about the "China challenge" improve the US economic or political situation, no more than China's worrying about "US hegemony" will solve China's internal problems. The United States needs to take care of its own business, with a sense of purpose that springs from its professed values and enormous material advantages. Let China's people and leaders worry about their country. They do; and as we have seen, they have plenty to worry about.

Some Remedial Steps

Specifically, what steps can be taken by the United States and China to reduce tensions, promote trust, and widen the basis for cooperation?

First, US military policy should change. The budget-driven reductions in US military spending, certain weapons acquisitions, and manpower that began in 2012 will be positive under at least four conditions relevant to Asia and to China in particular. The reductions must be accompanied by a change in US forward-deployment of forces and extended nuclear deterrence. They must eliminate or significantly cut back redundant weapons systems, nuclear as well as conventional. The United States—and Japan—must resist calls for Japan to become a more active security partner in response to China's rise.[4] And the reductions must affect missions, too; that is, unilateral US interventions to change regimes or build nations must be eliminated.

Secretary of State Clinton set the right tone when she said at a US-China dialogue meeting in 2012 that "no global player can afford to treat geopolitics as a zero-sum game" and that "if China's rising capabilities mean that we have an increasingly able and engaged partner in solving the threats we face to both regional and global security, that is all good."[5] Looking for ways to collaborate militarily seems like a better bet than reenacting Cold War–style deterrence scenarios. In Africa, for example, the US and PRC navies might regularly carry out joint antipiracy operations.[6]

Unfortunately, none of these conditions seems likely to be met, for no sooner were the budget reductions mentioned than President Obama and Secretary of Defense Leon Panetta reassured one and all that despite the reductions, a leaner, smaller US military would still maintain "full-spectrum capabilities," "military superiority," and the ability to defeat "more than one enemy" at a time. Panetta said the United States would continue working toward a positive relationship with China because of common interests, but "maintaining our military presence in Asia" and "enhancing" the US presence in the Pacific were mentioned in the same breath.[7] In fact, Panetta's Pentagon had already begun developing an "Air-Sea Battle Plan" with Chinese forces explicitly in mind.[8]

This China-focused "pivot" or "rebalancing" should be reconsidered. It is currently being played out in the South China Sea, where creating an anti-China coalition seems to be the US strategy.[9] Quietly boosting the security confidence of allies in case of serious trouble is one thing, but it is hard to see how new force deployments and threatening postures will benefit the long-term interests of Australia, Japan, or ASEAN in maintaining positive relations with China. To the contrary, as two former Australian prime ministers have argued, the Obama administration's emphasis on military strength in Asia needlessly risks alienating Beijing and does not serve their country's interests.[10] Moreover, the policy undercuts professed US hopes for gaining China's cooperation on international issues and establishing strategic stability in relations with it.

Second, policy regarding Taiwan is out-of-date and should change. The extent of economic integration that has occurred between Taiwan and the PRC is extraordinary: around $200 billion in investments in the mainland by some eighty thousand Taiwan firms, annual trade above $150 billion, and one million or more Taiwanese living on the mainland. The close economic relationship, coupled with the apparent political consensus on Taiwan that it will not seek de jure independence, presents an opportunity for the United States to honorably remove itself from its long-standing position between the two parties.[11] Donald Gross has suggested one way to do so:[12] negotiation of a US-PRC Framework Agreement that would reduce US forces near China in return for China's reduction and redeployment of its missile and other forces opposite Taiwan, a Chinese guarantee of respect for Taiwan's political system in return for reaffirmation of the "1992 PRC-Taiwan consensus" on the one-China principle and reduced US arms sales to Taiwan as promised in 1982 under President Reagan pending agreement on reunification,[13] and conclusion of a bilateral free-trade agreement. One can imagine many variations of this agreement, as well as interim steps not involving the United States. For example, to build trust and promote conflict prevention, the PRC (see Appendix, document 5) has proposed creating a "military security mechanism" with Taiwan, a project that interests some in the Taiwan defense community.[14]

The essential point is that any agreement should incorporate the "one China, but not now" formula that has unofficially prevailed for some time.[15] This would allow Beijing and Taipei to make their own decisions about their political relationship on their own schedule, so long as Taiwan refrains from pushing for de jure independence and China agrees to refrain from the use of force or threat against Taiwan.

Third, China and the United States should lead the way toward creating a new security dialogue mechanism (SDM) for Northeast Asia.[16] Formats such as the Six Party Talks on North Korea's nuclear weapons, writes one Chinese specialist, might "gradually become a more regular and systematic mechanism" for regional security.[17] Rather than focus exclusively (and only periodically) on North Korea's nuclear weapons, as the Six Party Talks do, the SDM would be a permanent institution devoted to many other regional security issues, including environmental and territorial disputes. The SDM would have the authority to convene on the call of any member. It would be "an early warning and crisis management system," as the Chinese specialist said. His comment suggests a larger point: as China becomes increasingly comfortable working within multilateral groups, US diplomacy with China might profit from doing the same in order to arrive at a common position on regional security issues.

Fourth, a code of conduct that prevents the kinds of dangerous confrontations that have occurred at sea and in the air between the United States and China in recent years would be enormously beneficial. (A specific agreement to prevent "incidents at sea," such as the United States and the Soviet Union concluded in 1972, would also be desirable so long as it included nonmilitary as well as military vessels.) Reducing and redeploying US forces involved in close surveillance of the China coast would be an essential element of any such negotiation. As one

Chinese analyst has concluded in a study of two prominent incidents—the Belgrade bombing and the EP-3 air collision near Hainan—the factors in each country's management of a crisis do not bode well for the future. China, he wrote, puts great emphasis on symbolic gestures, the question of responsibility, and national dignity, while the United States, particularly the military, "demonstrates a strong utilitarian tendency; that is to say, how to advance its objectives and maximize its interest in a crisis."[18] Understanding these differences is surely the first step to overcoming them.

Fifth, the United States and China should launch collaborative projects for human development. Given its human-development needs, Africa would be a good place to start. Though China has in the past rejected EU proposals for a cooperative approach in Africa, early in 2012 a senior foreign ministry official in African affairs (Lu Shaye, director-general of the Department of African Affairs in the foreign ministry) advocated conducting development projects jointly with the West. He defended China against charges of neocolonialism (perhaps a reason for the proposal) and pointed to PRC humanitarian assistance to "build roads, bridges, hospitals and schools."[19] US development aid targets public health and education, too, providing opportunities for cooperation.

Sixth, the two countries should seek a closer understanding of how and when humanitarian intervention—"the responsibility to protect"—should be endorsed by the UN Security Council. China, while upholding the doctrine of the absolute sovereignty of states, has sometimes altered its position, such as when it decided not to veto Security Council resolutions on Libya and Côte d'Ivoire that authorized military strikes. Some writers see the Chinese as distinguishing between support for a Security Council resolution that upholds intervention as a last resort against genocide and crimes against humanity, such as in Côte d'Ivoire, and (as in Security Council resolutions on Syria, for instance) opposition to an international intervention that amounts to regime change and defense of human rights.[20] That distinction may be too abstract, however: in the Syria case, a UN report in February 2012 found the Assad regime guilty of crimes against humanity, yet China's position (as well as Russia's) against sanctions or other international involvement did not change. Still, there may be times when international military intervention to save large numbers of lives will bring the United States and China together, and that is an objective worth working on.

Seventh, the ethical side of US-China business relations needs attention. The usual business topic is the huge US trade deficit with China—$273 billion in 2011, or about 55 percent of the total US trade deficit. That needs correcting, though it is hard to see how the deficit can be dramatically reduced when the US consumer sees "Made in China" on virtually everything. Less often discussed are two ethical issues: theft of US technology by Chinese companies and improper labor and other practices by US firms operating in China. Theft of trade secrets costs US and other countries' companies doing business in China billions of dollars annually. It is in this domain that the notion of the Chinese "eating our lunch" very specifically applies.[21] Obtaining legal recourse in China is now on the US-PRC agenda and will be a test of China's willingness to play by the rules.

US corporate activities in China also have to answer for certain practices. Foxconn is the Taiwan-based manufacturer of Apple's iPad and other devices in China. But Foxconn's assembly lines have been poorly monitored, resulting in unsafe working conditions and serious injuries to Chinese workers, including cases of suicide. Early in 2012, Apple hired a labor-rights monitoring organization to provide an independent audit of working conditions at Foxconn. US trade with China that involves the export of technology with military applicability or the import of goods that might originate with prison labor should stop. US information-technology firms should not cave in to Chinese censors, as Microsoft and Yahoo have done. Nor should they assist China's security apparatus to track people's movements, such as by selling it video-surveillance technology, as Cisco Systems has done for the city of Chongqing, or by raising money, as US investment companies and banks have done to manufacture a chip-implanted residence card in Shenzhen.[22] The usual corporate response that pleads ignorance of how the customer uses or abuses its product, or treats workers, simply will not wash. What is needed is "naming and shaming" of these corporations to move them to pay attention to the social consequences of their production.

The eighth policy recommendation concerns energy. China and the United States are the world's leading energy consumers, and demand can only go one way: up. A global energy compact should be negotiated alongside agreement on global warming. The focus of cooperative efforts—and since 2009 a jointly financed clean-energy research center has been available—should be on sustainability and conservation rather than continued exploitation of oil, gas, and coal to meet ever increasing demand. While joint ventures on energy may sometimes be desirable from a political and business point of view, all they accomplish is more drilling, more mining, more consumption, and of course more global warming. Both countries are hunting for new domestic sources of oil, but reliance on imports is likely to remain heavy well into the future. The coal and natural-gas pictures for China are similar: rapidly increasing demand and the need to rely increasingly on imports as well as on alternative energy sources such as nuclear and hydropower. From the point of view of public health, China should have a strong interest in working simultaneously with the United States on environmental protection and clean energy sources.

A Final Thought

"Whose century?" is really the wrong question. The right one is: How do world leaders go about creating a legitimate and effective framework for cooperative security—one that lays the groundwork for addressing the most serious *human*-security problems? For the United States, China, and the other countries with global reach, the answer must include practicing new forms of leadership, deepening cooperation with each other, and embracing *common* security as the touchstone of *national* security. They must recognize that the greatest security challenges of our time are poverty—and violence in response to poverty—and destruction of the environment, and that these challenges can be effectively met only by making them a common priority. Military buildups and resort to force or threat are irrelevant to the solution of such problems. If China and the United States can find common ground on cooperative security, both can truly lay claim to being responsible great powers.

Notes

1. As Thomas L. Friedman and Michael Mandelbaum write in *That Used to Be Us: How America Fell Behind in the World It Invented and How We Can Come Back* (New York: Farrar, Straus & Giroux, 2011), p. 54: "Our biggest problem is not that we're failing to keep up with China's best practices but that we've strayed so far from our own best practices."

2. Ed O'Keefe, "Mullen: Despite Deal, Debt Still Poses the Biggest Threat to U.S. National Security," *Washington Post*, August 2, 2011; at www.washington post.com/blogs/checkpoint-washington/post/mullen-despite-deal-debt-still-a-risk-to -national-security/2011/08/02/gIQAhSr2oI_blog.html.

3. National Intelligence Council, *Global Trends, 2025: A World Transformed* (November 2008); at www.dni.gov/nic/PDF_2025/2025_Global_Trends _Final_Report.pdf.

4. For example, Richard L. Armitage and Joseph S. Nye, "The U.S.-Japan Alliance: Anchoring Stability in Asia," report of the Center for Strategic and International Studies, Washington, DC, August 2012; at http://csis.org/files /publication/120810_Armitage_USJapanAlliance_Web.pdf.

5. "Remarks at U.S.-China Strategic and Economic Dialogue Opening Session," Beijing, May 3, 2012; at www.state.gov/secretary/rm/2012/05/189213.htm.

6. Brown, *Hidden Dragon, Crouching Lion*, p. 97. A joint counterpiracy exercise involving a US guided-missile destroyer and a Chinese navy frigate did take place in September 2012 in the Gulf of Aden. See www.cpf.navy.mil /news.aspx/040006.

7. Interview with Jeffrey Brown, Oregon Public Broadcasting news broadcast of January 5, 2012.

8. Representative J. Randy Forbes, "America's Pacific Air-Sea Battle Vision," *Diplomat*, March 8, 2012; at http://thediplomat.com/2012/03/08/americas-pacific -air-sea-battle-vision/. The main idea behind the plan is to provide US commanders in the Pacific with the capabilities to deal with any Chinese attempt to deny US forces access to the region in a crisis.

9. Refer again to the October 2012 speech by Deputy Secretary of Defense Ashton Carter cited in n. 53, Chapter 3.

10. Both former prime ministers argued for US emphasis on a cooperative relationship with China. See Malcolm Fraser, "Obama's China Card?" Project-Syndicate, July 11, 2012; at www.project-syndicate.org/commentary/obama-s-china -card; and Paul Keating, cited by Greg Earl, "US Wrong on China: Keating," *Australian Financial Review*, August 6, 2012; online at http://afr.com /p/national/us_wrong_on_china_keating_Bjp2FY9i9j5ahuD7iGsQBP.

11. See Daniel Lynch, "Why Ma Won the Elections and What's Next for Taiwan and China," *Foreign Affairs*, January 15, 2012; at www.foreignaffairs.com /articles/137029/daniel-lynch/why-ma-won-the-elections-and-whats-next-for-tai-wan-and-china.

12. Donald G. Gross, "Transforming the U.S. Relationship with China," pp. 78–89.

13. In mid-2011 the Obama administration announced it would not proceed with the sale to Taiwan of F-16 fighter jets, an action that immediately drew criticism from Republicans despite the fact that Obama approved other military sales to Taiwan valued at $5.8 billion.

14. See Sue-Chung Chang and Chung-Yuan Yao, "Possible Variables for Establishing a Military Confidence-Building Mechanism Across the Taiwan Strait," *Asian Perspective* 36, no. 4 (2012): 725–734.

15. Chas Freeman, "Preventing War in the Taiwan Strait: Restraining Taiwan— and Beijing," *Foreign Affairs* 77, no. 4 (1998): 6–11.

16. See my "Averting War in Northeast Asia: A Proposal," *Asia-Pacific Journal* 9, no. 2 (2011); at http://japanfocus.org/-Mel-Gurtov/3467.

17. Wang Yizhou, "China's Path," p. 16.

18. Wu Xinbo, "Understanding Chinese and U.S. Crisis Behavior," *Washington Quarterly* 31, no. 1 (2007–2008): 61–76.

19. Li Liangxing, "China Keen to Cooperate with West in Africa," *China Daily*, January 12, 2012; at http://usa.chinadaily.com.cn/china/2012-01/12 /content_1425697.htm.

20. Amitai Etzioni, "Changing the Rules," *Foreign Affairs* 90, no. 6 (2011): 172–175.

21. One person directly involved in reviewing cases of technology theft noted that US companies have "got renminbi dancing in their eyes" when they allow such theft to go on. "But nine years later," he said, "the Chinese are eating your lunch": Jonathan Weisman, "U.S. to Share Cautionary Tale of Trade Secret Theft with Chinese Official," *New York Times*, February 15, 2012, p. A10.

22. Keith Bradsher, "China Enacting a High-Tech Plan to Track People," *New York Times*, August 12, 2007, online ed. Other US corporations that have sold China surveillance-related technology are United Technologies, Honeywell, and IBM.

Appendix

Selected Documents

Document 1

Wang Jisi, "Inside China" (2010)

For obvious reasons, most China-watchers outside the country are more concerned about China's external relations and behavior than its domestic affairs. However, the key to understanding China's international policies and practices, including economic ones, is to see where its domestic trends are heading. As Zhang Baijia, a leading historian of the Chinese Communist Party (CCP), once observed, "China has always influenced the world by changing itself."

In retrospect, domestic politics have defined and confined foreign relations at every stage in the history of the People's Republic of China (PRC). The numerous political campaigns under Mao Zedong's leadership against "class enemies" were consistent with China's direct participation in the Korean War and indirect participation in the Vietnam War against "US imperialism." In the early 1960s and during the Cultural Revolution, the class struggles aimed at digging out "capitalist roaders" and "revisionists" within the CCP predetermined a radical foreign policy and impeded China's foreign trade.

After 1978, Deng Xiaoping and the rehabilitated party leaders linked economic reforms at home with opening the country to the outside world. Beijing then normalized diplomatic relations with all the countries important to it. The decisions made by President Jiang Zemin and Premier Zhu Rongji in the 1990s to deepen the reforms ensured China's accession to the World Trade Organization (WTO) and further moderated its foreign policy. Today, China's national security strategy, trade policy, international monetary policy and reactions to climate change, as well as other non-traditional security issues, are all conditioned on its main domestic considerations and how they are prioritized.

This is the main portion of an introduction to a special issue on China of *Global Asia* (vol. 5, no. 2 [Summer 2010]: 8–9). Professor Wang is dean of the School of International Studies at Beijing University. Reprinted with permission of *Global Asia*.

149

There seems to be a consensus among Chinese social elites that domestic problems, rather than challenges from abroad, are posing greater threats to China's political order, social cohesion, national unity, sustainable economic growth, financial stability, individual livelihood, morality and the natural environment. However, it is hard to find a consensus on what constitutes the root causes of these domestic problems, not to mention solutions to them. In observing present-day China, it is most important to bear in mind the plurality of views and expectations among Chinese themselves. For one thing, under an extraordinarily powerful Party leadership and with omnipresent government intervention in social life, few people can confidently define what the Chinese value system is, or whether a coherent value system exists besides "getting rich," "enjoying life" and "patriotism."

It is also essential to recognize the diversity of interests in China among regions, localities, industrial sectors, government agencies and social spectra. It is the competing interests that are generating different views and underlying policy debates every day in the Chinese media and on the Internet. No close watcher of China would fail to notice the pace of change in people's thinking and behavior, which is occurring as fast as new construction projects around the country. No wonder each time I have chatted with Thomas Friedman, a distinguished columnist for the *New York Times*, he would reiterate the warning that when in China, "fasten your seatbelt!"

Few Chinese would understand such a warning, and fewer would heed it. However, the top leadership—headed by President Hu Jintao and Premier Wen Jiabao—has recognized, in their own way, the need to rein in the horse after three decades of galloping economic growth. In recent years, two political slogans in China are especially worth noting. The first is to build up a "harmonious society," which should be based on fairer redistribution of wealth, improved social welfare, better education and enhanced social justice. Many policy adjustments have been made to reduce social tensions, though with varying degrees of success.

The second slogan is to "apply the scientific outlook on development," which means "putting people first and aiming at comprehensive, coordinated and sustainable development." To translate it in plainer language, the central leadership is calling for more attention to the needs and anxieties of the population rather than the simple indexes of economic growth. The government should also make greater efforts to narrow the gaps between urban and rural areas, different regions, and social spectra, and to protect the environment.

Furthermore, in the framework of "scientific outlook on development," the Chinese government has recently stressed the urgent task of "speeding up the transformation of the economic development mode." Essentially, this means to turn China's economic expansion from quantity-based to quality-oriented development by facilitating indigenous innovation. This also means to make energy savings and emission reductions a top priority. A salient feature of the continued development mode is the dependence on foreign investment and trade, and the required transformation emphasizes domestic consumption and social welfare of both the urban and rural populations.

Document 2

China's National Defense in 2010 (2011, excerpts)

Preface

In the first decade of the 21st century, the international community forged ahead in a new phase of opening up and cooperation, and at the same time faced crises and changes. Sharing opportunities for development and dealing with challenges with joint efforts have become the consensus of all countries in the world. Pulling together in the time of trouble, seeking mutual benefit and engaging in win-win cooperation are the only ways for humankind to achieve common development and prosperity.

China has now stood at a new historical point, and its future and destiny has never been more closely connected with those of the international community. In the face of shared opportunities and common challenges, China maintains its commitment to the new security concepts of mutual trust, mutual benefit, equality and coordination. By connecting the fundamental interests of the Chinese people with the common interests of other peoples around the globe, connecting China's development with that of the world, and connecting China's security with world peace, China strives to build, through its peaceful development, a harmonious world of lasting peace and common prosperity.

Looking into the second decade of the 21st century, China will continue to take advantage of this important period of strategic opportunities for national development, apply the Scientific Outlook on Development in depth, persevere on the path of peaceful development, pursue an independent foreign policy of peace and a national defense policy that is defensive in nature, map out both economic development and national defense in a unified manner and, in the process of building a society that is moderately affluent on a general basis, realize the unified goal of building a prosperous country and a strong military.

Excerpts from Information Office of the State Council of the PRC, March 31, 2011, at www.china.org.cn/government/whitepaper/node_7114675.htm.

The Security Situation

The international situation is currently undergoing profound and complex changes. The progress toward economic globalization and a multi-polar world is irreversible, as is the advance toward informationization of society. The current trend toward peace, development and cooperation is irresistible. But, international strategic competition and contradictions are intensifying, global challenges are becoming more prominent, and security threats are becoming increasingly integrated, complex and volatile.

On the whole, the world remains peaceful and stable. The international community has reaped the first fruits in joint efforts to respond to the global financial crisis. All countries have stepped up to adjust their strategies and models for economic development, and no effort has been spared in attempting to foster new economic growth points. Scientific and technological innovations are breeding new breakthroughs. And economic globalization has achieved further progress. The international balance of power is changing, most notably through the economic strength and growing international status and influence of emerging powers and developing countries. Prospects for world multi-polarization are becoming clearer. The prevailing trend is towards reform in international systems. Steady progress is being made in the establishment of mechanisms for management of the global economy and finance. G20 [the Group of 20 major economies] is playing a more outstanding role. The international spotlight has turned to the reform of the UN and other international political and security systems. Profound realignments have taken place in international relations; economic interdependence among various countries has been enhanced; shared challenges have been increasing; and communication, coordination and cooperation have become mainstream in relationships among the world's major powers. As factors conducive to maintaining peace and containing conflict continue to grow, mankind can look forward to a future that on the whole is bright.

The international security situation has become more complex. International strategic competition centering on international order, comprehensive national strength and geopolitics has intensified. Contradictions continue to surface between developed and developing countries and between traditional and emerging powers, while local conflicts and regional flashpoints are a recurrent theme. In a number of countries, outbreaks of unrest are frequently triggered off by political, economic, ethnic, or religious disputes. In general, world peace remains elusive. Deep-seated contradictions and structural problems behind the international financial crisis have not been resolved. World economic recovery remains fragile and imbalanced. Security threats posed by such global challenges as terrorism, economic insecurity, climate change, nuclear proliferation, insecurity of information, natural disasters, public health concerns, and transnational crime are on the rise. Traditional security concerns blend with non-traditional ones and domestic concerns interact with international security ones, making it hard for traditional security approaches and mechanisms to respond effectively to the various security issues and challenges in the world.

International military competition remains fierce. Major powers are stepping up the realignment of their security and military strategies, accelerating military reform, and vigorously developing new and more sophisticated military technologies. Some powers have worked out strategies for outer space, cyber space and the polar regions, developed means for prompt global strikes, accelerated development of missile defense systems, enhanced cyber operations capabilities to occupy new strategic commanding heights. Some developing countries maintain the push towards strengthening their armed forces, and press on with military modernization. Progress has been made in international arms control, but prevention of the proliferation of weapons of mass destruction remains complex, there is still much to do to maintain and strengthen the international non-proliferation mechanism.

The Asia-Pacific security situation is generally stable. Asia has taken the lead in economic recovery, and its growth as a whole has been sustained. With an enhanced sense of shared interests and destiny, Asian countries have seized the opportunities presented by economic globalization and regional economic integration, and maintained a commitment to promoting economic development and regional stability. They have persisted in multilateralism and open regionalism, actively developed bilateral and multilateral cooperation with countries inside and outside the region, and endeavored to build economic and security cooperation mechanisms with regional features. The Shanghai Cooperation Organization (SCO) is playing a growing role in promoting regional stability and development. The integration of the Association of Southeast Asian Nations (ASEAN) is moving ahead. There is growing cooperation in such mechanisms as China-ASEAN, ASEAN Plus Three (China, Japan and the Republic of Korea) and China-Japan-ROK. The Asia-Pacific Economic Cooperation (APEC) continues to make progress.

Nevertheless, Asia-Pacific security is becoming more intricate and volatile. Regional pressure points drag on and without solution in sight. There is intermittent tension on the Korean Peninsula. The security situation in Afghanistan remains serious. Political turbulence persists in some countries. Ethnic and religious discords are evident. Disputes over territorial and maritime rights and interests flare up occasionally. And terrorist, separatist and extremist activities run amok. Profound changes are taking shape in the Asia-Pacific strategic landscape. Relevant major powers are increasing their strategic investment. The United States is reinforcing its regional military alliances, and increasing its involvement in regional security affairs. . . .

The Chinese government has formulated and implemented principles and policies for advancing peaceful development of cross-Strait relations in the new situation, promoted and maintained peace and stability in the area. Significant and positive progress has been achieved in cross-Strait relations. On the basis of opposing "Taiwan independence" and adhering to the "1992 Consensus," the two sides have enhanced political mutual trust, conducted consultations and dialogues, and reached a series of agreements for realizing direct and bilateral exchanges of mail, transport and trade, as well as promoting economic and financial cooperation across the Straits. The peaceful development of cross-Strait relations accords with the interests and aspirations of compatriots on both sides of the Straits, and is widely applauded by the international community.

China is meanwhile confronted by more diverse and complex security challenges. China has vast territories and territorial seas. It is in a critical phase of the building of a moderately prosperous society in an all-round way. Therefore, it faces heavy demands in safeguarding national security. The "Taiwan independence" separatist force and its activities are still the biggest obstacle and threat to the peaceful development of cross-Strait relations. Further progress in cross-Strait relations is still confronted by some complicating factors. Separatist forces working for "East Turkistan independence" and "Tibet independence" have inflicted serious damage on national security and social stability. Pressure builds up in preserving China's territorial integrity and maritime rights and interests. Non-traditional security concerns, such as existing terrorism threats, energy, resources, finance, information and natural disasters, are on the rise. Suspicion about China, interference and countering moves against China from the outside are on the increase. The United States, in the defiance of the three Sino-US joint communiques, continues to sell weapons to Taiwan, severely impeding Sino-US relations and impairing the peaceful development of cross-Strait relations . . . .

National Defense Policy

China pursues a national defense policy which is defensive in nature. In accordance with the Constitution of the People's Republic of China and other relevant laws, the armed forces of China undertake the sacred duty of resisting foreign aggression, defending the motherland, and safeguarding overall social stability and the peaceful labor of its people. To build a fortified national defense and strong armed forces compatible with national security and development interests is a strategic task of China's modernization, and a common cause of the people of all ethnic groups.

The pursuit of a national defense policy which is defensive in nature is determined by China's development path, its fundamental aims, its foreign policy, and its historical and cultural traditions. China unswervingly takes the road of peaceful development, strives to build a harmonious socialist society internally, and promotes the building of a harmonious world enjoying lasting peace and common prosperity externally. China unswervingly advances its reform and opening up as well as socialist modernization, making use of the peaceful international environment for its own development which in return will contribute to world peace. China unswervingly pursues an independent foreign policy of peace and promotes friendly cooperation with all countries on the basis of the Five Principles of Peaceful Coexistence. China unswervingly maintains its fine cultural traditions and its belief in valuing peace above all else, advocating the settlement of disputes through peaceful means, prudence on the issue of war, and the strategy of "attacking only after being attacked." China will never seek hegemony, nor will it adopt the approach of military expansion now or in the future, no matter how its economy develops.

The two sides of the Taiwan Strait are destined to ultimate reunification in the course of the great rejuvenation of the Chinese nation. It is the responsibility of the Chinese people on both sides of the Straits to work hand in hand to end the history of hostility, and to avoid repeating the history of armed conflict between fellow countrymen. The two sides should take a positive attitude toward the future, and strive to create favorable conditions to gradually resolve, through consultation on an equal footing, both issues inherited from the past and new ones that emerge in the development of cross-Strait relations. The two sides may discuss political relations in the special situation that China is not yet reunified in a pragmatic manner. The two sides can hold contacts and exchanges on military issues at an appropriate time and talk about a military security mechanism of mutual trust, in a bid to act together to adopt measures to further stabilize cross-Strait relations and ease concerns regarding military security. The two sides should hold consultations on the basis of upholding the one-China principle to formally end hostilities and reach a peace agreement.

The goals and tasks of China's national defense in the new era are defined as follows:

• Safeguarding national sovereignty, security and interests of national development. China's national defense is tasked to guard against and resist aggression, defend the security of China's lands, inland waters, territorial waters and airspace, safeguard its maritime rights and interests, and maintain its security interests in space, electromagnetic space and cyber space. It is also tasked to oppose and contain the separatist forces for "Taiwan independence," crack down on separatist forces for "East Turkistan independence" and "Tibet independence," and defend national sovereignty and territorial integrity. National defense is both subordinate to and in service of the country's development and security strategies. It safeguards this important period of strategic opportunities for national development. China implements the military strategy of active defense of the new era, adheres to the principles of independence and self-defense by the whole nation, strengthens the construction of its armed forces and that of its border, territorial sea and territorial air defenses, and enhances national strategic capabilities. China consistently upholds the policy of no first use of nuclear weapons, adheres to a self-defensive nuclear strategy, and will never enter into a nuclear arms race with any other country.

• Maintaining social harmony and stability. The Chinese armed forces loyally follow the tenet of serving the people wholeheartedly, actively participate in and support national economic and social development, and safeguard national security and social stability in accordance with the law. Exercising to the full their advantageous conditions in human resources, equipment, technology and infrastructure, the armed forces contribute to the building of civilian infrastructure and other engineering construction projects, to poverty-alleviation initiatives, to improvements in people's livelihood, and to ecological and environmental conservation. They organize preparations for military operations other than war (MOOTW) in a scientific way, work out pre-designed strategic programs against non-traditional security threats, reinforce the building of specialized forces for emergency response, and enhance capabilities in counter-terrorism and stability maintenance, emergency rescue, and the protection of security. They resolutely undertake urgent, difficult, dangerous, and arduous tasks of emergency rescue and disaster relief, thereby securing lives and property of the people. Taking the maintenance of overall social stability as a critical task, the armed forces resolutely subdue all subversive and sabotage activities by hostile forces, as well as violent and terrorist activities. The Chinese armed forces carry on the glorious tradition of supporting the government and cherishing the people, strictly abide by state policies, laws and regulations and consolidate the unity between the military and the government and between the military and the people.

• Accelerating the modernization of national defense and the armed forces. Bearing in mind the primary goal of accomplishing mechanization and attaining major progress in informationization by 2020, the People's Liberation Army (PLA) perseveres with mechanization as the foundation and informationization as the driving force, making extensive use of its achievements in information technology, and stepping up the composite and integrated development of mechanization and informationization. The PLA has expanded and made profound preparations for military struggle, which serve as both pull and impetus to the overall development of modernization. It intensifies theoretical studies on joint operations under conditions of informationization, advances the development of high-tech weaponry and equipment, develops new types of combat forces, strives to establish joint operation systems in conditions of informationization, accelerates the transition from military training under conditions of mechanization to military training in conditions of informationization, presses ahead with implementation of the strategic project for talented people, invests greater efforts in building a modern logistics capability, and enhances its capabilities in accomplishing diversified military tasks in order to win local wars under the conditions of informationization, so as to accomplish its historical missions at the new stage in the new century. The state takes economic development and national defense building into simultaneous consideration, adopts a mode of integrated civilian-military development. It endeavors to establish and improve systems of weaponry and equipment research and manufacturing, military personnel training, and logistical support, that integrate military with civilian purposes and combine military efforts with civilian support. China vigorously and steadily advances reform of national defense and the armed forces, strengthens strategic planning and management, and endeavors to promote the scientific development of the national defense and armed forces.

• Maintaining world peace and stability. China consistently upholds the new security concepts of mutual trust, mutual benefit, equality and coordination, advocates the settlement of international disputes and regional flashpoint issues through peaceful means, opposes resort to the use or threat to use of force at will, opposes acts of aggression and expansion, and opposes hegemony and power politics in any form. China conducts military exchanges with other countries following the Five Principles of Peaceful Coexistence, develops cooperative military relations that are non-aligned, non-confrontational and not directed against any third party, and promotes the establishment of just and effective collective security mechanisms and military confidence-building mechanisms. China adheres to the concepts of openness, pragmatism and cooperation, expands its participation in international security cooperation, strengthens strategic coordination and consultation with major powers and neighboring countries, enhances military exchanges and cooperation with developing countries, and takes part in UN peace-keeping operations, maritime escort, international counter-terrorism cooperation, and disaster relief operations. In line with the principles of being just, reasonable, comprehensive and balanced, China stands for effective disarmament and arms control, and endeavors to maintain global strategic stability. . . .

Nuclear Disarmament

China has always stood for the complete prohibition and thorough destruction of nuclear weapons. China maintains that countries possessing the largest nuclear arsenals bear special and primary responsibility for nuclear disarmament. They should further drastically reduce their nuclear arsenals in a verifiable, irreversible and legally-binding manner, so as to create the necessary conditions for the complete elimination of nuclear weapons. When conditions are appropriate, other nuclear-weapon states should also join in multilateral negotiations on nuclear disarmament. To attain the ultimate goal of complete and thorough nuclear disarmament, the international community should develop, at an appropriate time, a viable, long-term plan with different phases, including the conclusion of a convention on the complete prohibition of nuclear weapons.

China holds that, before the complete prohibition and thorough destruction of nuclear weapons, all nuclear-weapon states should abandon any nuclear deterrence policy based on first use of nuclear weapons, make an unequivocal commitment that under no circumstances will they use or threaten to use nuclear weapons against non-nuclear-weapon states or nuclear-weapon-free zones, and negotiate an international legal instrument in this regard. In the meantime, nuclear-weapon states should negotiate and conclude a treaty on no-first-use of nuclear weapons against each other.

China has played a constructive role in the review process of the Treaty on the Non-Proliferation of Nuclear Weapons (NPT). Together with other signatories to the NPT, China is willing to sincerely implement the positive achievements of the Eighth NPT Review Conference in 2010. China supports the early entry into force of the Comprehensive Nuclear Test Ban Treaty (CTBT) and the early commencement of negotiations on the Fissile Material Cut-off Treaty (FMCT) at the Conference on Disarmament (CD) in Geneva.

As a permanent member of the UN Security Council and a nuclear-weapon state signatory of the NPT, China has never evaded its obligations in nuclear disarmament and pursues an open, transparent and responsible nuclear policy. It has adhered to the policy of no-first-use of nuclear weapons at any time and in any circumstances, and made the unequivocal commitment that under no circumstances will it use or threaten to use nuclear weapons against non-nuclear-weapon states or nuclear-weapon-free zones. China has never deployed nuclear weapons in foreign territory and has always exercised the utmost restraint in the development of nuclear weapons, and has never participated in any form of nuclear arms race, nor will it ever do so. It will limit its nuclear capabilities to the minimum level required for national security. . . . China consistently supports the efforts of non-nuclear-weapon states in establishing nuclear-weapon-free zones, has already signed and ratified all the relevant protocols which have been opened for signature of any nuclear-weapon-free zone treaties, and has reached agreement with the ASEAN countries on relevant issues under the Protocol of the Treaty on the Southeast Asia Nuclear-Weapon-Free Zone. China supports the Treaty on a Nuclear-Weapon-Free Zone in Central Asia and its protocols signed by Central Asian countries, and supports the establishment of a nuclear-weapon-free zone in the Middle East. . . .

China advocates resolving the nuclear issue in the Korean Peninsula peacefully through dialogues and consultations, endeavoring to balance common concerns through holding six-party talks in order to realize the denuclearization on the Korean Peninsula and maintain peace and stability of the Korean Peninsula and Northeast Asia. China, always considering the whole situation in the long run, painstakingly urges related countries to have more contacts and dialogues in order to create conditions for resuming six-party talks as early as possible. China is for the peaceful resolution of the Iranian nuclear issue through dialogue and negotiation, and for maintaining the peace and stability of the Middle East. China has been dedicated to promoting dialogue and negotiation, and has actively engaged with relevant parties to promote non-proliferation. China has attended the meetings of foreign ministers and political directors of the P5+1, and has participated in the deliberations on the Iranian nuclear issue at the UN Security Council and at the International Atomic Energy Agency (IAEA) in a constructive manner. . . .

Prevention of an Arms Race in Outer Space

The Chinese government has advocated from the outset the peaceful use of outer space, and opposes any weaponization of outer space and any arms race in outer space. China believes that the best way for the international community to prevent any weaponization of or arms race in outer space is to negotiate and conclude a relevant international legally-binding instrument.

In February 2008, China and Russia jointly submitted to the Conference on Disarmament (CD) a draft Treaty on the Prevention of the Placement of Weapons in Outer Space and the Threat or Use of Force against Outer Space Objects (PPWT). In August 2009, China and Russia jointly submitted their working paper responding to the questions and comments raised by the CD members on the draft treaty. China is looking forward to starting negotiations on the draft treaty at the earliest possible date, in order to conclude a new outer space treaty. . . .

Document 3

Charter 08
(2008, excerpts)

I. Foreword

A hundred years have passed since the writing of China's first constitution. 2008 also marks the sixtieth anniversary of the promulgation of the Universal Declaration of Human Rights, the thirtieth anniversary of the appearance of the Democracy Wall in Beijing, and the tenth anniversary of China's signing of the International Covenant on Civil and Political Rights.

We are approaching the twentieth anniversary of the 1989 Tiananmen massacre of pro-democracy student protesters. The Chinese people, who have endured human rights disasters and uncountable struggles across these same years, now include many who see clearly that freedom, equality, and human rights are universal values of humankind and that democracy and constitutional government are the fundamental framework for protecting these values.

By departing from these values, the Chinese government's approach to "modernization" has proven disastrous. It has stripped people of their rights, destroyed their dignity, and corrupted normal human intercourse. So we ask: Where is China headed in the twenty-first century? Will it continue with "modernization" under authoritarian rule, or will it embrace universal human values, join the mainstream of civilized nations, and build a democratic system? There can be no avoiding these questions. . . .

Victory over Japan in 1945 offered one more chance for China to move toward modern government, but the Communist defeat of the Nationalists in the civil war thrust the nation into the abyss of totalitarianism. The "new China" that emerged in 1949 proclaimed that "the people are sovereign" but

---

Translated from the Chinese by Perry Link, at www.charter08.eu/2.html. Published on the 60th anniversary of the UN Human Rights Declaration, December 10, 2008.

in fact set up a system in which "the Party is all-powerful." The Communist Party of China seized control of all organs of the state and all political, economic, and social resources, and, using these, has produced a long trail of human rights disasters, including, among many others, the Anti-Rightist Campaign (1957), the Great Leap Forward (1958–1960), the Cultural Revolution (1966–1969), the June Fourth [Tiananmen Square] Massacre (1989), and the current repression of all unauthorized religions and the suppression of the weiquan rights movement [a movement that aims to defend citizens' rights promulgated in the Chinese Constitution and to fight for human rights recognized by international conventions that the Chinese government has signed]. During all this, the Chinese people have paid a gargantuan price. Tens of millions have lost their lives, and several generations have seen their freedom, their happiness, and their human dignity cruelly trampled.

During the last two decades of the twentieth century the government policy of "Reform and Opening" gave the Chinese people relief from the pervasive poverty and totalitarianism of the Mao Zedong era, and brought substantial increases in the wealth and living standards of many Chinese as well as a partial restoration of economic freedom and economic rights. Civil society began to grow, and popular calls for more rights and more political freedom have grown apace. As the ruling elite itself moved toward private ownership and the market economy, it began to shift from an outright rejection of "rights" to a partial acknowledgment of them.

In 1998 the Chinese government signed two important international human rights conventions; in 2004 it amended its constitution to include the phrase "respect and protect human rights"; and this year, 2008, it has promised to promote a "national human rights action plan." Unfortunately most of this political progress has extended no further than the paper on which it is written. The political reality, which is plain for anyone to see, is that China has many laws but no rule of law; it has a constitution but no constitutional government. The ruling elite continues to cling to its authoritarian power and fights off any move toward political change. The stultifying results are endemic official corruption, an undermining of the rule of law, weak human rights, decay in public ethics, crony capitalism, growing inequality between the wealthy and the poor, pillage of the natural environment as well as of the human and historical environments, and the exacerbation of a long list of social conflicts, especially, in recent times, a sharpening animosity between officials and ordinary people.

As these conflicts and crises grow ever more intense, and as the ruling elite continues with impunity to crush and to strip away the rights of citizens to freedom, to property, and to the pursuit of happiness, we see the powerless in our society—the vulnerable groups, the people who have been suppressed and monitored, who have suffered cruelty and even torture, and who have had no adequate avenues for their protests, no courts to hear their pleas—becoming more militant and raising the possibility of a violent conflict of disastrous proportions. The decline of the current system has reached the point where change is no longer optional. . . .

[Section II. Our Fundamental Principles is omitted here.]

III. What We Advocate

Authoritarianism is in general decline throughout the world; in China, too, the era of emperors and overlords is on the way out. The time is arriving everywhere for citizens to be masters of states. For China the path that leads out of our current predicament is to divest ourselves of the authoritarian notion of reliance on an "enlightened overlord" or an "honest official" and to turn instead toward a system of liberties, democracy, and the rule of law, and toward fostering the consciousness of modern citizens who see rights as fundamental and participation as a duty. Accordingly, and in a spirit of this duty as responsible and constructive citizens, we offer the following recommendations on national governance, citizens' rights, and social development:

1. A New Constitution. We should recast our present constitution, rescinding its provisions that contradict the principle that sovereignty resides with the people and turning it into a document that genuinely guarantees human rights, authorizes the exercise of public power, and serves as the legal underpinning of China's democratization. The constitution must be the highest law in the land, beyond violation by any individual, group, or political party.

2. Separation of Powers. We should construct a modern government in which the separation of legislative, judicial, and executive power is guaranteed. We need an Administrative Law that defines the scope of government responsibility and prevents abuse of administrative power. Government should be responsible to taxpayers. Division of power between provincial governments and the central government should adhere to the principle that central powers are only those specifically granted by the constitution and all other powers belong to the local governments.

3. Legislative Democracy. Members of legislative bodies at all levels should be chosen by direct election, and legislative democracy should observe just and impartial principles.

4. An Independent Judiciary. The rule of law must be above the interests of any particular political party and judges must be independent. We need to establish a constitutional supreme court and institute procedures for constitutional review. As soon as possible, we should abolish all of the Committees on Political and Legal Affairs that now allow Communist Party

officials at every level to decide politically sensitive cases in advance and out of court. We should strictly forbid the use of public offices for private purposes.

5. Public Control of Public Servants. The military should be made answerable to the national government, not to a political party, and should be made more professional. Military personnel should swear allegiance to the constitution and remain nonpartisan. Political party organizations must be prohibited in the military. All public officials including police should serve as nonpartisans, and the current practice of favoring one political party in the hiring of public servants must end.

6. Guarantee of Human Rights. There must be strict guarantees of human rights and respect for human dignity. There should be a Human Rights Committee, responsible to the highest legislative body, that will prevent the government from abusing public power in violation of human rights. A democratic and constitutional China especially must guarantee the personal freedom of citizens. No one should suffer illegal arrest, detention, arraignment, interrogation, or punishment. The system of "Reeducation through Labor" must be abolished.

7. Election of Public Officials. There should be a comprehensive system of democratic elections based on "one person, one vote." The direct election of administrative heads at the levels of county, city, province, and nation should be systematically implemented. The rights to hold periodic free elections and to participate in them as a citizen are inalienable.

8. Rural–Urban Equality. The two-tier household registry system must be abolished. This system favors urban residents and harms rural residents. We should establish instead a system that gives every citizen the same constitutional rights and the same freedom to choose where to live.

9. Freedom to Form Groups. The right of citizens to form groups must be guaranteed. The current system for registering nongovernment groups, which requires a group to be "approved," should be replaced by a system in which a group simply registers itself. The formation of political parties should be governed by the constitution and the laws, which means that we must abolish the special privilege of one party to monopolize power and must guarantee principles of free and fair competition among political parties.

10. Freedom to Assemble. The constitution provides that peaceful assembly, demonstration, protest, and freedom of expression are fundamental rights of a citizen. The ruling party and the government must not be permitted to subject these to illegal interference or unconstitutional obstruction.

11. Freedom of Expression. We should make freedom of speech, freedom of the press, and academic freedom universal, thereby guaranteeing that citizens can be informed and can exercise their right of political supervision. These freedoms should be upheld by a Press Law that abolishes political restrictions on the press. The provision in the current Criminal Law

that refers to "the crime of incitement to subvert state power" must be abolished. We should end the practice of viewing words as crimes.

12. Freedom of Religion. We must guarantee freedom of religion and belief, and institute a separation of religion and state. There must be no governmental interference in peaceful religious activities. We should abolish any laws, regulations, or local rules that limit or suppress the religious freedom of citizens. We should abolish the current system that requires religious groups (and their places of worship) to get official approval in advance and substitute for it a system in which registry is optional and, for those who choose to register, automatic.

13. Civic Education. In our schools we should abolish political curriculums and examinations that are designed to indoctrinate students in state ideology and to instill support for the rule of one party. We should replace them with civic education that advances universal values and citizens' rights, fosters civic consciousness, and promotes civic virtues that serve society.

14. Protection of Private Property. We should establish and protect the right to private property and promote an economic system of free and fair markets. We should do away with government monopolies in commerce and industry and guarantee the freedom to start new enterprises. We should establish a Committee on State-Owned Property, reporting to the national legislature, that will monitor the transfer of state-owned enterprises to private ownership in a fair, competitive, and orderly manner. We should institute a land reform that promotes private ownership of land, guarantees the right to buy and sell land, and allows the true value of private property to be adequately reflected in the market.

15. Financial and Tax Reform. We should establish a democratically regulated and accountable system of public finance that ensures the protection of taxpayer rights and that operates through legal procedures. We need a system by which public revenues that belong to a certain level of government—central, provincial, county or local—are controlled at that level. We need major tax reform that will abolish any unfair taxes, simplify the tax system, and spread the tax burden fairly. Government officials should not be able to raise taxes, or institute new ones, without public deliberation and the approval of a democratic assembly. We should reform the ownership system in order to encourage competition among a wider variety of market participants.

16. Social Security. We should establish a fair and adequate social security system that covers all citizens and ensures basic access to education, health care, retirement security, and employment.

17. Protection of the Environment. We need to protect the natural environment and to promote development in a way that is sustainable and responsible to our descendants and to the rest of humanity. This means insisting that the state and its officials at all levels not only do what they

must do to achieve these goals, but also accept the supervision and participation of nongovernmental organizations.

18. A Federated Republic. A democratic China should seek to act as a
responsible major power contributing toward peace and development in the
Asian Pacific region by approaching others in a spirit of equality and fairness. In Hong Kong and Macao, we should support the freedoms that
already exist. With respect to Taiwan, we should declare our commitment to
the principles of freedom and democracy and then, negotiating as equals
and ready to compromise, seek a formula for peaceful unification. We
should approach disputes in the national-minority areas of China with an
open mind, seeking ways to find a workable framework within which all
ethnic and religious groups can flourish. We should aim ultimately at a federation of democratic communities of China.

19. Truth in Reconciliation. We should restore the reputations of all
people, including their family members, who suffered political stigma in the
political campaigns of the past or who have been labeled as criminals
because of their thought, speech, or faith. The state should pay reparations
to these people. All political prisoners and prisoners of conscience must be
released. There should be a Truth Investigation Commission charged with
finding the facts about past injustices and atrocities, determining responsibility for them, upholding justice, and, on these bases, seeking social reconciliation.

China, as a major nation of the world, as one of five permanent members of the United Nations Security Council, and as a member of the UN
Council on Human Rights, should be contributing to peace for humankind
and progress toward human rights. Unfortunately, we stand today as the
only country among the major nations that remains mired in authoritarian
politics. Our political system continues to produce human rights disasters
and social crises, thereby not only constricting China's own development
but also limiting the progress of all of human civilization. This must
change, truly it must. The democratization of Chinese politics can be put off
no longer.

Accordingly, we dare to put civic spirit into practice by announcing
Charter 08. We hope that our fellow citizens who feel a similar sense of crisis, responsibility, and mission, whether they are inside the government or
not, and regardless of their social status, will set aside small differences to
embrace the broad goals of this citizens' movement. Together we can work
for major changes in Chinese society and for the rapid establishment of a
free, democratic, and constitutional country. We can bring to reality the
goals and ideals that our people have incessantly been seeking for more
than a hundred years, and can bring a brilliant new chapter to Chinese civilization.

Document 4

Open Letter of Party Elders (October 11, 2010)

Dear members of the Standing Committee of the National People's Congress:

Article 35 of China's Constitution as adopted in 1982 clearly states that: "Citizens of the People's Republic of China enjoy freedom of speech, of the press, of assembly, of association, of procession and of demonstration." For 28 years this article has stood unrealized, having been negated by detailed rules and regulations for "implementation." This false democracy of formal avowal and concrete denial has become a scandalous mark on the history of world democracy.

On February 26, 2003, at a meeting of democratic consultation between the Standing Committee of the Political Bureau of the Central Committee of the Chinese Communist Party and democratic parties, not long after President Hu Jintao assumed office, he stated clearly: "The removal of restrictions on the press, and the opening up of public opinion positions, is a mainstream view and demand held by society; it is natural, and should be resolved through the legislative process. If the Communist Party does not reform itself, if it does not transform, it will lose its vitality and move toward natural and inevitable extinction."

On October 3, America's Cable News Network (CNN) aired an interview with Chinese Premier Wen Jiabao by anchor Fareed Zakaria. Responding to the journalist's questions, Wen Jiabao said: "Freedom of speech is indispensable for any nation; China's Constitution endows the people with freedom of speech; The demands of the people for democracy cannot be resisted."

In accord with China's Constitution, and in the spirit of the remarks made by President Hu Jintao and Premier Wen Jiabao, we hereupon repre-

---

"Enforce Article 35 of China's Constitution, Abolish Censorship and Realize Citizens' Right to Freedom of Speech and Freedom of Press: A Letter to the Standing Committee of the National People's Congress," taken from David Mandurski, China Media Project at the University of Hong Kong, at http://cmp.hku.hk/2010/10/13/8035/.

sent the following concerning the materialization of the constitutional rights to freedom of speech and of the press:

Concerning the Current State of Freedom of Speech and Press in Our Country:

We have for 61 years "served as master" in the name of the citizens of the People's Republic of China. But the freedom of speech and of the press we now enjoy is inferior even to that of Hong Kong before its return to Chinese sovereignty, to that entrusted to the residents of a colony.

Before the handover, Hong Kong was a British colony, governed by those appointed by the Queen's government. But the freedom of speech and freedom of the press given to residents of Hong Kong by the British authorities there was not empty, appearing only on paper. It was enacted and realized.

When our country was founded in 1949, our people cried that they had been liberated, that they were not their own masters. Mao Zedong said that, "From this moment, the people of China have stood up." But even today, 61 years after the founding of our nation, after 30 years of opening and reform, we have not yet attained freedom of speech and freedom of the press to the degree enjoyed by the people of Hong Kong under colonial rule. Even now, many books [on] political and current affairs must be published in Hong Kong. This is not something that dates from the [territory's] return, but is merely an old tactic familiar under colonial rule. The "master" status of the people of China's mainland is so inferior. For our nation to advertise itself as having "socialist democracy" with Chinese characteristics is such an embarrassment.

Not only the average citizen, but even the most senior leaders of the Communist Party have no freedom of speech or press. Recently, Li Rui met with the following circumstance. Not long ago, the *Collected Works in Memory of Zhou Xiaozhou* were published, and in it was originally to be included an essay commemorating Zhou Xiaozhou that Li Rui had written for the *People's Daily* in 1981. Zhou Xiaozhou's wife phoned Li Rui to explain the situation: "Beijing has sent out a notice. Li Rui's writings cannot be published." What incredible folly it is that an old piece of writing from a Party newspaper cannot be included in a volume of collected works! Li Rui said: "What kind of country is this?! I want to cry it out: the press must be free! Such strangling of the people's freedom of expression is entirely illegal!"

It's not even just high-level leaders—even the Premier of our country does not have freedom of speech or of the press! On August 21, 2010, Premier Wen Jiabao gave a speech in Shenzhen called, "Only By Pushing Ahead With Reforms Can Our Nation Have Bright Prospects." He said, "We must not only push economic reforms, but must also promote political reforms. Without the protection afforded by political reforms, the gains we have made from economic reforms will be lost, and our goal of modernization cannot be realized." Xinhua News Agency's official news release on August 21, "Building a Beautiful Future for the Special Economic Zone," omitted the content in Wen Jiabao's speech dealing with political reform.

On September 22, 2010, Premier Wen Jiabao held a dialogue in New York with American Chinese media and media from Hong Kong and Macao, and again he emphasized the importance of "political system reforms." Wen said: "Concerning political reforms, I have said previously that if economic reforms are without the protection to be gained by political reforms, then we cannot be entirely successful, and even perhaps the gains of our progress so far will be lost." Shortly after, Wen Jiabao addressed the 65th Session of the United Nations General Assembly, giving a speech called, "Recognizing a True China," in which he spoke again about political reform. Late on September 23 (Beijing time), these events were reported on China Central Television's Xinwen Lianbo and in an official news release from Xinhua News Agency. They reported only Wen Jiabao's remarks on the circumstances facing overseas Chinese, and on the importance of overseas Chinese media. His mentions of political reform were all removed.

For these matters, if we endeavor to find those responsible, we are utterly incapable of putting our finger on a specific person. [They are] invisible black hands. For their own reasons, they violate our constitution, often ordering by telephone that the works of such and such a person cannot be published, or that such and such an event cannot be reported in the media. The officials who make the call do not leave their names, and the secrecy of the agents is protected, but you must heed their phone instructions. These invisible black hands are our Central Propaganda Department. Right now the Central Propaganda Department is placed above the Central Committee of the Communist Party, and above the State Council. We would ask, what right does the Central Propaganda Department have to muzzle the speech of the Premier? What right does it have to rob the people of our nation of their right to know what the Premier has said?

Our core demand is that the system of censorship be dismantled in favor of a system of legal responsibility.

The rights to freedom of speech and the press guaranteed in Article 35 of our Constitution are turned into mere adornments for the walls by means of concrete implementation rules such as the "Ordinance on Publishing Control." These implementation rules are, broadly speaking, a system of censorship and approvals. There are countless numbers of commandments and taboos restricting freedom of speech and freedom of the press. The creation of a press law and the abolishment of the censorship system has already become an urgent task before us.

We recommend that the National People's Congress work immediately toward the creation of a Press Law, and that the "Ordinance on Publishing Control" and all of the local restrictions on news and publishing be annulled. Institutionally speaking, the realization of freedom of speech and freedom of the press as guaranteed in the Constitution means making media independent of the Party and government organs that presently control them, thereby transforming "Party mouthpieces" into "public instruments." Therefore, the foundation of the creation of a Press Law must be the enacting of a system of [post facto] legal responsibility [determined according to fair laws]. We cannot again strengthen the censorship system in the name of "strengthening the leadership of the Party." The so-called censorship system is the system by which prior to publication one must receive the approval of Party organs, allowing for publication only after approval and designating all unapproved published materials as illegal. The so-called system of legal responsibility means that published materials need not pass through approval by Party or government organs, but may be published as soon as the editor-in-chief deems fit. If there are unfavorable outcomes or disputes following publication, the government would be able to intervene and determine according to the law whether there are cases of wrongdoing. In countries around the world, the development of rule of law in news and publishing has followed this path, [enabling] a transition from systems of censorship to systems of legal responsibility. There is little doubt that systems of legal responsibility mark progress over systems of censorship, and this is greatly in the favor of the development of the humanities and natural sciences, and in promoting social harmony and historical progress. England did away with censorship in 1695. France abolished its censorship system in 1881, and the publication of newspapers and periodicals thereafter required only a simple declaration, which was signed by the representatives of the publication and mailed to the office of the procurator of the republic. Our present system of censorship leaves news and book publishing in our country 315 years behind England and 129 years behind France.

Our specific demands are as follows:

1. Abolish sponsoring institutions of media, allowing publishing institutions to independently operate; truly implement a system in which directors and editors in chief are responsible for their publication units.

2. Respect journalists, and make them strong. Journalists should be the "uncrowned kings." The reporting of mass incidents and exposing of official corruption are noble missions on behalf of the people, and this work should be protected and supported. Immediately put a stop to the unconstitutional behavior of various local governments and police in arresting journalists. Look into the circumstances behind the case of [writer] Xie

Chaoping. Liang Fengmin, the party secretary of Weinan city, must face party discipline as a warning to others.

3. Abolish restrictions on extra-territorial supervision by public opinion [and watchdog journalism] by media, ensuring the right of journalists to carry out reporting freely throughout the country.

4. The internet is an important discussion platform for information in our society and the voice of citizens' views. Aside from information that truly concerns our national secrets and speech that violates a citizen's right to privacy, internet regulatory bodies must not arbitrarily delete online posts and online comments. Online spies must be abolished, the "Fifty-cent Party" must be abolished, and restrictions on "tunneling/[anti-censorship]" technologies must be abolished.

5. There are no more taboos concerning our Party's history. Chinese citizens have a right to know the errors of the ruling party.

6. *Southern Weekly* and *Yanhuang Chunqiu* should be permitted to restructure as privately operated pilot programs [in independent media]. The privatization of newspapers and periodicals is the [natural] direction of political reforms. History teaches us: when rulers and deliberators are highly unified, when the government and the media are both surnamed "Party," and when [the Party] sings for its own pleasure, it is difficult to connect with the will of the people and attain true leadership. From the time of the Great Leap Forward to the time of the Cultural Revolution, newspapers, magazines, television and radio in the mainland have never truly reflected the will of the people. Party and government leaders have been insensitive to dissenting voices, so they have had difficulty in recognizing and correcting wholesale errors. For a ruling party and government to use the tax monies of the people to run media that sing their own praises, this is something not permitted in democratic nations.

7. Permit the free circulation within the mainland of books and periodicals from the already returned territories of Hong Kong and Macao. Our country has joined the World Trade Organization, and economically we have already integrated with the world—attempting to remain closed culturally goes against the course already plotted for opening and reform. Hong Kong and Macao offer advanced culture right at our nation's door, and the books and periodicals of Hong Kong and Macao are welcomed and trusted by the people.

8. Transform the functions of various propaganda organs, so that they are transformed from [agencies] setting down so many "taboos" to [agencies] protecting the accuracy, timeliness and unimpeded flow [of information]; from [agencies] that assist corrupt officials in suppressing and controlling stories that reveal the truth to [agencies] that support the media in monitoring Party and government organs; from [agencies] that close publications, fire editors and arrest journalists to [agencies] that

oppose power and protect media and journalists. Our propaganda organs have a horrid reputation within the Party and in society. They must work for good in order to regain their reputations. At the appropriate time, we can consider renaming these propaganda organs to suit global trends.

We pressingly represent ourselves, hoping for your utmost attention.

Sponsors:

Li Rui—former standing vice minister of the Organization Department of the CCP Central Committee, member of the 12th Central Committee of the CCP

Hu Jiwei—former director of *People's Daily*, standing committee member to the 7th National People's Congress, director of the Federation of Chinese Communication Institutes.

Jiang Ping—former head of the China University of Political Science and Law, tenured professor, standing committee member to the 7th National People's Congress, deputy director of the Executive Law Committee of the NPC

Li Pu—former deputy director of Xinhua News Agency

Zhou Shaoming—former deputy director of the Political Department of the Guangzhou Military Area Command

Zhong Peizhang—former head of the News Office of the Central Propaganda Department

Wang Yongcheng—professor at Shanghai Jiaotong University

Zhang Zhongpei—researcher at the Imperial Palace Museum, chairman of the China Archaeological Society

Du Guang— former professor at the Central Party School

Guo Daojun—former editor-in-chief of *China Legal Science*

Xiao Mo—former head of the Architecture Research Center of the Chinese National Academy of Arts

Zhuang Puming—former deputy director of People's Press

Hu Fuchen—former director and editor-in-chief at China Worker's Publishing House

Zhang Ding—former director of the China Social Sciences Press at the Chinese Academy of Social Sciences

Yu You—former editor-in-chief of *China Daily*

Ouyang Jin—former editor-in-chief of Hong Kong's *Pacific Magazine*

Yu Haocheng—former director of Masses Publishing House

Zhang Qing—former director of China Cinema Publishing House

Yu Yueting—former director of Fujian Television, veteran journalist

Sha Yexin—former head of the Shanghai People's Art and Drama Academy, now an independent writer of the Hui ethnic minority

Sun Xupei—former director of the News Research Institute at the Chinese Academy of Social Sciences

Xin Ziling—former director of the editorial desk at China National Defense University

Tie Liu—editor-in-chief of *Wangshi Weihen* (Scars of the Past) magazine.

Legal Counsel:

Song Yue—Chinese citizen, practicing lawyer in the State of New York, U.S.

Document 5

US-China Joint Statement (January 19, 2011, excerpts)

1. At the invitation of President Barack Obama of the United States of America, President Hu Jintao of the People's Republic of China is paying a state visit to the United States of America from January 18–21, 2011. During his visit, President Hu met with Vice President Joseph Biden, will meet with U.S. Congressional leadership, and will visit Chicago.

2. The two Presidents reviewed the progress made in the relationship since President Obama's November 2009 State Visit to China and reaffirmed their commitment to building a positive, cooperative, and comprehensive U.S.-China relationship for the 21st century, which serves the interests of the American and Chinese peoples and of the global community. The two sides reaffirmed that the three Joint Communiqués issued by the United States and China laid the political foundation for the relationship and will continue to guide the development of U.S.-China relations. The two sides reaffirmed respect for each other's sovereignty and territorial integrity. The Presidents further reaffirmed their commitment to the November 2009 U.S.-China Joint Statement.

3. The United States and China committed to work together to build a cooperative partnership based on mutual respect and mutual benefit in order to promote the common interests of both countries and to address the 21st century's opportunities and challenges. The United States and China are actively cooperating on a wide range of security, economic, social, energy, and environmental issues which require deeper bilateral engagement and coordination. The two leaders agreed that broader and deeper collaboration with international partners and institutions is required to develop and implement sustainable solutions and to promote peace, stability, prosperity, and the well-being of peoples throughout the world.

The White House, Office of the Press Secretary, at www.whitehouse.gov/the-press -office/2011/01/19/us-china-joint-statement.

Strengthening U.S.-China Relations

4. Recognizing the importance of the common challenges that they face together, the United States and China decided to continue working toward a partnership that advances common interests, addresses shared concerns, and highlights international responsibilities. The two leaders recognize that the relationship between the United States and China is both vital and complex. The United States and China have set an example of positive and cooperative relations between countries, despite different political systems, historical and cultural backgrounds, and levels of economic development. The two sides agreed to work further to nurture and deepen bilateral strategic trust to enhance their relations. They reiterated the importance of deepening dialogue aimed at expanding practical cooperation and affirmed the need to work together to address areas of disagreement, expand common ground, and strengthen coordination on a range of issues.

5. The United States reiterated that it welcomes a strong, prosperous, and successful China that plays a greater role in world affairs. China welcomes the United States as an Asia-Pacific nation that contributes to peace, stability and prosperity in the region. Working together, both leaders support efforts to build a more stable, peaceful, and prosperous Asia-Pacific region for the 21st century.

6. Both sides underscored the importance of the Taiwan issue in U.S.-China relations. The Chinese side emphasized that the Taiwan issue concerns China's sovereignty and territorial integrity, and expressed the hope that the U.S. side will honor its relevant commitments and appreciate and support the Chinese side's position on this issue. The U.S. side stated that the United States follows its one China policy and abides by the principles of the three U.S.-China Joint Communiqués. The United States applauded the Economic Cooperation Framework Agreement between the two sides of the Taiwan Strait and welcomed the new lines of communications developing between them. The United States supports the peaceful development of relations across the Taiwan Strait and looks forward to efforts by both sides to increase dialogues and interactions in economic, political, and other fields, and to develop more positive and stable cross-Strait relations.

7. The United States and China reiterated their commitment to the promotion and protection of human rights, even as they continue to have significant differences on these issues. The United States stressed that the promotion of human rights and democracy is an important part of its foreign policy. China stressed that there should be no interference in any country's internal affairs. The United States and China underscored that each country and its people have the right to choose their own path, and all countries should respect each other's choice of a development model. Addressing differences on human rights in a spirit of equality and mutual respect, as well

as promoting and protecting human rights consistent with international instruments, the two sides agreed to hold the next round of the U.S.-China Human Rights Dialogue before the third round of the Strategic and Economic Dialogue (S&ED).

8. The United States and China agreed to hold the next round of the resumed Legal Experts Dialogue before the next Human Rights Dialogue convenes. The United States and China further agreed to strengthen cooperation in the field of law and exchanges on the rule of law. The United States and China are actively exploring exchanges and discussions on the increasing role of women in society.

9. The United States and China affirmed that a healthy, stable, and reliable military-to-military relationship is an essential part of President Obama's and President Hu's shared vision for a positive, cooperative, and comprehensive U.S.-China relationship. Both sides agreed on the need for enhanced and substantive dialogue and communication at all levels: to reduce misunderstanding, misperception, and miscalculation; to foster greater understanding and expand mutual interest; and to promote the healthy, stable, and reliable development of the military-to-military relationship. Both sides noted the successful visit of Secretary of Defense Robert Gates to China earlier this month, and that the United States welcomed Chief of the PLA General Staff General Chen Bingde to the United States in the first half of 2011. Both sides reaffirmed that the Defense Consultative Talks, the Defense Policy Coordination Talks, and the Military Maritime Consultative Agreement will remain important channels of communication in the future. Both sides will work to execute the seven priority areas for developing military-to-military relations as agreed to by Secretary Gates and General Xu Caihou, Vice Chairman of the Central Military Commission in October 2009.

10. The United States and China agreed to take specific actions to deepen dialogue and exchanges in the field of space. The United States invited a Chinese delegation to visit NASA headquarters and other appropriate NASA facilities in 2011 to reciprocate for the productive visit of the U.S. NASA Administrator to China in 2010. The two sides agreed to continue discussions on opportunities for practical future cooperation in the space arena, based on principles of transparency, reciprocity, and mutual benefit.

11. The United States and China acknowledged the accomplishments under the bilateral Agreement on Cooperation in Science and Technology, one of the longest-standing bilateral agreements between the two countries, and welcomed the signing of its extension. The United States and China will continue to cooperate in such diverse areas as agriculture, health, energy, environment, fisheries, student exchanges, and technological innovation in order to advance mutual well-being.

12. The United States and China welcomed progress by the U.S.-China Joint Liaison Group on Law Enforcement Cooperation (JLG) to strengthen

law enforcement cooperation across a range of issues, including counterterrorism. The United States and China also agreed to enhance joint efforts to combat corruption through bilateral and other means. . . .

Addressing Regional and Global Challenges

16. The two sides believe that the United States and China have a common interest in promoting peace and security in the Asia-Pacific region and beyond, and agreed to enhance communication and coordination to address pressing regional and global challenges. The two sides undertake to act to protect the global environment and to work in concert on global issues to help safeguard and promote the sustainable development of all countries and peoples. Specifically, the United States and China agreed to advance cooperation to: counter violent extremism; prevent the proliferation of nuclear weapons, other weapons of mass destruction, and their means of delivery; strengthen nuclear security; eliminate infectious disease and hunger; end extreme poverty; respond effectively to the challenge of climate change; counter piracy; prevent and mitigate disasters; address cybersecurity; fight transnational crime; and combat trafficking in persons. In coordination with other parties, the United States and China will endeavor to increase cooperation to address common concerns and promote shared interests.

17. The United States and China underlined their commitment to the eventual realization of a world without nuclear weapons and the need to strengthen the international nuclear non-proliferation regime to address the threats of nuclear proliferation and nuclear terrorism. In this regard, both sides support early entry into force of the Comprehensive Nuclear Test Ban Treaty (CTBT), reaffirmed their support for the early commencement of negotiations on a Fissile Material Cutoff Treaty in the Conference on Disarmament, and agreed to work together to reach these goals. The two sides also noted their deepening cooperation on nuclear security following the Washington Nuclear Security Summit and signed a Memorandum of Understanding that will help establish a Center of Excellence on Nuclear Security in China.

18. The United States and China agreed on the critical importance of maintaining peace and stability on the Korean Peninsula as underscored by the Joint Statement of September 19, 2005 and relevant UN Security Council Resolutions. Both sides expressed concern over heightened tensions on the Peninsula triggered by recent developments. The two sides noted their continuing efforts to cooperate closely on matters concerning the Peninsula. The United States and China emphasized the importance of an improvement in North-South relations and agreed that sincere and constructive inter-Korean dialogue is an essential step. Agreeing on the crucial

importance of denuclearization of the Peninsula in order to preserve peace and stability in Northeast Asia, the United States and China reiterated the need for concrete and effective steps to achieve the goal of denuclearization and for full implementation of the other commitments made in the September 19, 2005 Joint Statement of the Six-Party Talks. In this context, the United States and China expressed concern regarding the DPRK's claimed uranium enrichment program. Both sides oppose all activities inconsistent with the 2005 Joint Statement and relevant international obligations and commitments. The two sides called for the necessary steps that would allow for early resumption of the Six-Party Talks process to address this and other relevant issues.

19. On the Iranian nuclear issue, the United States and China reiterated their commitment to seeking a comprehensive and long-term solution that would restore international confidence in the exclusively peaceful nature of Iran's nuclear program. Both sides agreed that Iran has the right to peaceful uses of nuclear energy under the Non-Proliferation Treaty and that Iran should fulfill its due international obligations under that treaty. Both sides called for full implementation of all relevant UN Security Council Resolutions. The United States and China welcomed and will actively participate in the P5+1 process with Iran, and stressed the importance of all parties—including Iran—committing to a constructive dialogue process.

20. Regarding Sudan, the United States and China agreed to fully support the North-South peace process, including full and effective implementation of Sudan's Comprehensive Peace Agreement. The two sides stressed the need for all sides to respect the result of a free, fair, and transparent referendum. Both the United States and China expressed concern on the Darfur issue and believed that further, substantive progress should be made in the political process in Darfur to promote the early, comprehensive, and appropriate solution to this issue. Both the United States and China have a continuing interest in the maintenance of peace and stability in the wider region.

21. The two sides agreed to enhance communication and coordination in the Asia-Pacific region in a spirit of mutual respect and cooperation, and to work together with other Asia-Pacific countries, including through multilateral institutions, to promote peace, stability, and prosperity.

Building a Comprehensive and Mutually Beneficial Economic Partnership

22. President Obama and President Hu recognized the vital importance of working together to build a cooperative economic partnership of mutual respect and mutual benefit to both countries and to the global economy. The two leaders agreed to promote comprehensive economic cooperation, and will develop further a framework of comprehensive economic cooperation,

relying on existing mechanisms, by the third round of the S&ED in May, based on the main elements outlined below.

23. The two sides agreed to strengthen macroeconomic communication and cooperation, in support of strong, sustainable and balanced growth in the United States, China and the global economy:

The United States will focus on reducing its medium-term federal deficit and ensuring long-term fiscal sustainability, and will maintain vigilance against excess volatility in exchange rates. The Federal Reserve has taken important steps in recent years to increase the clarity of its communications regarding its outlook and longer run objectives.

China will intensify efforts to expand domestic demand, to promote private investment in the service sector, and to give greater play to the fundamental role of the market in resource allocation. China will continue to promote RMB exchange rate reform and enhance RMB exchange rate flexibility, and promote the transformation of its economic development model.

Both sides agree to continue to pursue forward-looking monetary policies with due regard to the ramifications of those policies for the international economy.

The two sides affirmed support for efforts by European leaders to reinforce market stability and promote sustainable, long-term growth.

24. The two countries, recognizing the importance of open trade and investment in fostering economic growth, job creation, innovation, and prosperity, affirmed their commitment to take further steps to liberalize global trade and investment, and to oppose trade and investment protectionism. The two sides also agreed to work proactively to resolve bilateral trade and investment disputes in a constructive, cooperative, and mutually beneficial manner. . . .

Cooperating on Climate Change, Energy and the Environment

36. The two sides view climate change and energy security as two of the greatest challenges of our time. The United States and China agreed to continue their close consultations on action to address climate change, coordinate to achieve energy security for our peoples and the world, build on existing clean energy cooperation, ensure open markets, promote mutually beneficial investment in climate friendly energy, encourage clean energy, and facilitate advanced clean energy technology development.

37. Both sides applauded the progress made in clean energy and energy security since the launch of the U.S.-China Clean Energy Research Center, Renewable Energy Partnership, U.S.-China Joint Statement on Energy Security Cooperation, and Energy Cooperation Program (ECP). Both sides

reaffirmed their ongoing exchanges on energy policy and cooperation on oil, natural gas (including shale gas), civilian nuclear energy, wind and solar energy, smart grid, advanced bio-fuels, clean coal, energy efficiency, electric vehicles and clean energy technology standards.

38. The two sides commended the progress made since the launch of the U.S.-China Ten Year Framework on Energy and Environment Cooperation (TYF) in 2008. They agreed to further strengthen practical cooperation under the TYF, carry out action plans in the priority areas of water, air, transportation, electricity, protected areas, wetlands, and energy efficiency, engage in policy dialogues, and implement the EcoPartnerships program. The United States and China were also pleased to announce two new EcoPartnerships. The two sides welcomed local governments, enterprises, and research institutes of the two countries to participate in the TYF, and jointly explore innovative models for U.S.-China energy and environment cooperation. The two sides welcomed the cooperation projects and activities which will be carried out in 2011 under the TYF.

39. The two sides welcomed the Cancun agreements and believed that it is important that efforts to address climate change also advance economic and social development. Working together and with other countries, the two sides agreed to actively promote the comprehensive, effective, and sustained implementation of the United Nations Framework Convention on Climate Change, including the implementation of the Cancun agreements and support efforts to achieve positive outcomes at this year's conference in South Africa.

Expanding People-to-People Exchanges

40. The United States and China have long supported deeper and broader people-to-people ties as part of a larger effort to build a cooperative partnership based on mutual respect and mutual benefit. Both sides agreed to take concrete steps to enhance these people-to-people exchanges. Both sides noted with satisfaction the successful Expo 2010 Shanghai, and the Chinese side complimented the United States on its USA Pavilion. The two sides announced the launch of a U.S.-China Governors Forum and decided to further support exchanges and cooperation at local levels in a variety of fields, including support for the expansion of the sister province and city relationships. The United States and China also agreed to take concrete steps to strengthen dialogue and exchanges between their young people, particularly through the 100,000 Strong Initiative. The United States warmly welcomes more Chinese students in American educational institutions, and will continue to facilitate visa issuance for them. The two sides agreed to discuss

ways of expanding cultural interaction, including exploring a U.S.-China cultural year event and other activities. The two sides underscored their commitment to further promoting and facilitating increased tourism. The United States and China agreed that all these activities help deepen understanding, trust, and cooperation.

Conclusion

41. President Hu Jintao expressed his thanks to President Obama and the American people for their warm reception and hospitality during his visit. The two Presidents agreed that the visit has furthered U.S.-China relations, and both sides resolved to work together to build a cooperative partnership based on mutual respect and mutual benefit. The two Presidents shared a deep belief that a stronger U.S.-China relationship not only serves the fundamental interests of their respective peoples, but also benefits the entire Asia-Pacific region and the world.

Document 6

Joint Statement on the US-China Strategic and Economic Dialogue Outcomes of the Strategic Track (May 3–4, 2012, excerpts)

At the Fourth Round of the U.S.-China Strategic and Economic Dialogue (S&ED) May 3–4, 2012, Secretary of State Hillary Rodham Clinton, special representative of President Barack Obama, and State Councilor Dai Bingguo, special representative of President Hu Jintao, chaired the Strategic Track, which included participation from senior officials from across both governments. The two sides held in-depth discussions on major bilateral, regional, and global issues and reviewed progress over the four rounds of the S&ED in deepening strategic trust and advancing President Barack Obama and President Hu Jintao's shared vision for building a U.S.-China cooperative partnership based on mutual respect and mutual benefit. The dialogue on the Strategic Track produced the following specific outcomes and areas for further cooperation. The United States and China:

I. Promoting High-Level Exchanges

1. Reviewed President Barack Obama's meeting with President Hu Jintao on the margins of the Nuclear Security Summit in Seoul, the successful reciprocal visits of Vice President Joseph Biden and Vice President Xi Jinping, and other high-level engagement since the last round of the S&ED. The two sides noted that upcoming meetings such as the G-20 Summit and the East Asia Summit provide further opportunities for high-level engagement.

II. Bilateral Dialogues and Consultations

2. Held the second round of the China-US Strategic Security Dialogue (SSD) and had candid and in-depth exchange of views on issues relating to the strategic and comprehensive security of the two countries. The dialogue

US Department of State, Office of the Spokesperson, May 4, 2012, at www .state.gov/r/pa/prs/ps/2012/05/189287.htm.

was co-chaired by Deputy Secretary of State William Burns on the U.S. side and Vice Foreign Minister Zhang Zhijun on the Chinese side, who were joined by Acting Undersecretary of Defense James Miller, Deputy Chief of the General Staff of the PLA Ma Xiaotian and others from the relevant departments of the two countries. The two sides commented positively on the role of the SSD and decided to continue working together to develop the mechanism to increase mutual trust and manage differences between the two countries and look forward to holding another round next year.

3. Decided to hold a fourth round of the U.S.-China Asia-Pacific Consultations in the second half of 2012. Acknowledging our common interests and challenges in the region and shared goal of maintaining peace, stability, and prosperity, the two sides decided to further implement the program to carry out multilateral cooperation in such areas as food security, urban search and rescue, and disaster relief capacity building in the Asia-Pacific region reached by Secretary of State Hillary Clinton and Foreign Minister Yang Jiechi at the ASEAN Regional Forum in 2011.

4. Affirmed their commitment to continuing constructive bilateral dialogue on human rights on the basis of equality and mutual respect and decided to hold the bilateral Human Rights Dialogue in Washington, D.C., in summer 2012.

5. Noted the conclusion of the bilateral Legal Experts Dialogue in Beijing in April 2012 and confirmed their intention to hold the next round of the Legal Experts Dialogue in the United States in 2013.

6. Held the Policy Planning talks on the margins of the fourth round of the S&ED. The two sides decided to hold a U.S.-China consultation on Middle East affairs at a time and place to be decided. The two sides further decided to hold the next round of sub-dialogues on Policy Planning, Africa, Latin America, South Asia, and Central Asia on a regular basis and to enhance bilateral coordination and cooperation on regional and international issues.

7. Reaffirmed their intention to enhance communication and cooperation on major international security and other nonproliferation issues on the basis of mutual respect, equality, and mutual benefit. The two sides decided to hold the next rounds of the Security Dialogue and the Nonproliferation Dialogue on dates to be decided by both sides.

8. Decided to work to deepen and improve law enforcement cooperation to address issues of mutual concern. Both sides welcome the efforts of the U.S.-China Joint Liaison Group on Law Enforcement Cooperation (JLG) to achieve these objectives and will seek to arrange reciprocal visits to the Federal Law Enforcement Training Center and Public Security University, as well as other agencies and institutions, to improve information exchange. Both countries have decided to hold the tenth session of the JLG in the fall in China, and prioritize cooperation in intellectual property enforcement, fugitives, human smuggling, repatriation, cybercrime, counternarcotics, anti-corruption, legal assistance, and retrieving illicit funds.

9. Affirmed their support for the establishment of the U.S.-China Maritime Safety Dialogue Mechanism between the U.S. Coast Guard and the China Maritime Safety Administration and to hold the first dialogue this fall in China, in conjunction with a visit by U.S. Coast Guard Commandant Admiral Robert J. Papp, Jr.

10. Noted that the fourteenth U.S.-China Joint Commission meeting on Science and Technology Cooperation (JCM) was held in Beijing May 1, 2012. Dr. John P. Holdren, Assistant to the President for Science and Technology and Director of the White House Office of Science and Technology Policy, and Dr. Wan Gang, Minister of Science and Technology of China, co-chaired the meeting. Representatives from government science and technology ministries and agencies and from research institutes in energy, measurement science, agriculture, environment, health, and basic research attended the meeting. The two sides reviewed collaborative programs under the U.S.-China Agreement on Cooperation in Science and Technology, discussed future efforts, outlined areas for cooperation, and developed a work plan.

• Signed the Protocol between USDA and the Ministry of Science and Technology for Cooperation on Agricultural Flagship Projects.

• Signed Memorandum of Understanding between the National Science Foundation of the United States (NSF) and the Ministry of Science and Technology of People's Republic of China (MOST) on the establishment of a partnership.

11. Decided to hold the third Advanced Biofuels Forum, the third Renewable Energy Industry Forum, and the twelfth Oil and Gas Industry Forum in due course.

12. Noted the results of the Joint Coordinating Committee Meeting between the U.S. Department of Energy (DOE) and the Chinese Academy of Sciences in April 2012. The U.S. Department of Energy and Chinese Academy of Sciences met in April and discussed ongoing and potential new collaborative activities. The two sides decided to continue the successful ongoing collaborations in high-energy physics, nuclear physics, and fusion energy sciences, and explore potential new mutually beneficial collaborations in basic energy sciences including chemistry, materials research, and light source research and development.

13. Decided that under the U.S.-China Bilateral Forum on Combating Illegal Logging and Associated Trade, the two governments are cooperating and undertaking concrete activities to fulfill the objectives of the associated Memorandum of Understanding, including through exchange of information, the research program on wood legality verification options and strategies for U.S.-China trade in forest products and encouraging participation of the private sector and civil society in the Forum.

14. Announced that the U.S.-China Joint Working Group on Environmental Research is to be held in the United States in June 2012 by

the U.S. Environmental Protection Agency and China's Ministry of Science and Technology.

15. Decided to hold the tenth session of the Joint Working Group of U.S.-China Agricultural Science and Technology Cooperation in Shandong province in August 2012.

16. Decided to hold the third round of the Dialogue on Law of the Sea and Polar Issues in Beijing, May 22–23, 2012.

III. Addressing Regional and Global Challenges

17. Decided to enhance communication and coordination on regional and global issues to jointly address common challenges and to safeguard peace and stability, in particular using multilateral mechanisms such as peacekeeping operations. The two sides held in-depth discussions on the Korean peninsula, the Iranian nuclear issue, and Syria. The two sides reiterated their understandings on the Korean peninsula and the Iranian nuclear issue as expressed in the 2011 U.S.-China Joint Statement.

18. Decided to work together, including exploring ways of cooperation, to encourage the international community to assist developing countries, including in Africa, Latin America, and Asia, to support poverty reduction, development, regional integration, and food security, and to contribute to inclusive and sustainable economic growth. Regarding joint development projects in third countries, the two sides could first conduct joint feasibility studies on programs and projects agreed and selected by all parties, including the host country, in the fields of agriculture, health, and human resources.

19. Reaffirmed the importance of encouraging a peaceful relationship and a productive dialogue between the governments of Sudan and South Sudan on all bilateral issues, including settlement of the remaining post Comprehensive Peace Agreement issues, decided to maintain communication and consultation on the issue concerning Sudan and South Sudan, coordinate actions on the basis of respecting related parties' concerns, support the peaceful coexistence of the two countries and safeguard safety and stability in the region, including through full implementation of the UN peacekeeping missions there.

IV. Enhancing U.S.-China Bilateral Cooperation

20. Welcomed the continued deepening of subnational relations as envisioned in the Memorandum of Understanding Concerning the Establishment of the U.S.-China Governors Forum to Promote Sub-National Cooperation. Highlighted the success since the last S&ED of the inaugural U.S.-China Governors Forum held in Salt Lake City, the second dialogue held in Beijing, and the Governors Roundtable held in Los Angeles on the margins of Vice President Xi Jinping's official visit.

21. Decided to hold specific talks on the issuance of five-year multiple entry visas for businessmen, tourists, students, and other agreed-upon visa classes.

22. Reaffirmed their support for the National China Garden Foundation's efforts to construct a China Garden at the U.S. National Arboretum, expecting the Foundation to complete an Architect-Engineering Feasibility Study by the second half of 2012, develop the final design by the end of 2012, and begin construction in 2013.

23. Decided to continue to implement the Memorandum of Understanding between the Department of Homeland Security, U.S. Customs and Border Protection and the General Administration of Customs of the People's Republic of China Concerning Bilateral Cooperation on Supply Chain Security and Facilitation and the Action Plan. Three Customs-Trade Partnership Against Terrorism (C-TPAT) joint validations are to be conducted this year in China, which will further U.S.-China Customs cooperation on supply chain security and facilitation. In the meantime, the comparative studies of "Authorized Economic Operator (AEO)" systems will be carried out in conjunction with the joint validations in order to achieve the goal of mutual recognition of AEO as early as possible.

24. Reiterated commitments to combating illegal trafficking of nuclear and other radioactive materials. The Radiation Detection Training Center for China Customs jointly established by both sides is to be put into use in the second half of this year.

25. Decided to sign the Letter of Intent between the U.S. Customs and Border Protection and the General Administration of Customs of the People's Republic of China and on a Joint Training Program designed to facilitate the exchange of information and personnel, undertake joint operational exercises, and strengthen customs-to-customs cooperation to identify and interdict illegitimate and illicit materials traveling via air and maritime cargo.

26. Decided to strengthen communication between the U.S. Coast Guard and China's Ministry of Transport to improve the coordination of search and rescue operations at sea, consider a possible joint exercise to be conducted in Hawaii in September between the U.S. Coast Guard and a vessel from the China Maritime Safety Administration.

27. Welcomed the exchanges between senior law enforcement officials to advance the practical development of bilateral law enforcement cooperation, including the Director of the Office of National Drug Control Policy R. Gil Kerlikowske's visit to China in June 2012.

28. Reaffirmed commitment to cooperate on transportation safety and security through study tours arranged by the U.S. Trade and Development Agency on maritime safety and operations; transportation safety and disaster rescue coordination; and an eighth phase of aviation executive management training under the U.S.-China Aviation Cooperation Program.

V. Cooperation on Climate Change, Energy, Environment, Science, and Technology

29. Decided to continue the climate change policy dialogue and pragmatic cooperation. Decided to work together constructively to implement the outcomes reached in Cancun and Durban and to achieve a positive outcome at the UN Climate Conference in Doha, Qatar. Decided to further strengthen the mechanisms for bilateral climate change policy dialogues and related cooperation, strengthen communications at various levels, and exchange views on issues under international climate change negotiations and on domestic policies.

30. Will strengthen cooperation under the Global Alliance for Clean Cookstoves to help the Alliance reach its ambitious goals for the large-scale global adoption of clean stoves and fuels for cooking, and thereby realize the multiple goals of improved health, improved livelihoods, women's empowerment, energy conservation, and environmental protection. China announced its decision to join the Global Alliance for Clean Cookstoves.

31. Welcomed the progress made under the U.S.-China Ten-Year Framework (TYF) on Energy and Environment Cooperation. At the 8th Joint Working Group Meeting of the TYF held in April this year, both sides decided to continue to strengthen cooperation in the action plans under the TYF, including clean water, clean air, clean and efficient transportation, clean and efficient electricity, nature reserves/protected areas, wetlands cooperation, and energy efficiency, and to further implement the EcoPartnerships program. Both sides will promote the "sister lake" partnership program and launch joint study on groundwater pollution prevention and control; co-host a Regional Air Quality Management Conference, implement pilot work on air quality improvement, and engage in technological exchanges on pollutants control; implement the livable transportation project, and deepen cooperation on aviation bio-fuels, energy conservation and emissions reduction in the aviation sector, and vehicle pollution prevention and control; implement the Memorandum of Understanding between the NEA and FERC and hold the U.S.-China Smart Grid Forum in Shenzhen in 2012; implement projects and activities of Annex 11 to the Protocol on Cooperation and Exchanges in the Field of Conservation of Nature between the U.S. and China; facilitate the joint publication of a special issue of the journal "Wetlands," and hold the third U.S.-China Energy Efficiency Forum in Beijing in June 2012.

32. Held an EcoPartnerships signing ceremony during the 4th S&ED and announced the expansion of the EcoPartnerships program by admitting five new EcoPartnerships. By bringing together local governments, research institutions, universities and corporations from the U.S. and China, EcoPartnerships spur innovation, investment and cooperation on energy and environmental issues in both countries. Critical investment by and pragmat-

ic cooperation among EcoPartners at the subnational level translate the strategic goals of the action plans under the TYF into concrete actions.

33. Reaffirmed the commitments made in the U.S.-China Joint Statement on Energy Security Cooperation, which noted the two countries, as the world's largest producers and consumers of energy, share common interests and responsibilities to ensure energy security and face common challenges. The two sides decided to strengthen dialogue and planning in these areas. The United States and China pledged to strengthen cooperation and increased dialogue and exchange of information in several areas including stabilizing international energy markets, emergency responses, ensuring diversified energy supply, and a rational and efficient use of energy.

34. Reaffirmed the commitments made in the U.S.-China Memorandum of Understanding for Cooperation in Establishing a Center for Excellence in Nuclear Security to strengthen cooperation in nuclear non-proliferation, nuclear security, and combating nuclear terrorism. The two countries decided to continue supporting the cooperation on the project to establish a Center of Excellence, and the two countries decided to strengthen the cooperation in the field of radioactive waste management.

35. Reaffirmed the importance of ensuring the continued safe operation of their respective nuclear power facilities and of sharing their nuclear safety expertise and experience; reaffirmed their support for the Action Plan on Nuclear Safety approved by the IAEA Board of Governors and endorsed by the IAEA General Conference in 2011; and reaffirmed the importance of establishing a global nuclear liability regime. The two sides decided to cooperate in the field of nuclear liability regime.

36. Welcomed the recent completion of the first U.S.-China shale gas assessment and decided to build on recent progress and strengthen future cooperation concerning shale gas development and regulatory and environmental frameworks. The two sides decided to work within the established Memorandum of Cooperation on Shale Gas Resources between the State Department and the National Energy Administration to enhance dialogue on the commercial environment and to further encourage responsible production in both countries to enhance global energy security.

37. Decided to participate as partners in the Asia-Pacific Energy Regulatory Forum (APERF) to facilitate the sharing of information on energy regulatory and policy practice and experience in the Asia-Pacific region. China is to attend the U.S.-hosted APERF meeting in August 2012 in Washington, D.C., where participants plan to discuss (1) the transition to a low-carbon economy, (2) energy infrastructure and market regulatory arrangements, and (3) competition reform.

38. Welcomed the furthering of bilateral cooperation on clean energy, including the extension of the U.S.-China Clean Energy Exchange Program, under the action plan between the U.S. Trade and Development Agency (USTDA) and the National Energy Administration.

39. Announced that U.S.-China Clean Energy Research Center (CERC) has held an IPR workshop in China March 5–7, 2012, and will hold one other IPR workshop in the United States within a year. CERC will conduct mid-term assessment on the work progress of its industry-academia-research consortia this year. The United States and China announced the completion of the first U.S.-China Clean Energy Research Center Annual Report.

40. Welcomed the third year of progress under the U.S.-China Energy Cooperation Program, announced during the visit of President Obama to China in November 2009. Under this program, the two sides held consultations and selected sites for implementation of a joint pilot project on distributed energy and combined heat and power. The two countries decided to work together to organize workshops, study tours, and other activities covering energy policy.

41. Announced USTDA consideration for two studies to support mutually beneficial cooperation in the areas of 1) an integrated smart grid communication model; and 2) denitrification of power plant emissions. Considering that China has made related research deployment in the aforementioned areas, the two sides decided to conduct mutually beneficial cooperation in those areas.

42. Decided to strive to expand cooperation in the field of advanced biofuel and to explore further cooperation on development of aviation biofuel.

43. Welcomed the recent signing of a new Environmental Law Annex under the EPA-MEP Memorandum of Understanding on Scientific and Technical Cooperation in the Field of Environment. This annex is intended to strengthen cooperation in the field of environmental law. Building on 30 years of cooperation, the U.S. Environmental Protection Agency (EPA) and China's Ministry of Environmental Protection (MEP) proposed holding the next meeting of the Joint Committee on Environmental Cooperation (JCEC), in China in the second half of 2012.

44. Announced further collaboration on groundwater investigation including soil remediation, beginning with USTDA-supported technical workshops and study in the United States. Advanced cooperation on reducing air pollution through technical study tours organized by USTDA on mercury emissions controls and green cement production.

45. Decided to strengthen cooperation and exchange through the APFNet [Asia-Pacific Network for Sustainable Forest Management and Rehabilitation] and carry out and jointly promote sustainable forest management and conservation in the Asia-Pacific Region.

46. Decided to increase bilateral exchanges in science, technology, and policy to enhance the pragmatic cooperation between the United States and China on fronts such as food security, food safety, and sustainable agriculture.

47. Decided to jointly support wildlife enforcement efforts to combat illegal trafficking of endangered and protected wildlife. The United States

and China will participate in a Special Investigations Group meeting in Nanning, China, June 20–21, led by ASEAN-WEN, where wildlife investigators and forensic scientists will identify and recommend improved enforcement and inspection efforts.

48. Affirmed our mutual commitment to strengthening joint research between the National Oceanic and Atmospheric Administration (NOAA) and the China Meteorological Administration (CMA) through the U.S.-China Science and Technology Agreement to develop accurate and reliable capabilities for observing and understanding the behavior of greenhouse gases in the atmosphere.

49. Signed the Framework Plan for Ocean and Fishery Science and Technology Cooperation for 2011–2015 between NOAA and the State Oceanic Administration. The two sides decided to develop the implementation plan of the "Indian Ocean Southern Climate Change Observation, Reanalysis and Prediction" (ISOCORE) program.

VI. Breakout Sessions and Other Meetings

50. Held breakout sessions on Climate Change, Energy Security, Policy Planning, South Asia, Sudan–South Sudan, and Peacekeeping, and conducted a series of bilateral meetings between senior officials on a broad range of issues covering the entire strategic track of the U.S.-China relationship.

Bibliography

Alden, Chris. *China in Africa*. London: Zed Books, 2007.

Blanchard, Jean-Marc F., and Lu Fujia. "Thinking Hard About Soft Power: A Review and Critique of the Literature on China and Soft Power." *Asian Perspective* 36, no. 4 (2012): 565–590.

Brautigam, Deborah. *The Dragon's Gift: The Real Story of China in Africa*. London: Oxford University Press, 2009.

Brzezinski, Zbigniew. "The Group of Two That Could Change the World." *Financial Times*, January 13, 2009.

Chi, Eunju. "The Chinese Government's Responses to Use of the Internet." *Asian Perspective* 36, no. 3 (2012): 387–409.

Christensen, Thomas J. "The Advantages of an Assertive China: Responding to Beijing's Abrasive Diplomacy." *Foreign Affairs* 90, no. 2 (2011): 54–67.

Chu Shulong. *Zhongguo waijiao zhanlue he zhengci* (China's External Strategy and Policy). Beijing: Shishi chubanshe, 2008.

Chung, Jae Ho. "Korean Views of Korea-China Relations: Evolving Perceptions and Upcoming Challenges." *Asian Perspective* 36, no. 2 (2012): 219–236.

Deng Xiaoping, *Fundamental Issues in Present-Day China*. Beijing: Foreign Languages Press, 1987.

Dittmer, Lowell, and George T. Yu, eds. *China, the Developing World, and the New Global Dynamic*. Boulder, CO: Lynne Rienner Publishers, 2010.

Downs, Erica, and Suzanne Maloney. "Getting China to Sanction Iran: The Chinese-Iranian Oil Connection." *Foreign Affairs* 90, no. 2 (2011): 15–21.

Economy, Elizabeth. "The Great Leap Backward? The Costs of China's Environmental Crisis." *Foreign Affairs* 86, no. 5 (2007): 38–59.

———. *The River Runs Black: The Environmental Challenge to China's Future*. Ithaca, NY: Cornell University Press, 2004.

Fewsmith, Joseph. "Debating 'the China Model.'" *China Leadership Monitor*, no. 35 (2011); at http://media.hoover.org/sites/default/files/documents/CLM35JF.pdf.

Forsythe, David P., Patrice C. McMahon, and Andrew Wedeman, eds. *American Foreign Policy in a Globalized World*. New York: Routledge, 2006.

Freeman, Chas W., Jr. "Beijing, Washington, and the Shifting Balance of Prestige: Remarks to the China Maritime Studies Institute," Newport, RI, May 10, 2011.

Gill, Bates, and James Reilly. "The Tenuous Hold of China Inc. on Africa." *Washington Quarterly* 30, no. 3 (2007): 37–52.

Gurtov, Mel. "Averting War in Northeast Asia: A Proposal." *Asia-Pacific Journal* 9, no. 2 (2011); at http://japanfocus.org/-Mel-Gurtov/3467.

Huang, Yanzhong, "Is China Facing a Health Care Crisis?" at www.nytimes.com/roomfordebate/2011/11/01/is-china-facing-a-health-care-crisis/chinas-health-costs-outstrip-gdp-growth.

Ikenberry, G. John. "The Rise of China and the Future of the West." *Foreign Affairs* 87, no. 1 (2008): 23–37.

International Crisis Group. "China's Growing Role in UN Peacekeeping." Report no. 166, April 17, 2009.

———. "Stirring Up the South China Sea (II): Regional Responses." July 24, 2012; at www.crisisgroup.org/~/media/Files/asia/north-east-asia/229-stirring-up-the-south-china-sea-ii-regional-responses.pdf?utm_source=chinareport&utm_medium=pdf&utm_campaign=mremail.

Irvine, Roger. "Primacy and Responsibility: China's Perception of Its International Future." *China Security*, no. 18 (2010); at www.chinasecurity.us.

Jakobson, Linda, and Dean Knox. "New Foreign Policy Actors in China." SIPRI (Stockholm International Peace Research Institute) Policy Paper no. 26, September 2010.

Kan, Shirley A. "Taiwan: Major U.S. Arms Sales Since 1990." CRS Report RL30957, August 2, 2011; at www.fas.org/sgp/crs/weapons/RL30957.pdf.

Kennedy, Scott. "The Myth of the Beijing Consensus." *Journal of Contemporary China* 19, no. 65 (2010): 461–477.

Kim, Samuel S., ed. *The International Relations of Northeast Asia*. Lanham, MD: Rowman & Littlefield, 2004.

Kristensen, Hans M., and Robert S. Norris. "Chinese Nuclear Forces, 2011." *Bulletin of the Atomic Scientists* 67, no. 6 (2011): 81–87.

Lampton, David M., ed. *The Making of China's Foreign and Security Policy in the Era of Reform, 1978–2000*. Stanford, CA: Stanford University Press, 2001.

Li, Cheng. "China's Most Powerful 'Princelings': How Many Will Enter the New Politburo?" Brookings Institution paper, October 17, 2007; at www.brookings.edu/articles/2007/1017china.aspx.

Link, Perry. "China: From Famine to Oslo." *New York Review of Books*, January 13, 2011; at www.nybooks.com/articles/archives/2011/jan/13/china-famine-oslo/.

Lum, Thomas, Hannah Fischer, Julissa Gomez-Granger, and Anne Leland. "China's Foreign Aid Activities in Africa, Latin America, and Southeast Asia." CRS Report R-40361, February 25, 2009.

Nadkami, Vidya. *Strategic Partnerships in Asia: Balancing Without Alliances*. London: Routledge, 2010.

Nathan, Andrew J. "Present at the Stagnation: Is China's Development Stalled?" *Foreign Affairs* 85, no. 4 (2006): 177–182.

Norris, Robert S. "Chinese Nuclear Forces, 2011." *Bulletin of the Atomic Scientists* 67, no. 6 (2011): 81–87.

O'Rourke, Ronald. "China's Naval Modernization: Implications for U.S. Navy Capabilities—Background and Issues for Congress." CRS Report RL33153, July 22, 2011.

Packer, George. "The Broken Contract: Inequality and American Decline." *Foreign Affairs* 90, no. 6 (2011): 20–31.

Pei, Minxin. "The Paradoxes of American Nationalism." *Foreign Policy* (May–June 2003): 31–37; at www.foreignpolicy.com/articles/2003/05/01/the_paradoxes_of_american_nationalism.

Rice, Condoleezza. "Promoting the National Interest." *Foreign Affairs* 79, no. 1 (2000): 45–62.

Salidjanova, Nargiza. "Going Out: An Overview of China's Outward Foreign Direct Investment." U.S.-China Economic and Security Review Commission, Staff

Research Report, March 30, 2011; at www.uscc.gov/researchpapers /2011/GoingOut.pdf.

Sautman, Barry, and Yan Hairong. "Trade, Investment, Power, and the China-in-Africa Discourse." *Asia-Pacific Journal*, no. 52-3-09 (December 28, 2009); at http://japanfocus.org/-Yan-Hairong/3278.

Shirk, Susan L. *China: Fragile Superpower.* New York: Oxford University Press, 2007.

State Council Information Office, People's Republic of China. "China's Foreign Aid." April 2011; at http://news.xinhuanet.com/english2010/china/2011 -04/21/c_13839683.htm.

Sun, Yun. "Studying the South China Sea: A Chinese Perspective." Center for New American Security, East and South China Seas Bulletin, no. 1, January 9, 2012; at www.cnas.org/files/documents/flashpoints/CNAS_ESCS_bulletin1.pdf.

Swaine, Michael D., and M. Taylor Fravel. "China's Assertive Behavior, Part Two: The Maritime Periphery." *China Leadership Monitor*, no. 35 (2011): 1–32.

UN Development Programme. *Human Development Report, 2011: Sustainability and Equity, A Better Future for All.* New York: Palgrave Macmillan, 2011; at www.beta.undp.org/content/dam/undp/library/corporate/HDR/2011%20Global% 20HDR/English/HDR_2011_EN_Complete.pdf.

U.S.-China Economic and Security Review Commission. *2011 Report to Congress.* 112th Cong., 1st sess. Washington, DC: USCC, November 2011.

Valencia, Mark J. "Diplomatic Drama: The South China Sea Imbroglio." *Global Asia* 6, no. 3 (2011): 66–71.

Walzer, Michael. "On Humanitarianism: Is Helping Others Charity, or Duty, or Both?" *Foreign Affairs* 90, no. 4 (2011): 69–80.

Wang, Hongying, and James N. Rosenau. "China and Global Governance." *Asian Perspective* 33, no. 3 (2009): 5–39.

Wang Jisi. "China's Search for a Grand Strategy: A Rising Great Power Finds Its Way." *Foreign Affairs* 90, no. 2 (2011): 68–79.

———. "China's Search for Stability with America." *Foreign Affairs* 84, no. 5 (2005): 39–60.

Wang Jisi, and Kenneth Lieberthal. "Addressing U.S.-China Strategic Distrust." Beijing University International Strategy Research Institute, March 2012.

Wikileaks Archives, at www.wikileaks.org/wiki/Main_Page.

World Bank. *World Development Indicators*; at www.google.com/publicdata.

Wu Xinbo, "Understanding Chinese and U.S. Crisis Behavior." *Washington Quarterly* 31, no. 1 (2007/2008): 61–76.

Xu Yi-chong. "Nuclear Power in China: How It Really Works." *Global Asia* 7, no. 1 (2012): 32–43.

Yan Xuetong. "How China Can Defeat America." *New York Times*, November 20, 2011; online ed.

Yang Yao. "The End of the Beijing Consensus." February 2, 2010; at www .foreignaffairs.com/print/65914?page=show.

Yee, Albert. "China's Macroeconomic Response to the Global Recession: Ideational Sources and Substantive Contents." *Asian Perspective* 36, no. 1 (2012): 1–42.

Zakaria, Fareed. "The Future of American Power: How America Can Survive the Rise of the Rest." *Foreign Affairs* 87, no. 3 (2008): 18–43.

Zhao, Suisheng. "China's Pragmatic Nationalism: Is It Manageable?" *Washington Quarterly* 29, no. 1 (2005–2006): 131–144.

Zheng Bijian. "China's 'Peaceful Rise' to Great-Power Status." *Foreign Affairs* 84, no. 5 (2005): 18–24.

Zweig, David, and Bi Jianhai. "China's Global Hunt for Energy." *Foreign Affairs* 84, no. 5 (2005): 25–38.

Index

About the Book

Mel Gurtov takes issue with the widespread view that China is on the way to rivaling or even displacing the United States as the dominant world power.

Gurtov identifies serious constraints that will keep the country's leadership focused for the foreseeable future on challenges at home. Arguing that China's economic rise has exacerbated problems of social inequality, environmental degradation, official corruption, and more—and that its military capabilities and ambitions are far more limited than many observers have suggested—he makes a strong case that the most productive US policy will be one of engagement on issues of common concern, rather than confrontation or containment.

Mel Gurtov is professor emeritus of political science at Portland State University and editor in chief of the journal *Asian Perspective*. His numerous publications include *Global Politics in the Human Interest* (also published in Spanish, Japanese, and Chinese), *Superpower on Crusade: The Bush Doctrine in US Foreign Policy*, and *Pacific Asia? Prospects for Security and Cooperation in East Asia*.